UNITED NATIONS, DIVIDED WORLD

UNITED NATIONS, DIVIDED WORLD

THE UN'S ROLES IN
INTERNATIONAL RELATIONS

EDITED BY

Adam Roberts

and

Benedict Kingsbury

CLARENDON PRESS · OXFORD
1988

Oxford University Press, Walton Street, Oxford OX2 6DP

Oxford New York Toronto
Delhi Bombay Calcutta Madras Karachi
Petaling Jaya Singapore Hong Kong Tokyo
Nairobi Dar es Salaam Cape Town
Melbourne Auckland

and associated companies in
Beirut Berlin Ibadan Nicosia

Oxford is a trade mark of Oxford University Press

Published in the United States
by Oxford University Press, New York

British Library Cataloguing in Publication Data
United Nations, divided world: The UN's roles in international relations.
1. United Nations—History
I. Roberts, Adam II. Kingsbury, Benedict
341.23'09 JX1977
ISBN 0-19-827544-7

Library of Congress Cataloging in Publication Data
United Nations, divided world.
1. United Nations. 2. International relations.
I. Roberts, Adam. II. Kingsbury, Benedict.
JX1977.U448 1988 341.23 87-24821
ISBN 0-19-827544-7

Set by Colset Pte Ltd, Singapore
Printed and bound in
Great Britain by Biddles Ltd,
Guildford and King's Lynn

ACKNOWLEDGEMENTS

THIS book is a revised and enlarged version of the Cyril Foster Lectures 1986, held at Oxford University between May and December 1986. Our first thanks go to the Managers of the Cyril Foster Fund, which financed this lecture series. We also thank Dr Erik Jensen, Director of the UN Office in London, for his encouragement and help in the preparation both of the lecture series and of the present book. Mr Marrack Goulding, UN Under-Secretary-General for Special Political Affairs, gave valuable advice in planning the lectures. Mr Alvaro de Soto, Special Assistant to the Secretary-General, was notably helpful in answering numerous queries. The typing of successive drafts and revisions in the arduous process of turning a lecture series into a book was undertaken principally by Mary Bügge in Balliol College, and Carole Charlton and Jo Webb in the Social Studies Faculty Centre: our appreciation of their help is heightened by our knowledge of the difficulties of the material with which they had to work. Finally, we thank the Master and Fellows of Balliol College for their help and hospitality.

A.R.
B.K.

Balliol College, Oxford
November 1987

CONTENTS

NOTES ON CONTRIBUTORS

MAURICE BERTRAND is a former Senior Counsellor at the Cour des Comptes, France. Member of the UN Joint Inspection Unit, 1968–85. Member of the Group of High-level Inter-governmental Experts to Review the Efficiency of the Administrative and Financial Functioning of the UN, 1986. His publications include *Refaire l'ONU: Un Programme Pour la Paix* (Geneva, 1986).

KENNETH DADZIE has been Secretary-General of UNCTAD since February 1986. He has held numerous posts in the Ghana Foreign Service and in the UN Secretariat. High Commissioner of Ghana in London, 1982–6. Has also served as a member of Ghanaian teams for negotiations with the IMF, World Bank, and other international institutions.

TOM J. FARER is Professor of Law at the University of New Mexico. He was previously Distinguished Professor of Law, Rutgers University, 1971–85. Special Assistant to the US Assistant Secretary of State for Inter-American Affairs, 1975. Member, Inter-American Commission for Human Rights, 1976–84. His publications include *The Grand Strategy of the United States in Latin America* (New Brunswick, 1987).

THOMAS M. FRANCK is Professor of Law and Director, Center for International Studies, New York University. Director of Research, UN Institute for Training and Research, 1981–3. His publications include *Nation Against Nation: What Happened to the UN Dream and What the US Can Do About It* (New York, 1985).

SIR MICHAEL HOWARD, D. Litt., FBA, is Regius Professor of Modern History, University of Oxford, and a Fellow of Oriel College. He was previously Professor of War Studies, King's College, London, 1963–8, and Chichele Professor of the History of War, Oxford University, 1977–80. His publications include *War in European History* (Oxford, 1976).

BENEDICT KINGSBURY is Snell Junior Research Fellow in Law, Balliol College, Oxford. A New Zealand citizen, he is doing research on indigenous peoples and international law. His publications include (ed. with Hedley Bull and Adam Roberts) *Hugo Grotius and International Relations* (Oxford, forthcoming).

EVAN LUARD is a writer on international affairs. He is a former delegate to the UN General Assembly, 1967–8. Parliamentary Under-Secretary of State, Foreign and Commonwealth Office, 1969–70 and 1976–9. Member of the Secretary-General's Committee of Experts on the Restructuring of the UN's Economic and Social Activities, 1975. His publications include *The United Nations: How it Works and What it Does* (London, 1979).

SIR ANTHONY PARSONS was UK Permanent Representative to the UN, 1979–82, and Adviser on Foreign Affairs to the Prime Minister, 1982–3. He was previously Counsellor, UK Mission to UN, 1969–71; and Ambassador to Iran, 1974–9. His publications include *The Pride and the Fall* (London, 1984).

JAVIER PÉREZ DE CUÉLLAR has been Secretary-General of the UN since 1 January 1982. Between 1944 and 1981 he held numerous posts in the Peruvian foreign service and in the UN, including Ambassador of Peru to the Soviet Union, Poland, Switzerland, and Venezuela; Permanent Representative of Peru to the UN, 1971–5; Special Representative of the UN Secretary-General in Cyprus, 1975–7; and Under-Secretary-General for Special Political Affairs, 1979–81. His publications include *Manual de Derecho Diplomatico* (1964).

ADAM ROBERTS is Montague Burton Professor of International Relations, University of Oxford, and a Fellow of Balliol College. He was previously Lecturer in International Relations, London School of Economics and Political Science, 1968–81. His publications include *Nations in Arms: The Theory and Practice of Territorial Defence* (2nd edn., London, 1986).

NAGENDRA SINGH has been President of the International Court of Justice since 1985, and a Member since 1973. He was previously a member of the Constituent Assembly of India, 1947–8, and Secretary to the Indian Ministries of Defence and Transport, and to the President of India. He is a corresponding member of the British Academy. His publications include *Nuclear Weapons and International Law* (London, 1959).

ABBREVIATIONS

These are the principal abbreviations used in this book; and all sixteen of the specialized agencies of the UN, which are marked by an asterisk *. The dagger † denotes a peacekeeping or observer force—for more information on these see Appendix D.

ACABQ	Advisory Committee on Administrative and Budgetary Questions
*FAO	Food and Agriculture Organization of the United Nations
ECOSOC	Economic and Social Council (of the UN)
GA	General Assembly
GATT	General Agreement on Tariffs and Trade
IAEA	International Atomic Energy Agency
*IBRD	International Bank for Reconstruction and Development (the World Bank)
ICJ	International Court of Justice
*IDA	International Development Association
*ICAO	International Civil Aviation Organization
*IFC	International Finance Corporation
*IFAD	International Fund for Agricultural Development
*ILO	International Labour Organization
*IMO	International Maritime Organization (formerly IMCO)
*IMF	International Monetary Fund
INSTRAW	International Research and Training Institute for the Advancement of Women
*ITU	International Telecommunication Union
JIU	Joint Inspection Unit
†ONUC	United Nations Operation in the Congo
OPEC	Organization of Petroleum Exporting Countries
SC	Security Council
SOLAS	International Convention for the Safety of Life at Sea
UN	United Nations
UNCLOS III	Third United Nations Conference on the Law of the Sea (1973–82)
UNCTAD	United Nations Conference on Trade and Development
†UNDOF	United Nations Disengagement Observer Force

UNDP	United Nations Development Programme
†UNEF I	United Nations Emergency Force (1956–67)
†UNEF II	United Nations Emergency Force II (1973–9)
UNEP	United Nations Environment Programme
*UNESCO	United Nations Educational, Scientific and Cultural Organization
†UNFICYP	United Nations Peacekeeping Force in Cyprus
UNHCR	Office of the United Nations High Commissioner for Refugees
UNICEF	United Nations Children's Fund
*UNIDO	United Nations Industrial Development Organization
†UNIFIL	United Nations Interim Force in Lebanon
†UNIPOM	United Nations India–Pakistan Observation Mission
UNITAR	United Nations Institute for Training and Research
†UNMOGIP	United Nations Military Observer Group in India and Pakistan
†UNOGIL	United Nations Observer Group in Lebanon
UNRWA	United Nations Relief and Works Agency for Palestine Refugees in the Near East
†UNSCOB	United Nations Special Committee on the Balkans
†UNSF	United Nations Security Force in West New Guinea
†UNTAG	United Nations Transition Assistance Group (Namibia)
†UNTSO	United Nations Truce Supervision Organization
†UNYOM	United Nations Yemen Observer Mission
*UPU	Universal Postal Union
*WHO	World Health Organization
*WIPO	World Intellectual Property Organization
*WMO	World Meteorological Organization

1

Introduction: The UN's Roles in a Divided World

ADAM ROBERTS AND BENEDICT KINGSBURY

THIS book is an assessment of the roles played by the United Nations in a world which has remained obstinately divided. It is about how the UN has changed since its foundation in 1945; about its successes, not the least of which is the mere fact of enduring for over forty years; about its equally notable failures; and about how it might address some of its current problems. Above all, it is an exploration of how to think about the UN, whose place in international relations has proved rather different from that envisaged both by its advocates and by its critics.

Our starting-point, as editors, has been dissatisfaction with many of the conventional views of the UN. Global international organizations which proclaim as their goal the radical restructuring of the unsatisfactory condition of international relations inevitably attract high hopes—and subsequent disappointment.[1] This has been true of the various communist internationals since the First International was founded in 1864, of the League of Nations founded in 1919, and now of the United Nations.

At the time of its foundation, the UN was seen by many as a prototype world government, or at least as a means of eliminating one of the major plagues of international life, namely war.[2] Further, the organization was and still is often seen in idealistic terms (sometimes reflecting the language of its Charter) as standing on a higher moral plane than the states of which it is composed, especially because of its advocacy of such principles as human rights, non-use of force, and disarmament.

---

[1] The pattern of vision and disillusion in the history of proposals for international organizations to maintain peace is traced in F. H. Hinsley, *Power and the Pursuit of Peace* (Cambridge, 1963). See also J. Ter Meulen, *Der Gedanke der Internationalen Organisation in seiner Entwicklung*, 2 vols. (The Hague, 1917 and 1929).

[2] See e.g. Clyde Eagleton, *International Government* (3rd rev. edn., New York, 1957).

Others have advanced more critical views. The UN is all talk and no action; it is an arena in which governments hypocritically proclaim one set of values while themselves practising another; it is a vehicle for the pursuit of power politics in disguise, not for their replacement. In the sober, even disillusioned, world of the late 1970s and early 1980s these critical views became more prevalent and more influential, especially in that country where idealism about the UN was once particularly strong—the USA.[3]

These two sets of views, diametrically opposed as they may appear to be, are but two sides of the same coin.[4] They both evaluate the UN in rather simple terms, they both assume that the UN must be judged by the high standards set for it in the Charter, and they both make few distinctions between the UN's numerous different roles. It is time to go beyond such views: to describe and take stock of the UN's actual performance in more than forty years in a wide variety of fields—from the maintenance of international peace to the protection of human rights, from the advocacy of self-determination to the codification of international law.

There is a further reason for taking stock of the UN in this way. An international organization can have many quite distinct roles, and these may be perceived differently at different times. In the period between the two world wars, the League of Nations was seen, rightly or wrongly, as concerned above all with the problem of peace, but in fact the more enduring achievements of the League era were in more specialized areas such as labour and health. In the early post-World War II period the UN was viewed similarly as being concerned with the maintenance of peace, but later its role in this area came to seem more marginal: especially in the era of *détente* when the two superpowers improved their mutual relations in negotiations outside the UN framework. Thus since the 1960s the UN's contribution has seemed to many to be less in the field of peace than in social

---

[3] See e.g. Daniel Patrick Moynihan, *A Dangerous Place* (London, 1979); and Burton Yale Pines (ed.), *A World Without a UN: What Would Happen if the UN Shut Down?* (Washington DC, Heritage Foundation, 1984).

[4] The relationship between these two approaches in the US debate is cogently analysed by Thomas M. Franck, *Nation Against Nation: What Happened to the UN Dream and What the US Can Do about It* (New York, 1985).

and economic improvement. The chapters in this book demonstrate, however, that the UN has retained or assumed important roles in each sphere. The purpose of this volume is realistically to appraise the value and appropriateness of these roles, and to assess the effectiveness of the UN in fulfilling them.

We asked the contributors to this book to provide, not just an account of particular aspects of UN activity addressed in each chapter, but also a rigorous and critical assessment: to look at failures as well as successes, to ask hard questions, and, where possible, to suggest directions for change. Many of the authors are, or have been, in positions of considerable responsibility in the UN system, but they have responded to our request for a candid view. It is a reflection of the growing maturity of ideas about the UN, as well as of the exigencies arising from the need to respond to the UN's persistent difficulties, that constructive candour is increasingly valued. It may yet supplant the traditional tendencies to utopianism, embittered cynicism, or, perhaps worst of all, blithe disregard in face of well-founded or politically damning criticism.

To take stock of the UN's roles in international relations is not easy. How is it possible methodically to determine, for instance, whether the UN has or has not contributed to peace and international stability? However, as some of our contributors show, in particular crises the UN has helped to defuse tension, and to make it possible for the participants to find an honourable way out. Furthermore, when one bears in mind the astonishing scope of changes in the world since 1945—the process of decolonization, the emergence of major new economic powers, the exploitation of resources under the seas, the rapid development of military technology—one cannot fail to be struck by the fact that developments which could easily have occasioned major wars often did not do so. While by no means all change has been peaceful, a great deal of peaceful change has been achieved. The UN does not deserve all the credit for this, but it certainly deserves some.

The picture which emerges from the various chapters is of a UN which, while operating in an evolving world, is not itself fundamentally concerned to restructure or replace the system of sovereign states so much as to ameliorate the problems spawned by its imperfections, and to manage the rapid changes in many distinct fields. The UN finds roles for itself in those areas of activity which are most appropriately tackled either on a truly multilateral basis, or by individuals representing, not a particular state, but the collectivity of states. Its agenda also undeniably includes many areas of activity in which states prefer rhetoric to real action.[5]

It is commonly said that the UN is nothing more than the sum of its members—those 159 sovereign states of which it is composed.[6] It was created by governments, and it can do nothing without their assent. Such a pragmatic view is a necessary antidote to the common illusions that the UN exists to supersede the states system, and that the UN ought to take strong action on its own initiative, irrespective of the views of states. But the pragmatic view, persuasive as it is, can easily lead to a neglect of the way in which all institutions, whatever their origins and power base, develop a life and an ethos of their own.[7] The UN is a singular example of this phenomenon: in fuelling the 'revolution of rising expectations' the UN has done much to ensure the genuine need for its own existence.

(a) Short Factual Description of the UN System

The term 'UN system' refers not just to the United Nations itself, as outlined in the Charter, but also the various subsidiary bodies and specialized agencies which operate under its auspices. Before attempting any kind of evaluation of this system, a few basic facts are in order.

The UN was formally established on 24 October 1945, when its basic constitutive instrument, the UN Charter, entered into force. It had fifty-one founder states. The first blueprints for the UN were drafted by the USA, the UK, the USSR, and their

[5] The importance of symbolic resolutions to coalition maintenance within the UN is demonstrated by M.J. Peterson, *The General Assembly in World Politics* (Boston, 1986), pp. 187 ff.

[6] To paraphrase former US Secretary of State Dean Rusk, 'the UN is 159 member states pursuing their national interests as they see them.' 'An Address to the Ninth Annual Conference on International Affairs', quoted in *Harvard International Law Journal*, 17 (1976), p. 606.

[7] See e.g. David Pitt and Thomas G. Weiss (eds.), *The Nature of United Nations Bureaucracies* (London, 1986); and Douglas Williams, *The Specialized Agencies and the United Nations—the System in Crisis* (London, 1987).

allies during World War II, reflecting their conceptions of the post-war international order. The Charter was finally adopted by fifty states meeting at San Francisco in June 1945. Although the nature and work of the UN has evolved considerably, the Charter has remained virtually unchanged.[8] The UN now has 159 members—virtually all the states of the contemporary world.[9] No member state has ever left the UN, although in 1965-6 Indonesia temporarily withdrew. In some cases the credentials of particular authorities to represent their state have not been accepted.

Six 'principal organs' of the UN were established by the Charter: the General Assembly, the Security Council, the Secretariat, the International Court of Justice (ICJ), the Trusteeship Council, and the Economic and Social Council (ECOSOC).

The General Assembly as the plenary body controls much of the work of the UN. It meets in regular session for approximately the last quarter of every year, and occasionally holds special or emergency sessions to consider specific issues. The General Assembly approves the budget, adopts priorities, calls international conferences, superintends the operations of the Secretariat and of numerous committees and subsidiary organs, and debates and adopts resolutions on major issues. The many subsidiary bodies created by the General Assembly include the United Nations Children's Fund (UNICEF), the Office of the United Nations High Commissioner for Refugees (UNHCR), the United Nations Conference on Trade and Development (UNCTAD), and the United Nations Development Programme (UNDP). Much of the work of the General Assembly is done in permanent or *ad hoc* committees responsible for particular fields of UN activity or deliberation.

The fifteen-member Security Council is dominated by its five permanent members (China, France, the UK, the USSR, and the USA), each of which has power to veto any draft resolution on substantive matters. The remaining ten members are elected for two-year periods by the General Assembly. The Security

---

[8] The text of the UN Charter is in Appendix A to this volume.

[9] A list of member states is in Appendix B. Non-members of the UN include North Korea, South Korea, Switzerland, Taiwan, a number of microstates, and dependent or non-self-governing territories.

Council has primary responsibility for the maintenance of international peace and security, and unlike the General Assembly is able to take decisions binding on all members of the UN. It meets frequently throughout the year, mainly to consider military conflicts and other situations or disputes where international peace and security are threatened. It is empowered to order mandatory sanctions, call for cease-fires, establish peace-keeping forces, and even to take military action on behalf of the UN. The veto power was intended to ensure that the UN could not act against the strong opposition of any of the most powerful states. Thus the Security Council could contribute little to the amelioration of armed conflicts in Suez (1956), Vietnam (1946–75), the Sino-Vietnamese clash (1979), and Afghanistan (1979–).

The Security Council has never ordered military 'enforcement' action (the closest approximation, the force in Korea in 1950–3, was merely an authorized force), and the agreements envisaged in the Charter placing national military units at the disposal of the UN have not been concluded. Significant binding sanctions were applied only to Rhodesia (1966–79) and to arms sales to South Africa (1977–). The Security Council has nevertheless played an important role in easing or containing numerous crises, and provides a high-level forum for discreet diplomatic contact and negotiation. Peacekeeping forces ranging from small observer units to large interposition or policing forces have been established by the Security Council in the Middle East, the Balkans, Kashmir, the Congo, Cyprus, and other areas. The General Assembly did create the United Nations Emergency Force in the aftermath of the Suez crisis in 1956 when the Security Council was prevented by veto from acting, and issued recommendations concerning UN forces in Korea and the Congo in similar circumstances, but control of peacekeeping has now returned firmly to the Security Council.[10] The Security Council also has a role, with the General Assembly, in the admission of new members to the UN, the appointment of the Secretary-General, and the election of judges to the ICJ.

The Secretary-General is head of the UN Secretariat, which

---

[10] A quick-reference list of UN peacekeeping operations is in Appendix D.

employs some 16,000 people at UN Headquarters in New York
and at other offices (the largest of which is Geneva). The Secretariat is part of the 50,000 strong international civil service
employed by agencies within the UN system at some 620 posts
throughout the world. The UN Charter requires that Secretariat staff be answerable only to the UN and stipulates that
merit is to be the paramount consideration in their employment,
but the UN has not always been able to adhere unswervingly to
these principles. While the nature and quality of the UN's work
depends greatly on the comparatively 'faceless' Secretariat, the
Secretary-General is also a significant figure in international
diplomacy.[11]

The Trusteeship Council superintended the transition of trust
territories to self-government, but the main pressure for decolonization has come from other UN quarters—the Special
Committee on Decolonization, dominated by 'Third World'
states, and the General Assembly's Fourth Committee.

The Economic and Social Council comprises fifty-four states
elected by the General Assembly. Many non-governmental
organizations also participate in its proceedings. It supervises
the work of numerous commissions, committees, and expert
bodies in the economic and social fields, and endeavours to
coordinate the efforts of the UN specialized agencies in this area.

The UN system extends beyond the six UN organs created by
the Charter, and the various subsidiary bodies established
subsequently by the UN, to include also a host of specialized
agencies with their own separate constitutions, memberships,
and budgets. These agencies constitute a distinct part of the UN
system. In the words of Article 57 of the UN Charter they
are 'established by intergovernmental agreement and having
wide international responsibilities, as defined in their basic
instruments, in economic, social, cultural, educational, health,
and related fields'. There are sixteen such specialized agencies
associated with the UN: apart from the financial agencies—the
main ones being the International Monetary Fund (IMF) and
the World Bank—the 'big four' are the International Labour
Organization (ILO), the Food and Agriculture Organization
(FAO), the United Nations Educational, Scientific and

[11] The Secretaries-General of the UN since 1945 are listed in Appendix C.

Cultural Organization (UNESCO), and the World Health Organization (WHO). Other intergovernmental organizations closely associated with the UN include the International Atomic Energy Agency (IAEA) and the General Agreement on Tariffs and Trade (GATT).

Expenditure by the UN system as a whole is substantial: on one calculation some US $4 billion per annum in the 1986-7 biennium. More than half of this is financed by voluntary contributions by states, with most of the remainder contributed by member states in accordance with binding assessments based mainly on gross and per capita national incomes. The regular assessed budget of the UN proper was some US $800 million in 1987. The UN has been in financial difficulties arising from non-payment of assessed contributions since the early 1960s, and the deficit increased sharply in the 1980s.[12]

(b) Myth and Reality in the UN System

Any serious assessment of the UN's successes and failures cannot neglect the importance of myth, symbol, and drama in the UN. The organization must be judged not just by what it does in particular fields of activity, or in particular crises, but also by the way in which, through its very existence, through the influence of its Charter, through the questions it addresses, and through its diplomatic rituals, it proclaims certain values and sets the terms of international debates.

The element of standard-setting and myth-making—of appealing to higher standards than those which commonly prevail in international relations, and of holding out the promise of a better-ordered world—is and always has been central to the UN. Many chapters in this book point to the significance of this role. The fact that it is always hard to quantify such a role, or enter it neatly into profit and loss columns of a UN balance sheet, does not mean that it can for a moment be neglected.

The very term 'United Nations' is a misnomer with a strong element of myth about it, and has been so ever since the foundation of the UN in 1945. The origins of the term are to be

---

[12] The UN's financial crisis is discussed in the chapters by Javier Pérez de Cuéllar and Maurice Bertrand.

found in the events surrounding the Washington Declaration of 1 January 1942, in which twenty-six Allied countries, which came to be called the 'United Nations', pledged themselves to employ their full resources against Germany, Italy, and Japan; and the Moscow Four-Nation Declaration of 30 October 1943 mentioned in Article 106 of the UN Charter.[13] The term 'United Nations' thus emerged in an atmosphere of wartime hyperbole; and it was partly to distinguish itself from the wartime alliance out of which it had grown that, in its early years, the UN was very widely known as the United Nations *Organization* (UNO). There is now no need for this formulation, except for the limited purpose of distinguishing the UN proper from the specialized agencies. Not only has the wartime alliance receded into the distant past, but when it is remembered, its members are usually called 'the Allies'. The term 'the United Nations' has been effectively appropriated by the international organization created in 1945.

One potentially misleading element in the term 'United Nations' is the claim to unity. Indeed, 'Divided Nations' might seem a more factually accurate, if less inspirational, term for the organization and its member states. While the very existence of the UN attests to a general unity of acceptance of an international society with certain agreed institutions, it is division, not unity, which has been the more conspicuous feature of the world since 1945, as indeed it was of the world before that date. This is not a matter of one division but of many. It is not just that division between East and West which has been widely perceived as the main cause of the UN's failure to exercise the more ambitious of its functions. It is also a matter of those other deep divisions between states which have caused so much conflict and cost so many lives: for example, divisions between India and Pakistan, between Israel and its neighbours, between Iran and Iraq. Some of these divisions have become more serious in the UN era than before—not least because the UN, somewhat paradoxically, has presided over perhaps the final phase in the triumphant advance of the idea of the 'sovereign

---

[13] The Washington Declaration, the Moscow Declaration, and other instruments of the wartime United Nations are conveniently reprinted in Royal Institute of International Affairs, *United Nations Documents 1941–1945* (London, 1946); and in Louise W. Holborn, *War and Peace Aims of the United Nations*, 2 vols. (Boston, Mass., 1943, 1948).

state'. In the wake of European decolonization the total number of such states has tripled. Many conflicts of our time have their origins in partitions and disputes which followed upon European decolonization, and the attendant uncertainties of new post-colonial regimes about their legitimacy, about the identity of their nation, and about their frontiers. With time, some of these problems may diminish. But facts must be faced: the world is, and is likely to remain, divided up into separate sovereign states, which have a capacity for making war, and which in their mutual relations will go on displaying at least some of those elements of rivalry and distrust which have always characterized the system of states.

A second misleading element in the term 'United Nations' has to do with the word 'nation'. Rather than 'Divided Nations', 'Divided States' might be an even more brutally accurate term. There is a dimension of inevitable mythology in the 'nations' part of the title 'United Nations'. If the term 'nation', properly used, refers to a people holding in common such attributes as ethnicity, history, culture, religion, language, and having a common perception of who their enemies are, then there are few 'nations' indeed among the member states of the United Nations. Many of these states are engaged in the difficult business of 'nation-building', and may indeed over time generate a sense of nationhood. Meanwhile there will continue to be deep divisions within states as well as between them—divisions of region, race, nationality, tribe, religion, and class. 'Nations' and 'states' are far from co-terminous; witness the phenomena of divided nations, of multinational states, and of states with irredentist claims. Indeed, many major wars of this century, including the two world wars, originated partly from these phenomena connected with the crucial difference between 'nation' and 'state'.[14] Yet the use of the term 'nation' as supposedly synonymous with 'state' or 'country' is deeply ingrained in contemporary usage, not just in the title of the UN itself, but in the very word 'international'. The important thing

---

[14] On the difference between 'nation' and 'state' see Hugh Seton-Watson, *Nations and States* (London, 1977). See also Benedict Anderson, *Imagined Communities: Reflections on the Origin and Spread of Nationalism* (London, 1983); José de Obieta Chalbaud, *El derecho humano de la autodeterminación de los pueblos* (Madrid, 1985); Anthony D. Smith, *The Ethnic Revival* (Cambridge, 1981); and Smith, *The Ethnic Origins of Nations* (Oxford, 1986).

is that such uses of the terms 'nation' and 'United Nations' should not cloud judgement by conveying an excessively simple image of those complex entities, sovereign states, of which our world is composed.

Sometimes the rhetoric of the UN does indeed cloud judgement. There are many elements in the ethos of the organization which need to be questioned from within as well as without. To take just one example, the UN has increasingly committed itself over the years to the goal of general and complete disarmament, and the General Assembly held two UN Special Sessions on Disarmament in 1978 and 1982. Yet there has been little analysis under UN auspices of why ambitious calls for disarmament, which have been a persistent feature of international life since 1899, have invariably failed. In particular, the possibility that the idea of general and complete disarmament as commonly proposed may contain some inbuilt defects (rather than merely face external 'obstacles') has seldom got a hearing. General and complete disarmament has the character of a myth to which the UN subscribes, but which it does little to describe or analyse. This disarmament approach, about which Michael Howard is notably sceptical in his chapter below, has several possible costs. First, it can contribute to verbal hostility between states, as they blame each other for the failure to achieve disarmament. Second, by presenting a mythological alternative to armaments it may distract attention from other possibly more fruitful approaches to the urgent problem of controlling and limiting military force—including many approaches in arms control and laws of war matters which the UN has pursued. And third, it risks having the same effect as did the League of Nations' commitment to disarmament in the 1920s and 1930s—namely not just that it will fail to produce results, but that in so doing it will weaken the international organization which had committed itself so deeply to this approach.[15]

In 1968, in *The United Nations: Sacred Drama*, which remains one of the most challenging books on the subject, Conor Cruise O'Brien suggested that the function of the UN was to act—not

---

[15] For a critical examination of the idea of 'general and complete disarmament' see Hedley Bull, *The Control of the Arms Race* (London, 1961); and John W. Spanier and Joseph L. Nogee, *The Politics of Disarmament* (New York, 1962). See also R. B. Byers and Stanley Ing (eds.), *Arms Limitation and the United Nations* (Toronto, 1982).

in the sense of taking executive action, but rather in the sense of acting in a theatre. He suggested that the UN Charter, and much UN activity, reflected

the feeling that the thing feared may be averted, and the thing hoped for be won, by the solemn and collective use of appropriate words. This prayer still converges on the United Nations—as on a holy place—at times when, as in the Cuban missile crisis in 1962, or the Middle Eastern crisis of the summer of 1967, the scourge of war seems once more to be about to descend. It is the prayer that makes the drama sacred.[16]

O'Brien saw the UN's espousal of certain ideas and principles—peace, decolonization, multiracialism among them—as its most important contribution to international life. He conceded, however, that the UN drama swings from tragedy to farce and back again, with neither bathos nor buffoonery alien to it. Two decades after he wrote this, the sacred character of the UN's drama seems to be more in doubt than ever. True, the People's Republic of China became a member in 1971, since which time the UN's claims to near-universalism have had real substance. On the other hand, the last two decades have seen greater criticism than ever before (whether or not it is justified is another matter) of the supposed 'double standards' of UN General Assembly resolutions; a failure by numerous states to pay their dues to the organization; allegations that staff assigned to the UN have engaged in espionage; controversy over the activities (or inactivity) in certain regions of humanitarian agencies such as the UNHCR; sharp disagreements about the UN's handling of human rights questions, leading to the departure in 1982 of the Director of the UN Human Rights Centre, Theo van Boven; and even, from 1986 on, accusations that Kurt Waldheim, UN Secretary-General 1972–81, had been involved in war crimes when he was with German occupation forces in Greece and Yugoslavia during World War II. One could not write a book about the UN in the late 1980s and call it *Sacred Drama*.

Yet why is this so? The current crisis is very much like what

[16] Conor Cruise O'Brien, *The United Nations: Sacred Drama* (London, 1968), p. 11. The theatrical metaphor was also used by Hernane Tavares de Sá, *The Play within a Play: the Inside Story of the UN* (New York, 1966).

has gone before. The collective security system has been thought to be in crisis almost since the day of its inauguration.[17] Accusations of 'double standards' were already rife by the time of the Suez crisis.[18] The need to reform or strengthen the UN has been argued with passion since its inception.[19] The fixation with compiling 'balance sheets' of achievements, to which the UN is subject to an extent almost unparalleled in any political system, seems as immutable as the Charter.[20] The first two Secretaries-General both ended their service on almost intolerably bad terms with one of the superpowers. The USSR and other states withdrew their cooperation from WHO in the early 1950s. McCarthyism and accusations of espionage had both cast a shadow over the Secretariat by 1950.[21] The first financial crisis began well over a quarter of a century ago with UNEF and ONUC, and has still not been fully resolved.

One answer, perhaps, is that the fate of the UN is often seen as being bound up with perceptions of the UN in the USA and, to a much lesser extent, the UK. The ideals and diplomacy of these countries certainly had much to do with the creation of the UN. Their power and their financial contribution, although diminishing, remain important. But the disproportionate attention paid to attitudes in these countries as a barometer of the health of the UN is perhaps due most to the international dominance of the news media of these countries. There is little to applaud in the fact that judgements as to sacredness or profanity are so heavily influenced by opinion in any one country. The chapters below bear witness to the impact of US views of the UN, but they also point to developments which are prompting the

---

[17] Note, for example, the work of an experienced Belgian Ambassador to the UN: Fernand van Langenhove, *La Crise du système de securité collective des Nations Unies 1946–1957* (The Hague, 1958).

[18] One illustration is L.C. Green, 'The Double Standard of the United Nations', *Year Book of World Affairs*, 11 (1957), pp. 104–37. The author is principally concerned to indict the USA and India for embracing double standards in their responses to the British role in the Suez crisis.

[19] e.g. Commission to Study the Organization of Peace, *Strengthening the United Nations* (New York, 1957). See also the reform proposals cited by Maurice Bertrand in his chapter in this book.

[20] Note the similarities in approach between Sir Alexander Cadogan, 'The United Nations: A Balance Sheet', *Year Book of World Affairs*, 5 (1951), pp. 1–11, and Juliana G. Pilon, *The United States and the United Nations: A Balance Sheet* (Heritage Foundation, Washington, 1982).

[21] See generally Shirley Hazzard, *Defeat of an Ideal: A Study of the Self-Destruction of the United Nations* (Boston, 1973).

replacement of shrill anti-UN rhetoric by more balanced appraisals.

(c) Role in Proclaiming International Principles and Standards

Even if the drama is sometimes profane, the UN has by no means lost its importance as a proclaimer, and upholder, of international standards. The UN and its agencies have had a formidable role, contributing greatly to those elements of common culture which can be detected across almost all the divisions of the world. The idea that colonialism is illegitimate was greatly reinforced, and the decolonization process assisted, by the UN. The universalism of the institutions of international diplomacy, and the codification of the rules attached thereto, owe much to the UN. The considerable (though by no means total) agreement about what states exist, and what governments represent those states, is due in part to the role of the UN as an intergovernmental body which admits (or refuses to admit) states members, and examines the credentials of the representatives of those states. The degree of acceptance throughout the world of certain social goals—literacy and birth control among them—owes much, not just to the work of UN agencies, but to the international ethos which the UN has helped to create.

The centre-piece of the UN's proclamation of international principles and standards remains even today the Charter of 1945. We may not go all the way with Nagendra Singh's view, expressed in this volume, that there is no ground at all for criticism of the new principles embodied in the Charter. But the importance of the document is undeniable. Indeed, it is a unique feature of our present era to have virtually all the states of the world agreeing, at least in their public utterances, to a single set of principles of international life.

The UN Charter may be a single agreed set of principles, but there are different interpretations of it. This is inevitable with a text more than forty years old which is accepted by 159 states. Two key differences relate to two of the most perennially sensitive issues of international politics: the right of states to use force, and their right to involve themselves in 'human rights' or similar questions within the jurisdiction of other states.

Articles 2(4) and 51 of the UN Charter largely restrict the right of states to use force (other than under UN auspices) to one circumstance: individual or collective self-defence. In the past, this has usually been interpreted to mean that states have the right to use force when there is an attack on a member state's territory—and presumably only then. All this is derived from the idea, which is perhaps too simple, that readily discernible 'aggression' is the main cause of war, and that stopping aggression will stop all war. But reality has proved more complex, and the practice of states has consequently been influenced by the words of the Charter only to a limited extent.[22] The UN era has seen many cases of the use of force by states which do not easily conform with this standard of self-defence: uses of force in pursuit of territorial claims, or in anticipation of a possible attack, or to stop unwanted political developments within a so-called 'sphere of influence', or by way of reprisal, or to rescue victims of aircraft hi-jackings. In April 1986, when US aircraft bombed targets in Libya in response to terrorist attacks on US citizens overseas, it was claimed that the US was acting in self-defence in conformity with the UN Charter.[23] While other states protested this interpretation, it exemplified the continuing tendency of states to expand the scope of self-defence beyond the literal limits of Article 51.

There are also different interpretations of the UN Charter on the vexed question of the right of states and international bodies actively to interest themselves in matters relating to the treatment of individuals or groups within other states—a subject most often discussed under the heading of 'human rights'.[24]

[22] See the commentaries by M. Virally on Article 2(4), and A. Cassese on Article 51, in J.-P. Cot and A. Pellet (eds.), *La Charte des Nations Unies* (Paris, 1985), pp. 113–25 and 769–91. The relationship between rhetoric and practice is also examined in Hedley Bull (ed.), *Intervention in World Politics* (Oxford, 1984).

[23] Speech by Vernon Walters, US Ambassador to the UN, on 15 Apr. 1986 during a debate in the UN Security Council. On 21 Apr. 1986 France, the UK, and the USA vetoed a draft resolution which would have condemned the armed attack by the US (*UN Chronicle* (New York), 23, no. 4 (Aug. 1986), pp. 46–7). See also the article by Abraham D. Sofaer, Legal Adviser to the US State Department, 'Terrorism and the Law', *Foreign Affairs*, 64 (1986), at pp. 921–2.

[24] Contrast, for instance, H. Lauterpacht, *International Law and Human Rights* (London, 1950), with J. S. Watson, 'Autointerpretation, Competence, and the Continuing Validity of Article 2(7) of the UN Charter', *AJIL*, 71 (1977), p. 60. See also the Declaration on the Inadmissibility of Intervention in the Domestic Affairs of States and the Protection of their Independence and Sovereignty—GA Res. 2131 (XX) of 21 Dec. 1965.

This is one matter on which both the Charter itself and the relevant UN bodies have been caught in unavoidable ambiguity. On the one hand, there is the principle of non-interference in the internal affairs of other states: on the other hand, certain human rights principles are proclaimed which would seem, at the very least, to justify international criticism of certain governments on account of their conduct towards their citizens. Not surprisingly, some states put more emphasis on the inviolability of sovereignty, some on the inviolability of human rights. The conventional view of the matter is that it is the Eastern bloc and Third World states which stress the principles of sovereignty and non-interference, and the Western powers which are leading the move away from the concept of the absolute supremacy of sovereignty. There is some truth in this but, as Tom Farer points out in his chapter, in many ways it is not the whole truth.

UN standard-setting instruments, and the bodies charged with their implementation, have prompted a convergence of the public pronouncements of states in a common international rhetoric of human rights. To a much smaller extent this convergence is mirrored in domestic practice. It remains the case that, despite the existence of many purportedly definitive agreements on the subject, different societies have very different conceptions of the content and importance of human rights. These different conceptions, reflecting different national experiences, are not likely to change quickly.[25]

In addition to these different interpretations of the Charter's actual provisions, there are different views of its whole ethos. Some, particularly those steeped in constitutionalist domestic polities such as the US, are inclined to find the solution to problems of all sorts in the interpretation and reinterpretation of the Charter provisions. This organic view of an expanding and diversifying UN, founded on an ethos of continuous progress, is sustained by teleological interpretations of the original Charter language. Although far from dormant, especially as a means of

---

[25] See generally Aldeeb Abu-Sahlieh *et al.* (eds.), *Universalité des droits de l'homme et diversité des cultures* (Fribourg, 1984); John Humphrey, *Human Rights and the United Nations—A Great Adventure* (Dobbs Ferry, New York, 1984); Jack Donnelly, *The Concept of Human Rights* (London, 1985); R. J. Vincent, *Human Rights and International Relations* (Cambridge, 1986).

accommodating revisionist demands, this approach has lost momentum in recent years.

Others view the Charter as an incorrigibly idealistic document, for example, in its apparent assumption that there would be unanimity between the great powers. But the provision that the Security Council must operate on the basis of unanimity of its permanent members is not necessarily the product of impractical idealism: on the contrary, it reflects a highly realistic belief that UN action will not be possible if one of the great powers seriously dissents from it.[26] There are other respects, too, in which the Charter is upon closer inspection a notably hard-headed document.[27] For example, it is extremely cautious in what it says about disarmament; and it contains no reference at all to the well-defined, but highly problematic, principle of 'national self-determination', preferring instead the much vaguer formulation, 'equal rights and self-determination of peoples', which is less haunted by ghosts from Europe's history between the two world wars.[28] To some extent the Charter anticipated the growth of concern with economic and social matters, the advent of regional security organizations, and the process of decolonization. The memoirs of some of those who helped frame the Charter confirm that they knew what they were doing when, in ways such as these, they skilfully took account of changing realities while avoiding hitching the UN wagon too rigidly to unrealistic procedures or impossible ideals.[29]

[26] A permanent member of the Security Council can avoid having to make direct use of the veto power if it is sure that the proposal in question will not in any event obtain the requisite two-thirds majority. The Western states, in particular, were frequently able to use this tactic in the early years of the UN. The changing pattern of use of the veto as between the two superpowers is illustrated by Robert C. Johansen, 'The Reagan Administration and the UN: The Costs of Unilateralism', *World Policy Journal*, 3 (1986), p. 605: 1946–50—US 0, USSR 47; 1951–5—US 0, USSR 30; 1956–60—US 0, USSR 15; 1961–5—US 0, USSR 11; 1966–70—US 1, USSR 2; 1971–5—US 11, USSR 4; 1976–80—US 10, USSR 4; 1981–5—US 20, USSR 2.

[27] Note the remarks of Ian Brownlie, 'The United Nations as a Form of World Government', *Harvard International Law Journal*, 13 (1972), p. 421.

[28] See generally A. Rigo Sureda, *The Evolution of the Right to Self-Determination* (Leiden, 1973).

[29] The UN Charter provision for unanimity among the permanent members of the Security Council (the veto) was the result of extensive discussion, including at Dumbarton Oaks (Aug.–Oct. 1944) and Yalta (Feb. 1945). The evidence is that the UK, USA, USSR, and France all favoured the principle of unanimity, and that they were

Despite marked divergences in the interpretation of specific provisions and indeed of its whole ethos, the UN Charter does affect the behaviour of states. It has reinforced the idea that there is a strong presumption in most cases against the legitimacy of the uninvited use of force by a state outside its accepted international frontiers.[30] For example, the fact that in the years after 1973 there was no attempt by Western European countries, Japan, or the USA to seize oil resources on which they were heavily dependent, the price of which had increased phenomenally, is evidence not just of the possible adverse physical consequences which would have ensued, but also of the strength of the principle of non-intervention. It is certainly hard to answer positively the hypothetical question: In what previous era would such a situation not have resulted in interventions by some of these states?[31]

Perhaps the UN has sometimes been too rigid in its adherence to certain principles, including even non-intervention. The tendency of UN General Assembly resolutions in recent decades has been to condemn most invasions and occupations, irrespective of their motives or results. In the USA there was much criticism of the UN on account of its condemnation of the US-led invasion of Grenada in 1983.[32] This condemnation was not in essence an act of political partiality. Thus the UN has been even more critical of the Soviet intervention in Afghanistan since December 1979; and it has criticized the use of force by states from the Group of 77—by Argentina, for instance, in

motivated in this by a hard-headed concern to protect their own sovereign rights and national interest. See e.g. Winston S. Churchill, *The Second World War*, vol. 6, *Triumph and Tragedy* (London, 1954), pp. 181–2 and 308–13; Harry S. Truman, *Year of Decisions: 1945* (London, 1955), pp. 194–5, 201, and 206–7; Charles de Gaulle, *War Memoirs: Salvation 1944–1946—Documents*, tr. Murchie and Erskine (London, 1960), pp. 94–5. Truman, who became President of the USA in Apr. 1945, went so far as to write in his memoirs: 'All our experts, civil and military, favoured it, and without such a veto no arrangement would have passed the Senate' (p. 207).

[30] UN practice also evinces doubt about the legitimacy of large-scale uses of force even where an invitation has been issued by the government concerned. See Louise Doswald-Beck, 'The Legal Validity of Military Intervention by Invitation of the Government', *British Year Book of International Law 1985*, pp. 198–252.

[31] Although the so-called Kissinger doctrine did foreshadow the possibility of intervention to protect supplies vital to Western security, no such intervention ensued, at least until the exceptional naval involvements in the Gulf in 1987.

[32] The armed intervention in Grenada was deplored as 'a flagrant violation of international law' in GA Res. 38/7 of 2 Nov. 1983.

the Falklands/Malvinas invasion.[33] Rather, it seems to have reflected a view widely held in the international community that force should be avoided wherever possible, and the UN should not rush to applaud even good consequences of the use of force. This idea, that there should be a taboo on the use of force, or at least on its first use, is thoroughly understandable in a world which is grossly over-armed. But it may be that the UN as a body, and its member states, could give more thought both to the facts of each case under discussion, and to the general circumstances in which some kinds of interventions may be, if not desirable, at least defensible.[34]

Although the UN has tended to deplore most uses of force, it has in any case, and quite unavoidably, got caught up in many of the complexities which surround the whole question of the use of force in international relations. For example, the UN may condemn what is seen by a majority as a first or illegitimate use of force; but this very condemnation may, consciously or otherwise, give some encouragement to the use of counter-force. Thus the UN's criticisms of military incursions—for example, the Israeli occupation of Arab territories since 1967, the Soviet intervention in Afghanistan after 1979, and the Argentine invasion of the Falkland Islands in 1982—have all in their way had the effect of lending some legitimacy to the subsequent armed struggles to reverse these interventions. Furthermore, the implicit endorsement by the UN of such principles of justice as the retrocession of colonial enclaves may have encouraged certain decisions to resort to force. Thus preoccupation with principles by no means leads inevitably to a reduction in the use of force. On the contrary, it may (whether rightly or wrongly) help justify certain uses of force: and part of the concern about developments in the UN in the 1970s and 1980s was due to a fear that this was indeed proving to be so.

[33] See e.g. GA Res. 2 (ES-VI) of 14 Jan. 1980, on Afghanistan; and SC Res. 502 of 3 Apr. 1982 on the Falklands/Malvinas. On the relative impartiality of General Assembly criticism of users of force see Franck, *Nation Against Nation*, n. 4 above, pp. 224–31.

[34] For a discussion of the problems concerning the legitimacy of humanitarian intervention see R. Lillich (ed.), *Humanitarian Intervention and the United Nations* (London, 1973); Thomas Franck and Nigel Rodley, 'After Bangladesh: the Law of Humanitarian Intervention by Military Force', *American Journal of International Law*, 67 (1973), p. 275; Michael Akehurst, 'Humanitarian Intervention' in H. Bull (ed.), *Intervention in World Politics* (Oxford, 1984), pp. 95–118.

The UN has sometimes been involved in the advocacy of principles which are undefined, contradictory, or hotly controversial. One example relates to the principles which were recognized in the charter and judgment of the International Military Tribunal at Nuremberg in 1945–6, at which German war criminals were convicted. On 11 December 1946 the UN General Assembly unanimously adopted a resolution affirming these Nuremberg principles. However, subsequent attempts by the International Law Commission and other bodies to define exactly what these principles are have not gained general acceptance by states, partly no doubt because of the sensitivity of states about recognizing the legitimacy of disobeying superior orders.[35]

Another example of the difficulties for the UN in developing and espousing coherent principles has been in connection with an age-old question of international law and relations: In what circumstances are people entitled to engage in armed struggle against an existing state? And in what circumstances may other states assist such rebels? There are no neat general answers to these questions, and states have traditionally been careful (though far from consistently so) in guarding their monopoly of the right to use force.[36] The UN, due largely to the advent of new Third World members who were naturally critical of certain offspring of European colonialism, went a long way in the 1970s towards recognizing the legitimacy of the use of force by non-state bodies. Thus in 1970 the General Assembly approved the 'Declaration on Principles of International Law Concerning Friendly Relations and Cooperation Among States in Accord-

---

[35] The affirmation of the principles of international law recognized at Nuremberg is in GA Res. 95(I) of 11 Dec. 1946. The International Law Commission's formulation of the Nuremberg principles is in *Yearbook of the International Law Commission*, 1950, vol. 2, pp. 374–8. The General Assembly's non-committal response to this formulation is in GA Res. 488 (V) of 12 Dec. 1950. On the subsequent history of this issue see also *Yearbook of the International Law Commission*, 1954, vol. 2, pp. 150–2; and GA Res. 897 (IX) of 4 Dec. 1954.

[36] Questions related to the use of force by non-state groups are discussed in John Norton Moore (ed.), *Law and Civil War in the Modern World* (Baltimore, 1974); Michael Bothe, Karl Partsch, and Waldemar Solf, *New Rules for Victims of Armed Conflicts: Commentary on the Two 1977 Protocols Additional to the Geneva Conventions of 1949* (The Hague, 1982), pp. 36–52 and 232–58; Michel Veuthey, *Guérilla et Droit Humanitaire* (2nd edn., Geneva, 1983); J. A. Barberis, 'Nouvelles questions concernant la personalité juridique internationale', *Recueil des Cours*, 179 (1983), pp. 145–304.

ance with the Charter of the U N' which contained the remarkable formula:

Every State has the duty to refrain from any forcible action which
deprives peoples . . . of their right to self-determination and freedom
and independence. In their actions against, and resistance to, such
forcible action in pursuit of the exercise of their right to self-determination, such peoples are entitled to seek and to receive support in
accordance with the purposes and principles of the Charter.[37]

The problem with such a formulation is not that it is flawed in
its application to every case—plainly it is not—but rather (a) it is
worded so generally that it could be seen as legitimizing almost
any rebellion in the name of self-determination; (b) it says
nothing about whether any restraints, including laws of war
rules, should govern the methods used in self-determination
struggles—a highly topical question in an age of terrorism; and
(c) it appears to be in conflict with another statement earlier in
the same Declaration:

Every State has the duty to refrain from organizing, instigating, assisting or participating in acts of civil strife or terrorist acts in another State
or acquiescing in organized activities within its territory directed
towards the commission of such acts, when the acts referred to in the
present paragraph involve a threat or use of force.

The differences of view on this point, leading to the enunciation of apparently contradictory principles, were not
confined to this 1970 document. Exactly the same criticisms can
also be made of the 1974 Definition of Aggression.[38] The UN
seemed to be going a long way in encouraging self-determination struggles. For example, the Palestine Liberation
Organization was one of several national liberation movements
accorded observer status in the General Assembly and in other
UN-sponsored conferences in 1974.[39] The UN's pro-PLO
stance was confirmed in 1975 when the General Assembly

---

[37] This Declaration was approved by, and annexed to, GA Res. 2625 (XXV) of
24 Oct. 1970.
[38] The Definition of Aggression was approved by, and annexed to, GA Res. 3314
(XXIX) of 14 Dec. 1974. See especially Articles 3(g) and 7.
[39] GA Res. 3237 (XXIX) of 22 Nov. 1974. Already on 13 Nov. 1974 the PLO Chairman, Mr Yasser Arafat, had addressed the UN General Assembly: with the exception of
Pope Paul in 1965, he was the first such person not representing the government of a UN
member state to do so.

passed a resolution equating Zionism with 'racism and racial discrimination'.[40] These developments, justifiable as they may have been in the eyes of many, cast doubt on the independence and impartiality of the UN, and contributed greatly to the subsequent criticisms of the organization in the USA and elsewhere.[41] However, in recent years the UN has mitigated some of the concomitants of its stance, especially through its increasing criticism of international terrorism.[42]

Although it has been embroiled in controversy on matters to do with the principles it espouses, as well as in other areas of its activities, the UN has by no means lost either its own legitimacy, or its capacity to confer legitimacy.[43] Participation in UN activities has helped confer legitimacy on new states which might otherwise be uncertain of their status; on particular regimes within states; and on certain non-state entities, such as the Palestine Liberation Organization and the African National Congress.[44] UN endorsement lends legitimacy to doctrines and ideas, as with those concerning development assistance, the 'common heritage of mankind' in the deep sea-bed and outer space, and the formal equality (however limited) among sovereign states. UN endorsement may also legitimize compromise

[40] GA Res. 3379 (XXX) of 10 Nov. 1975.

[41] See e.g. Moynihan, *A Dangerous Place*, n. 3 above, pp. 181–205.

[42] UN efforts to achieve consensus on aspects of terrorism include GA Res. 3166 (XXVIII) of 14 Dec. 1973, adopting the text of the 1973 Convention on the Protection and Punishment of Crimes against Internationally Protected Persons, including Diplomatic Agents, (which entered into force on 20 Feb. 1977); GA Res. 34/146 of 17 Dec. 1979, approving the text of the 1979 International Convention Against the Taking of Hostages (which entered into force on 3 June 1983); and GA Res. 40/61 of 9 Dec. 1985, in which the General Assembly 'condemns as criminal all acts, methods and practices of terrorism wherever and by whomever committed'.

[43] An early study of the importance of the UN's role in conferring legitimacy is Inis Claude, 'Collective Legitimization as a Political Function of the United Nations', *International Organization*, 20 (1966), p. 367.

[44] National liberation movements recognized by the Organization of African Unity or the League of Arab States were granted observer status in the UN Conference on the Representation of States in Their Relations with International Organizations by the General Assembly 'in accordance with the practice of the United Nations'—GA Res. 3247 (XXIX) of 29 Nov. 1974. Numerous other resolutions and administrative decisions also confer status on such groups: the African National Congress (ANC), the PLO, the Pan-Africanist Congress of Azania (PAC), and the South West Africa People's Organization (SWAPO) were permitted, for instance, to sign the Final Act of the Third UN Conference on the Law of the Sea in 1982, though not to sign the Convention accompanying it. The UN Council for Namibia, as a UN creation, has greater formal status within the UN than, for instance, SWAPO.

solutions reached in particular international disputes and crises—a point developed in Anthony Parsons' chapter.

The UN serves an important function in shaping the international agenda, and in both facilitating and conditioning the articulation of new political demands. The necessities of coalition maintenance may lead to compromises, or to the agglomeration of demands in such grand abstractions as the 'New World Information and Communication Order'.[45] In many respects this agenda-setting function may be more important than the UN's role in the making and implementation of binding decisions.[46]

(d) Innovations in UN Practice

In many ways the UN has, in the course of forty years, gone beyond the confines of the Charter. Indeed, in matters relating to war and peace it has gone so far that it would be wrong to evaluate the UN's achievements exclusively with reference to the Charter's terms. This is particularly true so far as two related matters—peacekeeping forces, and the role of the Secretary-General—are concerned.

Peacekeeping forces, in the form in which they have developed, were not envisaged in the Charter. Yet especially since 1956, with the deployment of the UN Emergency Force (UNEF I) at the end of the Suez War, such forces have become a regular part of international life: perhaps the most conspicuous single physical manifestation of the UN's role in the world. These forces generally consist of separate national contingents carrying out, in the name of the UN, such tasks as the monitoring of cease-fires, observation of frontier lines, interposition between belligerents, and the maintenance of government and public order. Such forces have been used in international conflicts (as between Israel and its neighbours), and in internal conflicts with international complications (as in the Congo and Cyprus).

Although there has been a notable need for these forces, one cannot avoid being struck by the limited scope of their application. In almost all cases they have been used to tackle

---

[45] See Clare Wells, *The UN, UNESCO and the Politics of Knowledge* (London, 1987).
[46] See generally M.J. Peterson, *The General Assembly in World Politics* (Boston, 1986).

problems which have arisen in the wake of European decolonization. They have not yet been used in the central areas of
direct East–West rivalry—having had absolutely no role, for
example, in Hungary in 1956, in Czechoslovakia in 1968, in
Indo-China in all its upheavals since 1945, or in the various
conflicts in the Central American isthmus.

The results of UN peacekeeping efforts have been distinctly
limited. To mention just a few cases of controversy and failure:
in 1967, Secretary-General U Thant felt obliged to accede to the
Egyptian government's request for the withdrawal of UNEF,
even though it was widely understood that this action was a pro-
logue to the war between Israel and Egypt in June of that year; in
Lebanon, the presence of UN forces was unable to stop either
the country's slide into anarchy and communal warfare, or the
Israeli invasion in 1982. In Cyprus, the UN forces which existed
to keep the peace between the Greek and Turkish communities
could not prevent external involvement in that communal
conflict, culminating in the 1974 Turkish invasion of northern
Cyprus.

The cost of peacekeeping forces looms large in comparison to
the UN's regular budget. It is estimated that expenditures by
the UN on UNEF I (1956–67) were US $220 million, on UNEF
II (1973–9) $446 million, on the UN Operation in the Congo
(1960–4) $400 million. Total expenditure until 1984 on the five
forces still in place (UNTSO, UNDOF, and UNIFIL in the
Middle East, UNFICYP in Cyprus, and UNMOGIP in
Kashmir) was almost $2,400 million and rising.[47] Since the early
1980s some UN peacekeeping activities have been hampered by
severe financial crises, and more recently it also appears that the
demand for them has (perhaps temporarily) declined. However,
some of the *ersatz* substitutes in the 1980s for UN peacekeeping
forces have proven less successful and less enduring: witness the
short-lived and unlamented four-country Multi-National Force
in Lebanon in 1982–4.

Despite these limitations, the UN's peacekeeping activities
remain one of the most significant innovations of the organization, and their importance should not be discounted. In many
matters to do with security, success is by definition almost

[47] United Nations, *The Blue Helmets: A Review of United Nations Peace-keeping* (New York, 1985), pp. 329–50.

unnoticed—and UN forces have had their successes, not least in helping to isolate conflicts from East–West rivalry. In the future there is not likely to be any shortage of occasions calling for the use of peacekeeping forces—whether or not under UN auspices.

The role of the Secretary-General has also developed very significantly since 1945. In their respective chapters, both Javier Pérez de Cuéllar and Thomas Franck show clearly how the Secretary-General has taken on—or has had forced upon him—a wide range of functions: fact-finding, mediating in disputes between states, and responding to rapidly moving crises in which other UN bodies, because of the pace of events, have only limited possibilities of doing anything.

In many other ways, too, the UN system has moved significantly beyond its original form and purposes. The advent of so many Third World states to UN membership in the 1960s had the effect, not just of undermining the previous Western dominance within the organization, but also of focusing attention on issues which had previously been soft-pedalled. As Kenneth Dadzie shows, economic development is one such issue, but the UN's handling of it has been subject to many of the same vicissitudes and disappointments as have plagued the UN—a mixture of proposals for utopian solutions, piety and reproachful looks covering gaps between expectation and reality, and the uncontrolled intrusion of political interests largely extraneous to development issues.

The imagery of a republican dethronement of the West has been especially evident in UNESCO. Some in the English-speaking West discerned an element of parricide when an organization founded on what was thought to be a uniquely Western vision came to embrace 'anti-Western' values. The withdrawal of the US and the UK in 1984–5 appeared as an attempt to deny the inheritance on these grounds, but the collective concerns of the broader 'Geneva group' of Western countries concentrated on administrative and budgetary issues. With Soviet and some Third World support, these countries succeeded in 1987 in ousting Director-General M'Bow.

(e) Is the UN Indispensable?

There are many major problems in contemporary international relations to which, for one reason or another, the UN is of distinctly limited relevance. For example, it has played little or no part in mediating or controlling any of the several serious disputes between communist states. Even on issues which the UN has addressed, its role should not be exaggerated, especially as in many cases there are other institutions and procedures available.

Over centuries, states have devised numerous means of harmonizing their interests, mitigating their conflicts, or at least preventing disputes from leading to total war. True, these means have been far from perfect—witness the outbreak of two world wars in this century. But many of the functions which the UN performs can be—and sometimes are—performed also by other entities. If the UN has mediated in some disputes, it is also true that in other conflicts other mediators or arbitrators have been used: for example, in 1979–84 it was papal mediation which settled the long-standing Beagle Channel dispute between Argentina and Chile.[48] If UN peacekeeping forces have been used in some conflicts, non-UN forces have helped settle other long-standing problems: for example, the Commonwealth forces which monitored the elections and transfer of power in Zimbabwe in 1980 following the Lancaster House agreement of the previous year. If the UN has contributed notably to the development of international law, it is also true that this body of law is very much older than the UN, is well rooted in the overlapping interests of states, develops outside as well as within UN auspices, and would continue to exist even if the UN were to disappear tomorrow.[49] If states have on occasion paid a high political price for ignoring UN principles and procedures (as the USSR did over Korea in June 1950), in many other cases the

[48] For a succinct summary of the papal mediation between Argentina and Chile see *Keesing's Contemporary Archives*, 1984, p. 32781; and 1985, p. 33517.

[49] Evidence of the vitality of legal development outside the UN framework may be gleaned, for instance, by reference to the fact that the four Geneva Conventions on the protection of victims of war, concluded by states under the auspices of the International Committee of the Red Cross rather than the UN, had 165 parties of 31 Dec. 1986—more than the total membership of the.UN. The work of The Hague Conference on Private International Law, of the Commonwealth, and of regional intergovernmental organizations may also be cited in this context. In *International Law in a Divided World* (Oxford, 1986), Antonio Cassese identifies a traditional 'Westphalia model' and a new 'UN Charter model' of international law (pp. 396–407), but finds that at present 'international law possesses two souls, and the second seems incapable of supplanting the first' (p. 4).

political restraints on state behaviour have operated quite independently of the UN.

In our own time, many states and groups of states have achieved a degree of stability in their international relations by means which have little to do with the UN. Many regional organizations, whether of a political, economic, or military character, have proved remarkably successful. Numerous governments, whether in NATO, the Warsaw Pact, South Asia, or elsewhere, are inclined to attribute the security they have enjoyed in the post-1945 period more to their individual or collective possession of military power, including even nuclear weapons in some cases, than to any benign influence of the UN.

However, the UN's historical role should properly be seen, not as a means of supplanting power politics, but rather as a means of complementing them, modifying them, and mitigating some of their worst effects. For example, it may well be true that the degree of peace which has prevailed in Europe since 1945 has owed something at least to the existence of nuclear weapons, but it is also true that the rival alliances in Europe have been made ethically defensible and more politically practicable by their treaty obligations, consciously reflecting the language of the UN Charter, to use force only in accord with Charter principles and procedures.

If this view of the UN's role contains at least a grain of truth, it does not mean that the UN is consigned for ever to a restricted scope of activity. On the contrary, the UN has already played a major part in establishing the universalism of certain principles and practices—a role which will no doubt continue. In addition to its many other functions in international society, there are obvious possibilities for it to expand its involvement in various activities to which a multilateral approach is especially suitable. These activities might well include, despite certain obvious difficulties, further measures for the prevention or control of pollution and environmental degradation, of certain forms of terrorism, and of the international trade in narcotics.

The deep crisis in which the UN has been plunged in the late 1980s may make proposals for an expanded role seem arcane. The budgetary crisis was only temporarily alleviated by the adoption of General Assembly resolution 41/213 of 19 December 1986 which set up a system of consensual decision-making on budgetary recommendations. Subsequent withholdings of assessed contributions, mainly by the USA, exacerbated the crisis and threatened to restrict the leverage of Western states seeking reform.

Nevertheless, the need for reform is widely acknowledged. In this book, Maurice Bertrand outlines an ambitious programme of reform, based on a very frank assessment of the organization's failures. Whether or not all his proposals can be implemented—and he insists that outside pressure will be necessary if they are to be—there is no doubt that the UN is in the process of changing, not least because of changes in the attitudes of its member states. As Evan Luard shows, the American complaint of a decade ago that the UN was dominated by an anti-Western Third World 'automatic majority' was always simplistic, and is now scarcely tenable. One might go further, and say that the UN's principal critics, the Western powers, have considerable opportunities at the UN for extending their influence while strengthening the roles and utility of the UN, provided they are prepared to embrace intellectually coherent and energetic policies to this end.[50]

Moreover, there have been some preliminary signs of Soviet willingness to countenance a wider range of positive cooperative activities within the UN. This was evidenced in General Secretary Gorbachev's sweeping proposals, launched in September 1987, for an increased role for the UN;[51] in Soviet Foreign Minister Shevardnadze's speech to the General Assembly in the same month; and in the Soviet Union's pledges to pay off its arrears in UN contributions, including those

[50] One such strategy for the US is enunciated by Franck, *Nation Against Nation*, n. 4 above, especially pp. 246–72.

[51] Mikhail Gorbachev, 'Reality and the Guarantees of a Secure World', *Pravda*, Moscow, 17 September 1987. In this long article the Soviet leader suggested *inter alia* setting up 'under the aegis of the UN a mechanism for extensive international verification of compliance with agreements to lessen international tension, limit arms and monitor the military situation in areas of conflict'. He proposed wider use of 'UN military observers and UN peacekeeping forces in disengaging the troops of warring sides and monitoring cease-fire.and armistice agreements'. With reference to the International Court of Justice, he said: 'The General Assembly and Security Council could approach it more often for consultative conclusions on international legal disputes. Its mandatory jurisdiction should be recognised by all on mutually agreed conditions.' This last statement, if ever translated into policy, would entail an important modification to a long-held Soviet unwillingness to submit to compulsory jurisdiction.

relating to peacekeeping. A possibility of greater East–West cooperation within the UN system was indicated by the consensus of the five Permanent Members of the Security Council in at least agreeing a form of words in resolution 598 of 20 July 1987 demanding a cease-fire in the Iran–Iraq war; and, in the symbolically important field of electoral politics, by the election in late 1987 of Federico Mayor to the post of UNESCO Director-General in lieu of Amadou Mahtar M'Bow.

'The tents have been struck, and the great caravan of humanity is once again on the march.' So said Jan Christian Smuts in 1919, at the time of the founding of the League of Nations.[52] It is tempting to dismiss such views as merely part of the inflated rhetoric which international organizations seem so often to attract. Yet the UN in particular is remarkable in several respects. The late Professor Hedley Bull, in a memorandum written shortly before his death in 1985 proposing the course of lectures on which the present work is based, drew attention to 'the achievements of the UN in the role of bringing about change in international law and institutions. This has been central to the survival of the conception of an international society that is universal. The idea of the universality of mankind has been preserved by the changes in international law brought about by the UN system.' One may agree with him that the sovereign state is here to stay; that, with or without the UN, the collectivity of states should be seen as forming some kind of society; and that the divisions of the world will endure.[53] But in our divided world, there is a need for an institution which can in some way, however imperfectly, articulate the twin ideas of a universal international society and the cosmopolitan universality of mankind.

[52] Quoted by R. N. Stromberg, 'The Idea of Collective Security', *Journal of the History of Ideas*, 17 (1956), p. 251.

[53] The concept of a global international society is examined in Hedley Bull, *The Anarchical Society* (London, 1977); and Hedley Bull and Adam Watson (eds.), *The Expansion of International Society* (Oxford, 1984).

2

The United Nations and International Security

MICHAEL HOWARD

THE concept of 'international security' implies a common interest in security transcending the particular interests of sovereign states. The recognition of that common interest carries with it the aspiration to create a communal framework to replace the need for unilateral national security measures. That aspiration had led the victorious powers, under the determined leadership of President Wilson, to create in 1919 a League of Nations whose collective action would provide for the security of each of its several members. The failure of the League to achieve that goal was taken by Anglo-Saxon political leaders in the Second World War as a reason, not to abandon the concept, but to try again.

(a) The System of the UN Charter

From the very outset the establishment of a new framework for international security was seen as the United Nations' primary task. President Roosevelt in particular welcomed the creation of the United Nations as the beginning of a new international order:

It spells—and it ought to spell—the end of the system of unilateral action, exclusive alliances, and spheres of influence, and balances of power, and all the other expedients which have been tried for centuries and always failed.[1]

That was certainly the intention of its founders. As early as November 1943 the representatives of Britain, the USA, the

[1] Quoted in Brian Urquhart, 'The Role of the UN in Maintaining and Improving International Security' (Alastair Buchan Memorial Lecture), *Survival*, 28 (Sept.–Oct. 1986), p. 388.

Soviet Union, and China promulgated a Declaration on General Security in which they recognized 'the necessity of establishing at the earliest practicable date a general international organization . . . for the maintenance of international peace and security'.[2] When the Charter came to be drafted, the Preamble committed the signatories to unite their 'strength to maintain international peace and security, and to ensure . . . that armed force shall not be used, save in the common interest'. And Article 1 of the Charter, on the purposes of the United Nations, begins:

To maintain international peace and security, and to that end: to take effective collective measures for the prevention and removal of threats to the peace, and for the suppression of acts of aggression or other breaches of the peace, and to bring about by peaceful means, and in conformity with the principles of justice and international law, adjustment or settlement of international disputes or situations which might lead to a breach of the peace.

Only later in Article 1 does the Charter speak of:

international cooperation in solving international problems of an economic, social, cultural, or humanitarian character, and in promoting and encouraging respect for human rights . . .

The term 'collective security' was not used: it smelled of the failures of the 1930s. But the same intention was expressed in the phrase 'to unite our strength to maintain international peace and security'. The assumptions underlying this declaration of intent deserve examination. In the first place, there was no hint of supranationalism. The sovereign state was still the building-block of the international order. The functioning of the system depended on the goodwill of its members. Secondly, a basic cultural and ideological compatibility was assumed to exist among those states, sufficient at least to make it possible to proceed by consensus. Thirdly, there was assumed a willingness on the part of the signatories, however powerful they might be and however circumstances might alter, never unilaterally to use force to defend their own interests. Finally, and most important, a general and equal interest was assumed in the preservation of the *status quo post bellum*. Change would be possible, but

[2] US Department of State, *Towards the Peace Documents* (Publication 2298, 1945), p. 6.

only by general consent. The post-war world was conceived, in fact, in somewhat static terms.

The settlement resembled that of 1814 in that it visualized a continuing coalition of the victorious powers to maintain the settlement created by their victory. It resembled that of 1918 to the extent that it recognized that new states might come into being, and that they should be made members of the club when they did. But executive power was firmly entrusted to those with the capacity to use it. The Security Council was basically a condominium of the victorious major Allies, who would jointly keep the rest in order. The General Assembly might hold discussions and make recommendations and call matters to the attention of the Security Council, but it had no power of decision for action. It was a *parlement*, rather than a Parliament. Article 39 of the Charter placed responsibility for action firmly on the Security Council:

The Security Council shall determine the existence of any threat to the peace, breach of the peace, or act of aggression and shall make recommendations, or decide what measures shall be taken . . . to maintain or restore international peace and security.

The core of the Charter lay in Chapter VII: 'Action with Respect to Threats to the Peace, Breaches of the Peace, and Acts of Aggression'—the 'teeth' which the League of Nations was deemed to have lacked. The Security Council was empowered, if it thought fit, to call upon the members of the United Nations to apply sanctions short of war; and if these failed, to 'take such action by air, sea, or land forces as may be necessary to maintain or restore international peace and security'. Members undertook to make available such forces or facilities as were required, and to 'hold immediately available national air-force contingents for combined international enforcement action'. (Bombing was evidently foreseen as the most effective means of deterring or punishing aggressors.) A Military Staff Committee, consisting of the Chiefs of Staff of the permanent members of the Security Council, stood ready to advise and assist.

(b) Changes in UN Practice and Assumptions

We all know what happened. The Military Staff Committee disagreed at once over the question, what kind of force was required and whether each member should provide the same size of contingent, and rapidly became a non-entity. In 1950 the procedure described in the Charter was put into effect to deal with the invasion of South Korea by North Korea; but this was feasible only because the Soviet Union was at the time boycotting the Security Council for its refusal to seat a representative from the People's Republic of China in place of the sitting member representing Chiang Kai-shek. When the Russians resumed their place they effectively prevented any further action. Their veto was circumvented on 3 November 1950 when the Western powers, by securing the passage of the 'Uniting for Peace' resolution in the General Assembly, created a new role for a General Assembly in which they commanded, and believed that they would continue to command, a majority supporting their views. This 'Uniting for Peace' resolution stated:

If the Security Council, because of lack of unanimity of the permanent members, fails to exercise its primary responsibility for the maintenance of international peace and security in any case where there appears to be a threat to peace, breach of the peace, or act of aggression, the General Assembly shall consider the matter immediately with a view to making appropriate recommendations to Members for collective measures, including in the case of a breach of the peace or acts of aggression the use of armed force when necessary, to maintain or restore international peace and security. If not in session at the time, the General Assembly may meet in emergency special session within twenty-four hours of the request therefor. Such emergency special session may be called if requested by the Security Council on the vote of any seven members, or by a majority of the Members of the United Nations.

All members of the General Assembly were asked to hold armed forces ready for action, available even if not formally called upon by the Security Council.[3]

This expedient, which was never accepted as legitimate by the

[3] GA Res. 377 (V) of 3 Nov. 1950. See also H.G. Nicholas, *The United Nations as a Political Institution* (3rd edn., Oxford, 1967), p. 53.

Soviet Union, implicitly acknowledged that the original concept expressed in the Charter, of international security being maintained by consensus among the Great Powers, was unworkable, as indeed it had proved after 1815; and replaced it by the use of a majority of votes to overrule a dissident minority. But ironically the next time it was used—and the occasion of its most spectacular success—was when, six years later, it was employed against two of its original sponsors, Britain and France, after they had vetoed any action by the Security Council over their attack on Egypt in 1956. The General Assembly then called for an immediate cease-fire, and the withdrawal of forces from the Suez Canal. Britain, followed by France, acquiesced; less out of any respect for or fear of the united strength of the United Nations than because of the effective economic muscle of the United States. But a similar and nearly simultaneous resolution by the General Assembly calling upon the Soviet Union to withdraw its forces from Hungary was ignored, and no action followed. This was not simply because France and Britain were 'persuadable' in a way that the Soviet Union was not. It was because in the case of the Soviet Union the UN did not dare do more than try to persuade, and the Russians knew it.

The lessons of 1956 were clear. First, the UN could take action against 'aggression' only if the two great powers were agreed, or if one of them was indifferent; second, there were only two powers who counted. So it has remained. Whatever resolutions may be passed in the General Assembly, the UN is no more likely to take action against the Soviet Union over, say, Afghanistan than it is against the United States over Nicaragua. Whatever measures of collective security may be created, the superpowers can effectively defy them, and any state enjoying the vigorous support of either can probably do the same.

Within a few years a further and even more significant development was to occur. The Assembly became at least as ready to 'unite for peace' against the United States as it was against the Soviet Union, if not more so. Whereas in the first ten years of its existence the General Assembly had a built-in majority hostile to the Soviet Union, the great influx of new members from the 'Third World' has produced a majority at least potentially hostile to the United States. The United States can no longer expect the Assembly automatically to endorse its policies; but though the Soviet Union may build up or exploit declaratory majorities against the United States, there can be no outcome from resolutions passed against the most powerful country in the world. The result has been to reduce the General Assembly to eloquent impotence, the more impotent among its members tending to be the most eloquent. With the General Assembly powerless and the Security Council deadlocked, an utterly disproportionate weight of responsibility falls on the shoulders of the third element in the structure, the Secretariat, and in particular the Secretary-General, who becomes the scapegoat for the shortcomings of the organization as a whole.

But of more fundamental importance than changes in the balance and structure of the UN has been the change which has occurred since 1945 in assumptions about the nature of international society. We have seen how the founding fathers of the UN visualized an essentially static world system: one incrementally developing through peaceful change but in which 'peace and security' implied the maintenance of a status quo which only 'aggressors' (criminals whose motivation was irrelevant) would disturb. Korea (1950) fitted neatly into this pattern. Suez and Hungary (1956) did not. Both the latter were unilateral actions by major powers to *preserve* a status quo threatened by disruptive and apparently irreversible change. The Soviet Union succeeded in re-establishing the status quo; Britain and France failed. But in the world that was taking shape in the 1950s, the colonial structure of the late 1940s was the last thing that the majority of states wanted to preserve. For the newly created nations—and even more, those still aspiring to nationhood—the world was dynamic rather than static. Peace was to be sought not in the maintenance of order but in the securing of justice. It was something to be achieved, if necessary fought for, rather than preserved.

The problem of reconciling this view with the world picture implicit in the Charter can be seen in the Declaration in the Final Document which emerged from the first special session of the General Assembly on disarmament in June 1978. This reiterated the obligations of the Charter with respect to

refraining from the threat or use of force against the sovereignty, territorial integrity or political independence of any state, but added

or against peoples under colonial or foreign domination seeking to exercise their right to self-determination and to achieve independence. (Emphasis added.)[4]

Here we have, simultaneously, an adjuration against the use of force, and an innovatory adumbration of the principles of the Just War. The attempts forcibly to prevent 'justifiable' changes in the status quo are equated with attempts, on another level, to disturb the status quo—two conflicting concepts of the nature of peace which are inherently almost impossible to reconcile.

(c) The Requirements of International Peace and Security

In such a world, what can 'international peace and security' really mean, and what part can the UN play in maintaining it? There are, surely, two minimal requirements. First, there is the prevention of armed conflict and the peaceful resolution of disputes between major powers; and, second, there is the containment, failing the reconciliation, of regional conflicts, to prevent them from escalating to the point where they might affect global stability. Let us examine each of these in turn.

1. Great power relations, and arms regulation

Relations between the major powers must inevitably be a matter of direct intercourse between them, however much others may oil the wheels by provision of mediation and general good offices. The creation of the United Nations in 1945 did not prevent the major powers from continuing to deal directly with one another on matters of primary importance to themselves. Nor, when those negotiations became soured by mutual suspicion, did it prevent them from seeking security in all the old expedients of alliances, armaments, and balance of power which the UN had been intended to replace. Such measures were indeed legitimized under Article 51 of the Charter, which specified 'the inherent right of individual or collective self-defence if an armed attack occurs against a Member of the United Nations'; but this was seen as a purely interim expedient

---

[4] Quoted in *The United Nations and Disarmament 1945-1985* (UN Department for Disarmament Affairs, New York, 1985), p. 6.

'until the Security Council has taken measures necessary to maintain international peace and security'. However, the interim nature of those measures was quickly lost to sight, and states have continued to make such provision for their own security as lies in their power.

It is true, however, that the security arrangements of the post-1945 world have been made compatible with the principles of the UN, especially in their emphasis on collective defence, and on the idea that defence is the only legitimate basis for the use of force. This is evident in the 1949 North Atlantic Treaty and the 1955 Warsaw Treaty, which refer in almost identical terms to UN Charter provisions. Both treaties begin with an acceptance of the principles of peaceful settlement of disputes and non-use of force contained in Articles 2(3) and 2(4) of the UN Charter. Both treaties also echo the provisions of Articles 51 and 52 on self-defence and regional arrangements. For example, Article 5 of the North Atlantic Treaty (which is closely mirrored in Article 4 of the Warsaw Treaty) states:

The Parties agree that an armed attack against one or more of them in Europe or North America shall be considered an attack against them all, and consequently they agree that, if such an armed attack occurs, each of them, in exercise of the right of individual or collective self-defence recognized by Article 51 of the Charter of the United Nations, will assist the Party or Parties so attacked by taking forthwith, individually and in concert with the other Parties, such action as it deems necessary, including the use of armed force, to restore and maintain the security of the North Atlantic area.

Any such armed attack and all measures taken as a result thereof shall immediately be reported to the Security Council. Such measures shall be terminated when the Security Council has taken the measures necessary to restore and maintain international peace and security.[5]

Regional security arrangements and UN Charter language generally have also been invoked in many collective military interventions, including in the Dominican Republic in 1965 and in Czechoslovakia in 1968. All this may be no more than lip-

---

[5] The text of the 1949 North Atlantic Treaty is in the *United Nations Treaty Series*, vol. 34, p. 243. The text of the 1955 Warsaw Treaty is in ibid., vol. 219, p. 3. Texts of both may also be found in T. B. Millar (ed.), *Current International Treaties* (London, 1984), pp. 440 and 464.

service, but it is evidence that UN Charter principles are seen as having some pertinence.

One important element in the preservation of peaceful relations between major powers has been—or so it is generally believed—the regulation of their armaments. It has been a truism in discourse about international politics, albeit one seldom critically examined, that the lower the level of their armaments, the better the relations between states is likely to be. But when the United Nations was established, disarmament as such was not seen as being necessarily in itself desirable. The lessons of the 1930s were too fresh in every mind. 'Uniting of strength' implied that there would be strength to unite. The Four Nations' Declaration of 1943 had agreed only on cooperation 'to bring about a practicable general agreement with respect to the *regulation* of armaments in the post-war period'.[6]

By Article 26 of the Charter, the Security Council was made responsible:

for formulating . . . plans to be submitted to the Members of the United Nations for the establishment of a system for the regulation of armaments.

At the same time, by Article 11, the General Assembly was empowered to:

consider the general principles of cooperation in the maintenance of international peace and security, including the principles governing disarmament and the regulation of armaments, and may make recommendations with regard to such principles to the Members or to the Security Council or to both.

It may be wondered how the UN progressed, or regressed, from these cautious and realistic guide-lines to the grandiose resolutions in favour of 'General and Complete Disarmament under effective international control' which the General Assembly, with the support of both superpowers, passed in 1959 and which have remained a substantial part of the UN agenda ever since. It was in fact in consequence of two events unanticipated at the time that the Charter was drafted: the explosion of the first nuclear weapons, and the onset of the Cold War.

The control of nuclear weapons was at once seen as a problem

---

[6] See n. 2 above.

of a different order of magnitude from the regulation of what became known as 'conventional' armaments; a problem both more important and, given the novelty of nuclear weapons and the monopoly initially enjoyed by the United States, more practicable. The first resolution of the General Assembly, when it met in January 1946, was to set up an Atomic Energy Commission with broad responsibilities. It was to provide, among other things, for control of atomic energy to the extent necessary to ensure its use only for peaceful purposes; for the elimination from national armaments of atomic 'and all other major weapons adaptable to mass destruction'; and 'for effective safeguards by way of inspection and other means to protect complying states against the hazards of violations and evasions': all matters which have remained on the international agenda ever since.[7]

In response to this challenge the United States produced the Baruch Plan, which was certainly imaginative and apparently generous. This provided for an international authority—indeed, since it would be veto-free, a supranational authority—to control the entire process of the production of nuclear weapons, from the uranium mines and the laboratories to the bombs themselves; an authority possessing total powers of inspection and enforcement throughout the world. The United States, however, refused to give up their own weapons until the new authority was established and in working order. The Soviet Union saw this as a blatant device for the perpetuation of a US-controlled monopoly, and countered with their own proposals. All states should bind themselves not to use, produce, or store nuclear weapons, and to destroy all existing stocks. International inspection should be limited to those stocks which the host government declared to exist. This the Americans saw as an equally blatant attempt to disarm them, with no assurance that the Russians were not building up stocks of their own.[8]

As the Cold War deepened, each side entrenched itself more firmly. The United States used its majority in the General Assembly to make the UN adopt the Baruch Plan. The Soviet

[7] US Department of State, *The International Control of Atomic Energy: Growth of a Policy* (Publication 2702, 1946), p. 127.

[8] Bernhard G. Bechhoefer, *Postwar Negotiations for Arms Control* (Washington DC, 1961), pp. 41 ff.

Union turned to extramural propaganda and mounted a massive Peace Offensive (dove designed by Picasso) demanding the complete prohibition of nuclear weapons and a one-third cut of conventional forces across the board. Since they made this proposal in September 1948 at the time of the Berlin blockade, when the Western powers were at their wits' end to find sufficient armed forces to balance the Soviet conventional superiority, this could be regarded only as a propaganda ploy. The 'Peace Offensive' reached its climax with the Stockholm Peace Appeal of March 1950, with its demand for 'the absolute banning of the atom weapon, arm of terror and mass extermination of populations'. Like Trotsky at Brest-Litovsk in 1918, the Soviet Union was shouting over the heads of governments to the peoples they represented. Disarmament had become a matter not for serious negotiation but for competitive propaganda.[9]

In the 1950s the situation improved. The acquisition of their own nuclear weapons put the Soviet Union in a more favourable frame of mind for realistic discussions, and after Stalin's death a leadership came into power concerned to restore a more reasonable relationship with the West. More important, the development by both sides of thermonuclear weapons made the prospect of nuclear war a thousandfold more terrible; yet at the same time, since more destruction could be achieved with a smaller quantity of fissile material, it made the problem of international inspection and control very much more difficult. So although serious discussions were resumed between the superpowers, they came to focus less on the ultimate goal of abolition and more on such preliminary and partial measures as the monitoring or suspension of nuclear tests, the cut-off of the production of fissile material, the non-proliferation of nuclear weapons, and the prevention of surprise attack.

These questions were initially discussed under the auspices of the UN in a Disarmament Commission which had been set up in 1952 to deal both with nuclear and conventional disarmament; matters which had hitherto been considered separately. That Commission was instructed to draft

---

[9] Ibid., pp. 155–62.

proposals to be embodied in a draft treaty (or treaties) for the regulation, limitation and balanced reduction of all armed forces and all armaments, for the elimination of all major weapons adaptable to mass destruction and for the effective control of atomic energy to ensure the prohibition of atomic weapons and the use of atomic energy for peaceful purposes only.[10]

But as the questions involved became increasingly technical and the discussions increasingly serious, so the negotiations shifted away from the Commission to bilateral dialogue between the superpowers, and such significant negotiations as the Surprise Attack Conference in 1958 took place outside the UN framework altogether. This development was not welcomed by a General Assembly increasingly consisting of non-aligned states who resented being left out of the discussions. In November 1958 it passed a resolution sponsored by India and Yugoslavia which enlarged the Disarmament Commission to include *all* members of the General Assembly; which of course made effective negotiation quite impossible.[11]

So in 1959 a pattern was established which has continued ever since. A General Assembly dominated by Third World states, resentful of their exclusion from effective power, seized on the disarmament issue as a stick with which to beat the superpowers. In that year it placed on the agenda at the behest of the Soviet Union the item 'General and Complete Disarmament under effective international control'. Ten years later it designated the 1970s as 'the First Disarmament Decade'. In 1976 it convened a Special Session on Disarmament 'intended to set a new course in international affairs and turn states away from the nuclear and conventional arms race by means of a global strategy for the future course of disarmament'. This was held from 23 May to 30 June 1978. In 1979 the General Assembly designated the 1980s as 'the Second Disarmament Decade'. In June–July 1982 it had a second Special Session on Disarmament. In this, according to the official UN handbook, 140 states took part and expressed their views, together with 3,000 representatives from 450 non-governmental organizations, while representatives of fifty-three non-governmental organizations and twenty-two research institutes made statements. 'In addition, thousands of

---

[10] Bechhoefer, op cit., p. 166.   [11] Ibid., p. 461.

communications, petitions and appeals with many millions of signatories were received by the UN from organizations, groups, and individuals all over the world.' Regrettably the Assembly 'was unable to reach consensus on any specific course of action' except the launching of a World Disarmament Campaign. It did however agree to convene another Special Session, not later than 1988.[12]

To plough through the huge body of literature engendered by all this is a deeply depressing experience. How far any of it had any bearing on the actual course of relations between the superpowers which were increasingly conducted bilaterally outside the framework of the UN, or to the various political agreements they succeeded in reaching through the Strategic Arms Limitation Talks, it is hard to judge. It would probably be fair to say that the activities of the UN maintain an atmosphere in which it is difficult for the superpowers and their allies to abandon the search for arms agreements. On the other hand, it is an atmosphere which provides a constant temptation for both sides to substitute grandiose and unrealistic declaratory policies for careful and unspectacular incremental agreements. And it is also one in which a totally disproportionate importance becomes attached to negotiations between the superpowers about arms control at the expense of discussions about more immediate and potentially explosive areas of conflict such as Central America, southern Africa, and the Middle East.

2. Containment of local conflicts

The other role of the UN is one about which little is said in the Charter, and which was inherited not so much from the League of Nations as from the Concert of Powers which kept order in Europe before 1914: the containment of local conflicts through peacekeeping, reconciliation, and good offices. This is discussed elsewhere in this volume, especially in the chapter by Sir Anthony Parsons.

United Nations Peacekeeping Forces, in the form in which they have emerged, were not envisaged in the UN Charter. As observer, interposition or buffer forces, they have developed in response to numerous crises within and between states: in Israel

---

[12] *The United Nations and Disarmament 1945–85*, pp. 5–8.

and neighbouring states (ever since 1948), in India and Pakistan (since 1949), in West Irian (1962–3), in the Congo (1960–4), in Yemen (1963–4), and in Cyprus (ever since 1964).[13] It is noteworthy that these peacekeeping operations have all been in post-colonial areas, where there were great uncertainties about the legitimacy of regimes and/or boundaries, and where the great powers were able, if not to agree on action, at least not to disagree so strongly as fatally to undermine the UN effort.

Peacekeeping, reconciliation, and good offices are of course activities of the highest importance. In the Middle East in particular, the intervention of the United Nations has repeatedly made possible the defusing of critical situations which threatened to erupt into major conflict. But the effect of this activity is limited. Sir Brian Urquhart, who had forty years' experience of peacekeeping in the UN Secretariat and was personally responsible for much of it, explained why in the 1986 Alastair Buchan Memorial Lecture in London. At best, he shows, UN intervention can freeze or contain conflicts. Seldom if ever can it resolve them. The reason for this is that the Security Council, because of its dissensions, has failed to create

a benevolent international framework to assist combatants to resolve their differences and to provide the necessary protective apparatus . . . without such a framework it is often impossible for the parties to a situation that is violent, deep-rooted and complex to make progress on their own and in the open.[14]

(d) Conclusion: the UN's Failure in its Primary Task

In short, because of the dissensions among its leading members, the UN has failed, or rather the nations composing it have failed, to create a framework of international security. And it is that failure, Urquhart points out, which has also rendered nugatory all the rhetoric and exhortation about disarmament:

It is now seldom recalled that the original Charter idea was that the collective security system of the UN would provide the sense of security

---

[13] On UN peacekeeping forces see especially the four volumes by Rosalyn Higgins on *United Nations Peacekeeping* (Oxford, 1969–81). For a list of such forces, see Appendix D below.

[14] Urquhart, n. 1 above, p. 393.

and mutual confidence which would allow disarmament and arms control to proceed under the auspices of the Security Council.[15]

It is indeed clear that unless such a sense of security can be established, the demands and proposals sponsored by the General Assembly will continue to be totally ineffective— however numerous, repetitive, and well-meant.

The United Nations has achieved much, and those achievements are discussed elsewhere in this volume. It has preserved those elements of international cooperation—the World Health Organization, the International Labour Organization, and the International Court of Justice—which already existed, and added to them many more. It has eased the transformation of the world from a Eurocentric to a truly global system, and can take much of the credit for the remarkably orderly and comparatively amicable fashion in which this took place. It provides a focus for world politics which enables the smallest and least considerable of its members to feel themselves part of a world community. But it has failed in its primary task. It has not created a new world order in which every state derives its security from the collective strength of the whole. It reflects the disorders, fears, and rivalries of the world as it is, and does what it can to mitigate them. But this provides no reason for us either to be ashamed of the past, or to despair of the future.

[15] Ibid.

The United Nations and the National Interests of States

ANTHONY PARSONS

THE United Nations as a peacemaking and peacekeeping
institution—I am not talking of its widespread economic, social,
and humanitarian activities—is in deep trouble. This is of
course nothing new, but it seems to me that the present situation
is more serious, more intractable than on previous occasions.
The reluctance of the superpowers to pay the full contributions
due from them has, in addition, precipitated a financial crisis
which is a dangerous symptom of the prevailing malaise. The
fact has to be faced that certain major powers, particularly the
United States, are taking a more negative attitude towards
the UN than hitherto and are questioning its value from the
perspective of their national interest.

(a) Is the UN Worth Preserving as a Guardian of Peace?

Over the past few years success has eluded the United Nations
over many issues of peace and war. The UN did nothing to
prevent war from breaking out between Iran and Iraq in
September 1980, or Israel from invading Lebanon in June 1982.
For all the efforts of the Secretary-General, the Security Council
failed to bring about a peaceful Argentine withdrawal from the
Falkland Islands. The attempts by the Secretary-General and
his representative to secure an agreement between the parties in
Cyprus and a Soviet withdrawal from Afghanistan have yet to
produce positive results. So perhaps the time has come to try to
answer the question—is the UN worth preserving in its role as a
guardian of international peace and security?

If you were to pose this question to different states and groups
of states, you would receive different answers. If you asked the
government of the Soviet Union, they would reply 'yes'. If they

were prepared to be frank, they would go on to say that the Soviet Union has for many years found the UN a most valuable forum in which to bid for the hearts and minds of the non-aligned majority by vigorously and unquestioningly espousing their causes, by posing as a champion of national liberation, and by putting the West at a corresponding disadvantage in these respects. They might go on to say that they have been able to pursue these diplomatic objectives at minimal cost. By pretending to a fundamentalist attitude towards the Charter, they have been able to avoid paying their share of the heavy expenses involved in UN peacekeeping operations, and by inventing the notion that North–South economic disparity is the result of 'Western' imperialism which should therefore pay the price of redressing the imbalance, they have got away with paying only derisory sums towards the UN's economic and humanitarian activities.

However, the Soviet Union may be beginning to suffer slight pangs of anxiety. Until 1979 they had become confident that the General Assembly majority would always give them the benefit of the doubt while denying it to the West—the famous 'double standard'. The massive non-aligned condemnation of the Russian invasion of Afghanistan, repeated in successive General Assemblies, has undoubtedly worried Moscow and may well have been a factor, not only in stimulating the Soviet Union into cooperating with the UN-sponsored attempt to bring about withdrawal of its troops and a peaceful settlement of the Afghan problem, but also in restraining Moscow in its reaction to the situation in Poland in 1981.

Were you to ask the Non-Aligned Movement collectively the same question, you would also receive the answer 'yes'. The smaller states would say, with perfect justification, that the UN is the only forum in the world where they can make their voices heard, and that it is important to them as a proof of international recognition of statehood. It is interesting in this context that, with the exception of Switzerland, all states which feel able to assume the financial and manpower obligations of membership have joined the organization and that only one, Indonesia, has left it for any length of time. In general the non-aligned states would argue that the UN is a useful place in which to mobilize international support for the causes to which they attach importance, especially in relation to the Arab–Israeli dispute and the problems of southern Africa in all their aspects. The non-aligned states can accumulate year by year in the Security Council and the General Assembly an increasing volume of votes for propositions such as economic sanctions against South Africa over apartheid and Namibia, the need for total Israeli withdrawal from the Arab territories occupied in 1967, the establishment of an independent Palestinian state, and so on. The trap here is the tendency to equate increased voting support with increased pressure on the states to which the resolutions are addressed. In practice, the periodic reiteration of the same or similar sentiments has tended to harden the attitudes of those states which find themselves on the receiving end.

The United States' response to the question would be more doubtful, particularly in the political climate created by the Reagan Administration. Your American interlocutor would be liable to express nostalgia for the 'good old days' in the UN when like-minded states, led by the United States, were in the majority—a parliamentary situation which has gone, never to return. He or she might well add that the UN has become a quarry for the mining of virulent anti-American rhetoric, particularly in the Arab–Israeli context; a place where problems are complicated rather than simplified; and an ineffective body which is best avoided by serious negotiators. Moreover, a fact which galls many Americans, the United States is expected to pay 25 per cent of the cost of the privilege of being a whipping-boy, and cannot even prevent the adoption of fresh (and often undesirable) programmes for which again they have to pay the lion's share.

Western Europe would respond to the question with a variety of voices, all of which would be generally positive albeit for different reasons. The spectrum would range from the high idealism of Scandinavia through the more hard-headed realism of the larger members of the European Community to the southern European attitude which would be closer to that of the Non-Aligned Movement. But all would agree that, although the performance of the UN has fallen far below the impossibly high standards of its rhetoric, it has no equal as a diplomatic forum (Guatemala and Britain for example have been able to meet and discuss their problems in the UN for many years in spite of having no diplomatic relations) and that it has great value as a place in which to develop coalitions of particular countries in pursuit of common aims—European Community coordination being a striking case in point.

What would my own answer be? I am not starry-eyed. I am not, I think, an idealist. I have served many years in the UN or in jobs closely related to the UN. No one knows better than I do the frustrations, the *longueurs*, even the absurdities of which the UN is capable. But I have over the past two or three years, for the first time since I went to school nearly sixty years ago, had a chance to sit back and think. I have come to certain conclusions about the nature of the UN and about its positive value to Britain—ours being a country which, for historical reasons, is still obliged to conduct a global foreign policy, although we are now no more than a medium-sized European power.

(b) Functions the UN Cannot Perform

It is important, to begin with, to understand what the UN is, and what it is not. Only thus can an effective use of its machinery be made and the frustrations arising from the disappointment of false expectations be avoided.

The UN is *not* an instrument for providing collective security on a world-wide basis. It was indeed conceived for that purpose, as a projection into peacetime of the wartime alliance. But, were this alliance to break down, the collective security function of the United Nations—the military structure contained in Chapter VII of the Charter—would collapse with it. As we all know, the alliance fell to bits within months of the end of the Second World War, and the coercive powers of the UN became a dead letter. It is only realistic to assume that they will not be revived. The world therefore has been obliged to fall back for its collective security on the historical pattern of regional alliances such as NATO and the Warsaw Pact. As a consequence the UN has become an instrument of *persuasion* only and, with the rapid decolonization of the European empires, an instrument of persuasion preoccupied with the problems of the newly independent majority, namely the dangerous disputes in the so-called Third World, principally in Asia and Africa. It is no use trying to blink these facts or to turn the clock back to the days when the

Americans 'led' the United Nations. It is to be expected, and accepted, that the majority should set the agenda—the Charter itself is a document grounded in Western democratic principles—and it is wrong that any single state, however powerful, should dictate to the majority. In contemporary terms, partly because of the erratic performance of the United States in the UN context, even the Western states do not accept American leadership and have formed an influential and autonomous group of their own, namely the European Community.

Furthermore, the UN is *not*, and should not try to be, a forum for the *solution* of disputes. If I have learned anything from my experience, it is that problems can ultimately be solved peacefully only through direct negotiations between the parties themselves. It is no use expecting outside bodies, including the UN, to draw up detailed blueprints and to impose them on recalcitrant parties to disputes. It simply does not work.

(c) Functions the UN Can Perform

What the UN can do is to ameliorate disputes, to defuse crises, and to act as a catalytic agent to persuade the parties to come together and negotiate.

Looked at in this light, it can be seen that the UN possesses effective machinery, if properly used, to fulfil these functions. First there is the *public diplomacy* of the Security Council and, to a lesser extent, the General Assembly. Through these instruments the UN can draw up guide-lines (not blueprints) for the settlement of disputes. It can also create the necessary atmosphere for peaceful negotiations by deploying its peacekeeping capability (not foreseen in the Charter), namely the blue helmets and blue berets with which the world has become familiar and which have perhaps proved to be one of the UN's most important functions.

Then there is the *private diplomacy* of the UN, the good offices of the Secretary-General, unique in their confidentiality, impartiality, and in commanding the confidence of the membership as a whole.

Third, and perhaps most important of all, the UN can function as an *escape-route* or rather a ladder down which states can climb when their policies have got them into dangerously high and exposed positions.

(d) Examples of an Effective UN Role in Crises

Over the past thirty years, these different functions of the UN have proved invaluable to the interests of Britain and in certain cases to the interests of global peace. Some examples follow.

1. The Suez crisis of 1956

Shortly after the Anglo-French forces had landed in the Canal Zone on 5 November 1956, it must have been clear to the governments in London and Paris that the operation would have to be called off. Virtually the whole world was opposed to it, including even our closest ally, the United States. Britain and France had succeeded in achieving the almost impossible, namely uniting the two superpowers at a time when one of them was actively repressing a small European country, Hungary. But how could Britain and France withdraw without unacceptable humiliation in the eyes of their own peoples? Public opinion in Britain was already showing signs of deep division, and a major domestic crisis was looming. To have pulled out the British units and for them to have been replaced by Egyptian forces would clearly have been politically intolerable. This was where the UN came in.

With the Security Council blocked by Anglo-French vetoes, the General Assembly authorized the UN Emergency Force (UNEF I). This was the first-ever United Nations peacekeeping force of the kind that has since became familiar in many parts of the world. It replaced the British and French, and eventually the Israeli, forces which were at the time occupying Sinai. To accept replacement by international forces from the organization of which Britain and France were themselves founder-members was politically tolerable, and withdrawal could take place with some honour and dignity. The UN had provided an escape-route for two major powers which had taken up an untenable position, and an even more serious crisis had been averted.

2. The Cuban missile crisis of 1962

During this crisis in October 1962, it quickly became clear to the Soviet Union that the US government would not tolerate the deployment of Russian ground-to-ground missiles only 70 miles from the continental United States. The Soviet Union faced the

choice of war with the United States or climbing down unilaterally. It has since become public knowledge that the Americans
would have delivered a pin-point conventional bombing attack
on the missile sites if the Soviet merchant ships carrying more
missiles and related equipment had not agreed to stop while still
some distance from Cuba. Had the American attack been
delivered, there were many who believed that the Soviet Union
would have retaliated with a similar attack on the American
Jupiter missile sites in Turkey. The next rung in the ladder of
escalation could have brought close a nuclear exchange.

Khrushchev's problem was how to climb down without
unacceptable loss of face *vis-à-vis* the Third World to which the
symbolic importance of the missile deployment was to demonstrate that the Soviet Union was prepared to underwrite any
friendly state threatened by 'Yankee imperialism'. He was
rescued from his dilemma by the Secretary-General of the UN
U Thant. Identical letters and responses from and to the
Secretary-General were drafted, agreed, and exchanged with
the parties. Khrushchev felt able to be seen deferring to a plea
from the highest official of the international community to take
action to defuse what had become a crisis immediately endanger-
ing world peace. The UN escape-route had worked.

3. Southern Rhodesia 1965–79

When Ian Smith declared unilateral independence in
November 1965, the British government was faced with two
equally unacceptable choices: to use force to crush the rebellion,
or to acquiesce in the new situation. The first was rejected for a
whole series of reasons, the second because of the catastrophic
effect it would have had on Britain's international relations.
But there was a third choice—recourse to the UN Security
Council—which enabled the government to escape from the
trap. UN involvement culminated in May 1968 in the
unanimous adoption by the Security Council of comprehensive
mandatory sanctions against the illegal regime. I am not
arguing that these sanctions were effective in bringing an end to
the rebellion.[1] They were not. But the searchlight of the Security

---

[1] A useful discussion of the effectiveness of economic sanctions can be found in Robin
Renwick, *Economic Sanctions* (Cambridge, Mass., 1981).

Council, trained as it was for nearly 15 years on Southern Rhodesia, not only enabled successive British governments to side-step the other unacceptable choices, but also discouraged creeping international recognition of the Smith regime until the time came when vigorous diplomacy, conducted bilaterally and through the Commonwealth, was at last in the autum of 1979 able to bring all parties round the same negotiating table, the essential prerequisite for the peaceful settlement of any dispute.

4. *The Iranian claim to Bahrain 1968–70*

When, at the beginning of 1968, the British government announced that British protection of the Arab states of the Lower Gulf would be terminated at the end of 1971, the most critical unsolved problem in the area was the Iranian claim to the Bahrain Islands. Historically Iran regarded Bahrain as an integral part of its territory and it was referred to as the 14th province: two seats in the Iranian parliament were reserved for Bahraini deputies. The emotional attitude in Iran towards Bahrain was analogous to the Argentine attitude towards the Malvinas. However, for nearly 200 years Bahrain had been ruled as an independent Arab state under an Arab dynasty, the Al Khalifah. During the century and a half of British protection, successive Shahs of Iran had been able to excuse themselves in the eyes of their people from forcibly restoring Bahrain to Iranian sovereignty by the presence there of a powerful European state—Britain. However, Iran had succeeded in inhibiting Bahraini commercial and economic development by refusing to have anything to do with foreign firms which had establishments in Bahrain.

When the announcement of the imminent withdrawal of British protection was made, the Shah faced two unacceptable choices. He could either prosecute his claim by force, thus precipitating a general war between Iran and the Arab world, or he could unilaterally drop the claim, thus attracting major criticism within Iran. The good offices of the UN Secretary-General provided a third course. The Shah made clear that, although he had no doubt that Bahrain was part of Iran, he would be prepared to accept that the people of Bahrain might have changed over the centuries; he would be ready to acquiesce in their wishes as to their future, provided that they were properly and impartially ascertained and confirmed by the international community. In short Iran, as a founder-member in good standing in the organization, felt able to accept the verdict of the UN.

Complex and, above all, confidential negotiations followed, culminating, in early 1970, in an ascertainment of Bahrain opinion carried out by a senior UN official representing the Secretary-General. His report, the conclusion of which was that the people of Bahrain overwhelmingly wished to be citizens of an independent Arab state, was submitted to the Security Council and unanimously adopted in May 1970.[2] The 200-year-old claim had been laid to rest, the threat to peace and the obstacle to Bahraini development had been removed, and Britain's task of winding up her long-standing relationship with Bahrain had been greatly eased.

This was a classic case of the UN providing the vehicle on which parties to a dispute could reach a settlement. The UN was crucial, but so was the willingness and statesmanship of the parties. The settlement has survived the Iranian revolution, and the fact that it was concluded is a testimonial to the wisdom of the late Shah who has been so severely criticized in recent years.

5. The October War of 1973

In the closing stages of the war in the Middle East in October 1973, Israeli forces in the southern sector had crossed the Suez Canal in a westerly direction and were bottling up an Egyptian formation of about 20,000 men—the Third Army—in the area of Suez town. A temporary cease-fire had broken down and the Soviet Union had alerted its airborne forces to fly into the battle zone to break the Israeli ring round the Third Army. The United States had responded by similarly alerting its airborne forces in Europe to fly in and face the Soviet units if they arrived. The world was unquestionably closer to a superpower confrontation—on an actual battlefield—than at any time since the Second World War, a situation even more dangerous than the Cuban missile crisis. What happened? After some back-stage consultation, the now much maligned non-aligned members of the Security Council tabled a resolution designed to bring about

---

[2] The report of the Secretary-General's representative is contained in UN doc. S/9772 of 30 Apr. 1970.

a cease-fire and the deployment of UN peacekeeping forces to separate the combatants and to create the peaceful conditions in which negotiations could be resumed. The superpowers had been provided with the ladder down which to climb from their dangerously exposed positions, and the crisis passed. It is awe-inspiring to contemplate what the outcome might have been if the superpowers had not had the United Nations alternative to bilateral action, or if they had not been in the mood to make use of the UN machinery when the chips were down.

6. *The Vietnamese boat people 1979*

Many people seem to have forgotten the humanitarian tragedy and the threat to stability in South-East Asia when the Vietnamese government suddenly decided to expel large numbers of people of Chinese origin from Vietnamese territory. It was a very real crisis, and the Vietnamese government appeared impervious to bilateral representation. However, at the initiative of the British government, the then Secretary-General of the UN called a conference of all the parties in Geneva. The Vietnamese felt able to be more flexible and accommodating when faced with representations from the Secretary-General who was, after all, as much their Secretary-General as anyone else's. Arrangements were quickly worked out which relieved the worst of the distress and reduced the tension in the surrounding states.

7. *The Falklands crisis of April–June 1982*

This is perhaps the most recent occasion on which the British national interest was well served by the UN. From 1 April 1982, the day before the Argentine surprise attack on the islands, the British government was able to use the Security Council as the focal point for mobilizing international support for the proposition that, regardless of the views of the majority of the membership on the question of sovereignty, the use of force to settle a political dispute was unacceptable. As a consequence, non-aligned backing was forthcoming for the British-sponsored Security Council Resolution 502 of 3 April 1982 which demanded Argentine withdrawal. Moreover, through the negotiations conducted under the aegis of the present Secretary-General, the British government was seen by the world to have exerted all efforts to achieve Argentine withdrawal peacefully.[3] This made it easier for Britain's friends and allies to provide moral and material support when she was left with the only alternative to redeem the aggression—military action. Had Britain failed to secure and to sustain this international support, matters might well have turned out very differently.

(e) Conclusion: The Uses of the UN

I hope that, by setting out these examples—and there are many more—I have provided convincing evidence that Britain, and the world as a whole, has derived an important dividend from the UN in terms of peace and security for a very small financial investment. Let us get the figures into perspective. The current budget of the central United Nations is only about £800 million of which Britain pays about £30 million. Compare this with a national defence budget of £18,000 million and the proportions become clear.

I believe it to be both wrong and ill-advised to treat the UN as a propaganda forum, or as an arena for scoring empty diplomatic victories, or as an object of dismissive contempt. I have tried to show that it can have unique value for the national interest of states and for world peace. Its machinery, if properly used, is well tried and effective: states should use it rather than avoid it for fear of unforeseeable complications.

I make a final plea for greater use of the Security Council as a vehicle for pre-empting crises before they explode into violence. We all know how much easier it is to prevent war than to stop it once it has broken out. In this context, I leave some questions in your minds.

First, in 1980, anyone who could read a newspaper could see that war between Iran and Iraq was imminent. Why did no member state of the Security Council, or the Secretary-General, bring the mounting tension between the two countries to the attention of the Council before it was too late? Would not the fact of the international searchlight being trained on the area have made it just a little more difficult for Iraq to roll its tanks across the Iranian frontier in September? Only in 1987, after seven

[3] A full account is contained in my article in *International Affairs*, 59, no. 2 (Spring), 1983.

years of brutal war, did the UN Security Council involve itself deeply in attempts at a settlement.

Second, from the beginning of 1982, the question being bandied about between the delegates was not whether or not Israel would invade Lebanon, but when the invasion would take place. However, no one stirred to activate the pre-emptive machinery of the UN. Why not? Look at Lebanon today with its daily toll of death and destruction. Could more not have been done by the international community to prevent this consummation?

In both these cases—Iran–Iraq and the Lebanon—individual members of the Security Council had good reasons of national policy for not taking the initiative. Iran was at that time holding hostage the staff of the American Embassy in Tehran and no state was disposed to take action which appeared to be favourable to the Iranian regime. As regards the Lebanon, the Council as a whole had become conditioned to the fact that the US government was not prepared to countenance the adoption of any resolution or other action which pointed the finger, however tentatively, at Israel. In such circumstances, with the membership neutralized, should not the Secretary-General have taken the initiative? I do not deny that, if a state is deter-mined to wage war in what it considers to be a just cause, par-ticularly if it believes that it will win, there is nothing the UN can do to guarantee prevention of conflict. But the UN can make it more difficult for states to act in such a way. Let us assume that, in the summer of 1980 over Iran–Iraq, and in the spring of 1982 over Lebanon, the Secretary-General had taken his courage in both hands, risked offending one or other super-power and, relying on his undoubted prestige amongst the non-aligned majority, had called the Council under the authority granted to him by Article 99 of the Charter.[4] Would the super-powers have refused to attend a meeting and gone on to destroy the Secretary-General politically as the Soviet Union destroyed Trygve Lie? I doubt it. They would have grumbled and threa-tened but would have reluctantly participated. If the Council had then trained the public international searchlight on the

[4] The full text of Article 99 is as follows: 'The Secretary-General may bring to the attention of the Security Council any matter which in his opinion may threaten the main-tenance of international peace and security.'

mounting tension between Iran and Iraq and on the Israeli build-up in south Lebanon, and kept it trained on these situations, would it not have been that much more difficult to roll tanks across international frontiers?

These are extreme cases but, to me, they raise yet another question. Successive Secretaries-General have taken the view that they must be able to work with the Permanent Members of the Security Council, in particular the US and the USSR. Hence they are extremely reluctant, in order not to put the office of Secretary-General at risk, to take initiatives unless they are confident in advance that such initiatives will be acceptable to both superpowers. This can and does lead to paralysis, and I believe that any UN Secretary-General should from time to time ask himself whether it is worth preserving an office which is bound hand and foot, or whether it would not be worth taking a chance and calling the bluff of the great powers.[5] Perhaps Secretaries-General would feel bolder if they knew that they had been elected for only one term of office, say, for five or six years, and that there was no question of securing and maintaining the approval of this or that state or group of states for re-election. Perhaps this 'one term only' principle could be usefully applied to the heads of all international organizations such as the specialized agencies.

Lastly a word on the problem of so-called state-sponsored terrorism. Would it not have been better—instead of addressing the question of terrorism in general terms in the UN context, as the General Assembly did in 1985—if states which had firm evidence of the involvement of other states, such as Libya, in terrorist activities had specifically arraigned them in the Security Council and sought to mobilize international support for the adoption of deterrent measures? I do not claim that this would necessarily have done the trick. But it might have, and if it had, there would have been no justification for American bombers to attack Libyan cities and many people now dead would be alive. Instead, the UN machinery was used in the wrong way and the United States acted unilaterally on the

[5] For further treatment of the Secretary-General's role see G.R. Berridge and A. Jennings (eds.), *Diplomacy at the UN* (London, 1985). See also the next two chapters (by Javier Pérez de Cuéllar and Thomas M. Franck) in the present volume.

mistaken basis that all international remedies against Libya had been exhausted.

In this very dangerous world, is it not wiser, regardless of the demands of one's own public opinion, to explore every conceivable international means of settling problems peacefully, as Britain did over the Falklands, before taking the ultimate step of raising the level of violence? I for one believe so.

Furthermore, I also believe that it is both inexpedient and, in the longer term, dangerous to try to tackle all international crises outside the UN framework. First, such attempts do not seem to work. The American insistence on removing the Namibia negotiations from the UN and on conducting them bilaterally with South Africa from 1981 has not produced any progress towards a settlement in the intervening years. The deployment of the Multi-National Force (MNF) around Beirut in 1982–3, as opposed to extending the UN peacekeeping role, was a costly and bloody fiasco. These are two examples showing that great power politics are no more effective than international action, often less so. Secondly, the more the crisis management machinery of the UN is allowed to fall into disuse, the less able the organization will be to cope with the next issue of war and peace in which the UN, and only the UN, will be the key element,[6] as it has been in every one of the past decades, as I have tried to demonstrate.

[6] On 28 July 1987 the Security Council adopted mandatory resolution 598 demanding, *inter alia*, a cease-fire in the Iran–Iraq war: the Secretary-General was delegated to negotiate implementation with the parties.

4

The Role of the UN Secretary-General*

JAVIER PÉREZ DE CUÉLLAR

I HAVE been asked to discuss a very contemporary subject. I am, of course, deeply involved in it personally. At first I thought it too limited for this occasion. But my reluctance was overcome by two considerations. First, my distinguished predecessor, the late Dag Hammarskjöld, spoke here in Oxford on a rather similar subject a quarter of a century ago.[1] His exposition was, of course, influenced by the difficult situation he faced at that time. But some of what he said seems to me to be worth re-saying in the perspectives of today. Second, the subject is relevant in many ways to a much larger theme. To understand correctly the role of the Secretary-General is to appreciate the whole mission of the United Nations. And that, in turn, is central to the way international life is organized.

In keeping with the spirit of Oxford University and the rigorously objective manner appropriate thereto, I shall try to discuss the role of the Secretary-General regardless of who may be Secretary-General at any point in time. Men come and go, but institutions remain.

The Charter of the United Nations contains a chapter (Chapter XV) devoted to the Secretariat. It consists of Articles 97 to 101. It assigns two different functions to the Secretary-General: one political and the other administrative. The political function, though much studied and discussed, has never been very precisely defined. The way it is used depends on the state of international relations at the time and also on the political character of the Secretary-General—on his (or, one day, perhaps, her) courage, prudence, and fidelity to the aims of

---

* This is the text of the Cyril Foster Lecture delivered in the Sheldonian Theatre, Oxford, 13 May 1986. Footnotes added later by the Secretary-General's office.

[1] Dag Hammarskjöld, *The International Civil Servant in Law and in Fact* (Clarendon Press, Oxford, 1961). Lecture delivered in the Sheldonian Theatre, Oxford, on 30 May 1961. Also published as UN DPI Press Release SG/1035 of 29 May 1961.

the Charter. This elasticity, if I may call it that, is not peculiar to this office: in varying degrees, it occurs in any institution which has to respond to the complexity of human affairs.

(a) The Secretary-General's Political Functions

Anyone who has the honour to be cast as Secretary-General has to avoid two extremes in playing his, or her, role. On one side is the Scylla of trying to inflate the role through too liberal a reading of the text: of succumbing, that is, to vanity and wishful thinking. On the other is the Charybdis of trying to limit the role to only those responsibilities which are explicitly conferred by the Charter and are impossible to escape: that is, succumbing to modesty, to the instinct of self-effacement, and to the desire to avoid controversy. There are, thus, temptations on both sides. Both are equally damaging to the vitality of the institution. I submit that no Secretary-General should give way to either of them.

The first, the temptation to aggrandizement, can discredit the institution of Secretary-General, and thus the organization as a whole, because it can lead the Secretary-General into courses of action which are not realistically sustainable. When, because of lack of support from the Security Council or the General Assembly, these courses of action have to be abandoned or reversed, the prestige of the organization is bound to suffer. The second, the temptation to extreme caution, can be equally discrediting because situations can, and do, arise when the Secretary-General has to exercise his powers to the full, as the bearer of a sacred trust, and as the guardian of the principles of the Charter. Moreover, in choosing the safer course, he risks causing, through disuse, paralysis of the peacemaking and other functions which the Charter vests in him.

The political functions of the Secretary-General are defined in Articles 98 and 99.[2] These authorize him, respectively, to make

---

[2] Article 98 of the Charter provides: 'The Secretary-General shall act in that capacity in all meetings of the General Assembly, of the Security Council, of the Economic and Social Council, and of the Trusteeship Council, and shall perform such other functions as are entrusted to him by these organs. The Secretary-General shall make an annual report to the General Assembly on the work of the Organization.' Article 99 of the Charter provides: 'The Secretary-General may bring to the attention of the Security Council any matter which in his opinion may threaten the maintenance of international peace and security.'

an annual report to the General Assembly on the work of the organization, and to bring to the attention of the Security Council any matter which, in his opinion, may threaten the maintenance of international peace and security. These functions cannot be fully understood unless we first identify how the Secretary-General fits into the scheme envisaged in the Charter.

Article 7 designates the Secretariat as one of what the founding fathers chose to call the principal organs of the UN. The Secretariat, in turn, is described in Article 97 as comprising a Secretary-General *and* such staff as the organization might require. However, it is the Secretary-General who appoints the staff and it is he alone who is accountable to the member states for the work of the Secretariat. This means that he is co-responsible with the other organs (the General Assembly, the Security Council, and so on) for achieving the organization's aims and purposes. He has thus a dual capacity: in addition to acting as chief administrative officer in the meetings of the General Assembly, the Security Council, the Economic and Social Council, and the Trusteeship Council, he has the independent responsibilities of 'a principal organ'. This may seem a rather fine constitutional point, but failure to understand it can have an adverse effect on attitudes and policies towards the UN.

Misunderstanding can arise from the associations of the word 'secretary' as used in such expressions as the secretary of a committee. Many of the founders of the UN wanted to give a different designation to the occupant of this office. Franklin Roosevelt wished to call him the World's Moderator;[3] some others proposed having a President and a Director-General for the UN.[4] This gives rise to a question: in choosing the less

[3] As one history of the UN Charter puts it: 'The President [Roosevelt] . . . brought up a suggestion that he wanted to see worked into the plan of organization, namely, provision for a head of the entire institution . . . [He] seems to have used the term "moderator" in describing his idea of this official.'—Ruth B. Russell and Jeanette E. Muther, *A History of the United Nations Charter* (Washington DC, 1958), p. 373. Secretary-General U Thant later said: 'President Roosevelt suggested that the chief officer of the United Nations should be called "moderator" and I know of no better single word to describe my own idea of the office.'—U Thant, *The Role of the Secretary-General*, address delivered at the Dag Hammarskjöld Memorial Scholarship Fund of the UN Correspondents' Association, 16 Sept. 1971.

[4] Under one proposed 'Possible Plan for a General International Organization': 'There would be two permanent international officials, the President and the Director-

high-sounding and more conventional term 'Secretary-General', and in entrusting to one person the leadership of the political, administrative, and constitutional functions of the Secretariat, did the framers of the Charter wish to limit the Secretary-General's rights and duties to those given to his predecessor in the League of Nations? I am sure that the answer is no. For they departed radically from the Covenant of the League by including Article 99 and part of Article 98, and thereby giving the Secretary-General the authority to take the initiative in apprising the Security Council of potential threats to international peace and security, and to make an annual report to the General Assembly.

This was not a fortuitous development. On the contrary, it was dictated by the experience of the League of Nations. The League's Covenant, and its practice, were based on a purely administrative conception of the post of Secretary-General. The calamitous events which led to the Second World War revealed that this had been a mistake. A dangerous void had existed: in a situation of dissent and disarray among the European powers, there was no one who could speak for the wider international interest, an interest greater than the sum of the interests of the member states. There was no one in a position to initiate timely intervention by the League to avert the collapse of the international system. The framers of the Charter were most anxious not to let such a void occur again. This explains the difference between Article 6 of the League Covenant and Articles 97 to 101 of the UN Charter. Sir Eric Drummond, the first Secretary-General of the League, is said to have remarked that if Article 99 of the Charter had been at his disposal, the position of his office—and, by implication, the influence of the League on events—would have developed differently.

Let me now return to Articles 98 and 99 of the Charter. Article 98 is the constitutional basis on which the Secretary-General makes an annual report to the General Assembly on the

General. The latter would confine himself to administrative functions. The President, "a person of widely recognized eminence", would preside over the executive council, and perform such other duties of a "general political character" as were entrusted to him by the general assembly or by the executive council.'—S.M. Schwebel, 'The Origins and Development of Article 99 of the Charter', *British Year Book of International Law 1951*, pp. 373–4.

work of the organization. This is not meant to be, and should never become, a mere rapporteur's job: 'the work of the organization' is a broad term. It includes, but is not confined to, whatever the organization has done, or has failed to do, or is required to do. Its submission is one of the ways in which the Secretary-General can act as an initiator and can galvanize the efforts of the other parts of the UN. I myself have sought to give a thematic focus to the annual reports submitted during my mandate;[5] I am grateful for the reception they have met, but most of the steps I have suggested are, in 1986, yet to be taken.

As for Article 99 of the Charter, this, as I have said, authorizes the Secretary-General to bring to the attention of the Security Council any matter which in his opinion may threaten the maintenance of international peace and security. This authority contains the three elements of right, responsibility, and discretion. The Secretary-General's right is apparent from the wording and has never been the subject of dispute. However, the other two elements—responsibility and discretion—are interrelated. In considering them, it is worth bearing in mind that, when the Charter was being drafted, a proposal to amend the Article so as to make its invocation a *duty* of the Secretary-General had to be withdrawn.[6]

Before invoking the Article, the Secretary-General has to consider carefully how his initiative will fare, given the agreement or lack thereof among the Permanent Members and also the positions of the Non-Permanent Members. A situation may in certain cases be aggravated and not eased if the Secretary-General draws attention, under Article 99, and the Security Council then does nothing. Situations that threaten the peace are usually highly complicated and require a flexible and finely tuned response from the Secretary-General. Hence the discretion allowed him by Article 99. Two situations with equally dangerous potential may have to be dealt with in two different ways, depending on how far they can be insulated from great

---

[5] Annual Reports by the present Secretary-General have the following DPI reference numbers: DPI/721-40992 (Sept. 1982); DPI/785-41191 (Sept. 1983); DPI/829-41364 (Sept. 1984); DPI/862-41361 (Sept. 1985); DPI/897-41114 (Sept. 1986).
[6] United Nations Conference on International Organization, San Francisco, 1945, *Documents*, vol. 7 (London, 1945), pp. 392 and 556.

power rivalries, how far the parties are susceptible to moral suasion, and, in some cases, whether one or both of them is reluctant to face exposure in the Security Council. It is worth adding that the possibility that invocation of Article 99 might displease a member state, whether or not a party to the dispute, most certainly ought *not* to be a consideration inhibiting the Secretary-General.

I have said earlier that the chastening failure of the League of Nations was much in the mind of the drafters of the UN Charter. Article 99 makes it clear that they envisage the Secretary-General, in addition to his other functions, as someone with the power to anticipate and prevent crises. The words 'in his opinion' and 'may threaten' clearly signify first that the right vested in him can be exercised in relation not only to actual but also to potential causes of conflict; and, second, that he is expected to evaluate constantly and independently all matters which have a bearing on peace and security. It is also noteworthy that the Article uses the much broader term 'matter' and not 'situation or dispute'. The term covers all developments which (to quote the words of the Preparatory Commission of the United Nations) 'could have serious political implications remediable only by political action'.

The Secretary-General is thus given a reservoir of authority, a wide margin of discretion, which requires the most careful political judgement and is limited only by prudence. The ways in which this authority would be exercised and this discretion used could not have been anticipated at the time the Charter was framed. Nor did the drafters of the Charter foresee the circumstances in which Article 99 would be invoked. They had relied on a scheme of collective security predicated on agreement among the Permanent Members of the Security Council. When this basic assumption of great power unanimity broke down, indecision or inaction in the Council was often the result. Over the years, therefore, the practice grew for the Secretary-General himself to help to moderate conflicts or negotiate solutions, without, of course, detracting in any way from the Council's primary role. This kind of action by the Secretary-General does not necessarily require a formal invocation of Article 99. In my own experience, it has usually had to be discharged without such invocation. A topical instance is the reported use of chemical weapons in the Iran–Iraq war.[7]

Article 99 is concerned with action by the Secretary-General *vis-à-vis* the Security Council. He is given comparable powers *vis-à-vis* the General Assembly by the rule which accords him the right to place on the Assembly's provisional agenda all items which he deems necessary.[8] In both these cases, this function of the Secretary-General is not merely an attribute of his office but also one of the essential ways in which the UN can respond to the demands of the international situation. In the present state of international affairs, the Security Council is often unable to adopt a resolution because of division among its Permanent Members. Equally often, it makes a recommendation which is rejected by one of the parties, or it adopts a resolution which is not supported, or is perceived as not being supported, by some important states directly or indirectly involved. In all such cases, the Secretary-General has to act as the main intermediary between the parties, and to help pave the way, if he can, for an eventual accommodation or agreement between them. In 1986, the Secretary-General remains the only channel of communication between the parties involved in questions relating to Afghanistan, the Iran–Iraq war, Cyprus, and south Lebanon. In such efforts, the Secretary-General has to improvise, and may sometimes feel compelled to suggest means other than those which had been envisaged by the Security Council in its original discussions of the matter. The same is true with the General Assembly. Controversy often persists after the Assembly adopts a resolution. Here again, it becomes the duty of the Secretary-General to ensure, as far as he can, that the parties remain open to dialogue.

A caveat, however, must be entered here. It is of great importance that trust should be placed in the Secretary-General by the Security Council, by the General Assembly, and by governments, but delegation of responsibility to him should not be a way for member states to escape the responsibilities placed on them by the Charter. We must cling to the Charter concept of collective action for peace and security, and we must do nothing

---

[7] See the following Reports of the Secretary-General: S/16433 (26 Mar. 1984); S/17127 (17 Apr. 1985); S/17911 (12 Mar. 1986).

[8] Rule 13(G) of the General Assembly Rules of Procedure (UN publication sales no. E.85.I.13).

to weaken the chances of eventually putting it into practice. It cannot be repeated too often that it is the Security Council which bears the primary responsibility for such action. Disharmony between the different organs does not help the effective development of the UN. Moreover, it would gravely harm the interests of peace if the Secretary-General were ever to become a façade, behind which there was only deadlock and disagreement. He must not become an alibi for inaction. No authority delegated to the Secretary-General, and no exercise by him of this authority, can fill the existing vacuum in collective security. This vacuum is due to dissension among the Permanent Members of the Security Council, to the failure of member states to resort to the Charter's mechanisms for the settlement of disputes, and to their lack of respect for the decisions of the Security Council.

When the Secretary-General exercises his good offices, under the specific mandates given him, and within the general purview of Article 33 of the Charter which requires the parties to a dispute to seek a solution by peaceful means, the UN is using quiet diplomacy, the diplomacy of reconciliation. There does not seem to be enough appreciation of the advantages of the UN in this respect. This is indicated by the many instances today where the UN is bypassed.

Multilateral diplomacy of the kind in which the Secretary-General is frequently engaged differs from traditional diplomacy in several ways. As it is conducted in accordance with the principles of the Charter, it does not place the weaker party in an unfavourable position. It seeks an objective and lasting settlement of a dispute and not merely one which responds to the expediencies of the day. In a multilateral approach, all the member states of the UN have a direct or indirect influence: this can assure, as much as anything can, that the vital interests of all parties are taken into account. Such an approach can spot points of potential agreement which may not be obvious at first sight or in the context of power-political interests. The aim of traditional diplomacy was often limited to a stable balance of power: whether the balance conformed to justice was a lesser concern. But peace as envisaged by the UN Charter is a just peace: take that moral dimension away and we are back to the disorder and the injustice of power politics.

If quiet diplomacy is to succeed, it needs the confidence of all parties. And that means that the Secretary-General must not only be impartial but must be perceived to be so. He must not allow his independence of judgement to be impaired or distorted by pressures from governments. He should have no part in any diplomatic deal or undertaking which ignores the principles of the Charter or the relevant pronouncements of the competent organs of the UN.

However, moral concern must not become moral hubris. The Secretary-General must not allow himself to be influenced by his own judgement of the moral worth of either party's position or, for that matter, by what the leaders or media of one country glibly say about the position of the other. Subjective attitudes must not be allowed to hinder progress towards mutual understanding between the parties.

This is perhaps the severest demand the job makes on the Secretary-General. It is hard to suppress one's sympathies and preferences and harder still to endure the frustrations and discouragements which quiet diplomacy entails. But the Secretary-General does not have the option of being partial or of being discouraged. In saying that, however, I do not claim that the Secretary-General has at his disposal moral resources greater than his fellow men. What I do assert is that he cannot shoulder the burden of his office without unlimited patience, and an unfailing sense of justice and humanity.

When states are in conflict, the Secretary-General has to try to understand the roots of insecurity, the fears and resentments and the legitimate aspirations which inspire a people or a state to take the positions they do. International conflicts often occur when one party and its supporters ignore the fears of the other. If a third party is to succeed in resolving the conflict, he has to address the fears of each with empathy and imagination.

This process is not equally helpful in all cases, and should not be endless in any case. Sometimes the leadership of a state takes a stubborn stand and seems immune to rational persuasion. In such a case, the Secretary-General should go on as far as the point at which further exercise of his good offices can only disguise the reality: he should then state the facts plainly, without denunciation but without hiding the facts.

Apart from the exercise of good offices, the Secretary-General is often entrusted with other functions by the main organs of the

UN. Often a report is requested from him. I strongly believe that such requests should not be made as a matter of routine or to cover up the failure of the body concerned to agree on effective action. Another common occurrence is for the Secretary-General to be asked to secure compliance with a resolution. Difficulties can then arise if there is disagreement amongst the member states about how the resolution is to be interpreted. There are very few absolutes in international affairs. The principles of the Charter no doubt command everyone's assent. But, because of different perceptions and values, there is often controversy about how they should be applied in a complicated situation. In such a case, the powers delegated to the Secretary-General do not always provide the answer. All he can do is to interpret as faithfully as he can the directives of the competent bodies, and the rights and obligations of the UN under international law.

Impartiality is thus the heart and soul of the office of the Secretary-General. His impartiality must remain untainted by any feeling of indebtedness to governments which may have supported his appointment. I attach the greatest importance to this point and I therefore suggest that we should re-establish the healthy convention that no person should ever be a candidate, declared or undeclared, for this office. It is a post that should come *unsought* to a qualified person. However impeccable a person's integrity may be, he cannot in fact retain the necessary independence if he proclaims his candidacy and conducts a kind of election campaign, overt or covert. Some promises are bound to be made during his canvassing. But the only promise a future Secretary-General can properly make is to fulfil his duties under the Charter. There is no reason to fear that the convention I propose would make it more difficult for the member states to select a Secretary-General. Governments will always have a list of persons whom they consider qualified for the office. If it was a firm rule that such persons and their governments should go no further than answering enquiries about their availability, this would, I am sure, reinforce the moral authority which any Secretary-General must have.

In today's world, neither the functions of the Secretary-General nor multilateral diplomacy should be limited to good offices or negotiation. One of the UN's duties in a crisis is to be alert to all the nuances, and to use its contacts with governments to try to allay the underlying fears and suspicions. If it is successful in this, it may elicit concessions which the adversaries, left to themselves, would never consider. However, this requires a conscious decision on the part of the member states to strengthen the role of the Secretary-General and to provide him with better means to keep a watch over actual and potential points of conflict. At present, the UN lacks independent sources of information: its means of obtaining up-to-date information are primitive by comparison with those of member states—and indeed of most transnational corporations. To judge whether a matter may threaten international peace and security, the Secretary-General needs more than news reports and analyses made by outside experts: he needs full and impartial data, and he needs to be able to monitor developments world-wide. To enable the Secretariat to do this would in no way alter the distribution of functions and powers between the principal organs of the UN. Strengthening the institutional basis of preventive diplomacy would not diminish the role of the Security Council: on the contrary, it would enhance its effectiveness. The Secretary-General is, after all, a collaborator of the Security Council and not its competitor.

(b) The Secretary-General's Administrative Role

I have so far concentrated on the political role of the Secretary-General, as this is the part of his responsibilities which attracts the most interest. But equally important is his administrative function under Article 97 of the Charter which designates him as the chief administrative officer of the organization.

The responsibilities of the UN are now so widespread in the political, economic, social, and humanitarian fields that the Secretariat requires a staff highly qualified in most of the modern scientific and cultural disciplines. Articles 100 and 101 of the Charter saw the Secretariat as a genuinely international civil service, responsible only to the organization, and gave the Secretary-General the exclusive power of appointing the staff, bearing in mind the need for the highest standards of efficiency, competence, and integrity.

It is ironic and unfortunate that, while there has been a

dramatic rise in the Secretary-General's political responsibilities, his powers in the administrative field have been steadily eroded over the years. First of all, governments profess their dedication to the principle of an independent international civil service, but few refrain from trying to bring pressure to bear in favour of their own particular interests, especially on the personnel side. Second, the distribution of functions between the legislature and the executive, so essential to sound management, tends to be blurred when increasingly detailed directives about management policy are issued by the General Assembly. All this raises serious questions of organizational responsibility. The member states cannot ignore these if they want an efficient apparatus at their disposal to fulfil the purposes of the Charter. The problem has been aggravated by the financial crisis caused by the withholding of part of their contributions by a number of member states. The morale of the staff, the efficient execution of programmes, and the orderly management of the organization—all are jeopardized by the member states' failure to agree on a budgetary process and a scale of contributions acceptable to all.

The General Assembly reconvened its fortieth session on 28 April 1986 at my request to address this question urgently, for it threatens the viability and the very existence of the organization.[9] I proposed to the Assembly a package of measures to deal with this emergency and to preserve the operational effectiveness of the UN. At the same time, I made it clear that the Assembly was faced with questions about the future—the future of a UN sound in structure and enjoying the wide confidence and support which it must have to accomplish its great tasks. I am happy to say that the Assembly broadly endorsed my proposals; but the long-term problem remains.[10]

[9] Paragraph 13 of the Report of the Secretary-General on the Current Financial Crisis of the United Nations submitted to the General Assembly on 12 Apr. 1986 (UN doc. A/40/1102) summarized the situation as follows:

A. Arrears as at 1 Jan. 1986	$242.4 million
B. Amount of 1986 assessments	$735.6 million
C. Total payments due (A + B)	$978 million
D. *Less* expected payments in 1986	$715 to $703 million
E. Arrears projected at 31 Dec. 1986 (C – D)	$263 to $275 million
F. *Less* estimated reserves projected to 31 Dec. 1986	$199.2 million
G. Resulting shortfall projected to 31 Dec. 1986 (E – F)	$63.8 to 75.8 million

[10] On 9 May 1986 the General Assembly accepted budgetary proposals along the lines proposed by the Secretary-General.
On 19 Dec. 1986 the General Assembly decided that the recommendations of the

The international civil service is facing perhaps its most serious challenge ever. It would best be strengthened if member states would accept that the Secretary-General should carry out his functions as chief administrative officer without undue interference or political pressure. It must be recognized that it is the responsibility of the Secretary-General to ensure that the organization has at its disposal the staff necessary to perform all the functions given to it by the legislative bodies. It would be a refreshing change if the General Assembly and individual member states were to exercise more forbearance and give the Secretary-General the flexibility he needs to ensure the smooth and efficient functioning of the Secretariat.

(c) Priority Areas of International Concern

Over and above the administrative and political functions I have described, the Secretary-General's concerns must embrace the situation of the human community in general. Four areas at present demand priority.

The first is that of disarmament, particularly nuclear disarmament. The Secretary-General has the duty to stress the profound and incalculable danger that lies in the arms race. He has to avoid untimely interventions on specific issues, but he cannot remain a silent witness to a process by which a responsibility that belongs to all nations is monopolized by a few—the responsibility of assuring the survival of humanity and of organized society on this earth.

The second area of urgent concern is human rights. Frequent and sometimes massive violations of human rights are taking place in various parts of the world. Cruel penalties are inflicted on an untold number of people for no reason other than that they

Group of High-Level Intergovernmental Experts to Review the Efficiency of the Administrative and Financial Functioning of the UN (*GAOR*, supplement no. 49 (UN doc. A/41/49)) should be implemented by the Secretary-General taking into account a number of complementary points made by the Assembly (GA Res. 41/213). In the same resolution, the Assembly defined a revised procedure for determining the biennial budget and the longer-range medium-term plan.

On 11 Dec. 1986 the General Assembly had approved the continuation in 1987, with judicious adjustment, of the economy measures introduced in 1986 (GA Res. 41/204). This action was based on the Secretary-General's projection of possible further withholdings in 1987 and a resultant cash shortfall of US $85 million.

assert their basic rights. Human dignity is being denied and human lives and talent mutilated. Faced with these tragic realities, the Secretary-General must consider it one of his principal duties to help bring relief, whenever and wherever he can, to the victims of oppression. This is one of my daily preoccupations and a major anxiety. But in this area, too, great caution is needed: given the susceptibilities of governments, an indiscreet intervention, though morally satisfying, can have the opposite of the desired effect and serve only to aggravate the suffering of the persecuted. The main criterion must be the achievement of concrete results, whether or not a statement or report or silence by the Secretary-General serves the political interest of one side or another.

The third area is the shaming disparity of living standards between those who live in the developed world—the North—and their less fortunate brethren in the developing world—the South. This all-pervading problem touches on many of the Secretary-General's other concerns. For such disparities of wealth are unjust in themselves: and, in the world, as in individual countries, they provoke envy and strife, which, in turn, cause political conflict, with all the misery that flows from it. It has become a truism that a fraction of the resources spent on armaments could produce a radical improvement in the living standards of the developing world. These are questions that take up much of the General Assembly's time. Again, the Secretary-General's role is to do all he can to foster agreement between the North and the South on economic relations between them.

The fourth area of special concern is how the world should respond to natural or man-made disasters. The Secretary-General serves as a rallying point for its response. He should be the one who summons help on a systematic and organized basis. Recent and current action to relieve the plight of Africa demonstrates his role in this respect. I was inspired by the proof it gave of a sense of human solidarity. I hope that a response in the same spirit will be made to the dire situation now existing in Bolivia[11]

---

[11] The Secretary-General's actions in the case of Bolivia arose from a personal request in December 1982 by the President of the newly installed democratic government of Bolivia. The President requested that the Secretary-General use his good offices to mobilize financial support from the international community to assist the Bolivian government in its efforts to resolve the severe economic and social difficulties which it

and Haiti,[12] not only to relieve suffering, but also to encourage political and social progress.

(d) The Special Position of the Secretary-General

All this goes to show that the Secretary-General has a constituency unlike any other. It is a two-tier constituency. On the one hand, he is elected by the governments of 159 sovereign states, and it is to them that he is answerable for the way he discharges his mandate. But every one of those governments is attached to its own perceptions of its national interests, which means that the Secretary-General could not perform his duties under the Charter if he did not sometimes act above and beyond national positions.

Of course the Secretary-General is supposed to represent the member states' common interest in implementation of the principles laid down in the Charter. But the problem is that common interest does not always exist—or, rather, is not always perceived to exist. As I said earlier, when there are conflicting interpretations of these principles in a particular situation, the Secretary-General can be pulled in opposite directions by the member states. When agreement does not exist among governments, the first-tier constituency—the governments which elected him—can offer the Secretary-General little strength and support. It is then that he sometimes has to think of his second-tier constituency, namely the peoples for whom those governments act—all the peoples of the world who together form a single constituency for peace.

inherited on assuming office and which, if unresolved, were of sufficient gravity to undermine the democratic process so recently restored. To this end, the Secretary-General immediately appointed a special representative for Bolivia, and subsequently convened numerous special meetings of representatives of UN member states and of international financial institutions. His most recent initiative has been to assist in the establishment of a social emergency fund destined for specific programmes in support of economic reactivation and improved living conditions to offset the inevitable social impact of the 1985 economic stabilization programme.

12 The former President of Haiti, Jean-Claude Duvalier, left the country on 7 Feb. 1986. A new government was then constituted under General Henri Namphy. The Secretary-General paid an official visit to Haiti later in 1986. His actions in the case of Haiti took place against the economic and social background described in the *Programme interimaire de développement 1986–88*, published by the Commissariat à la promotion régional et à l'administration publique, Port au Prince, Oct. 1986: in particular, ch. 1.

It is, therefore, not only the right but also the duty of the Secretary-General to maintain contact as best he can with the adherents of the principles of the UN Charter who exist in every society in the world. Time and the meagre resources at his disposal limit him severely in this respect. He must, nevertheless, do all he can to expound the principles of the United Nations, and what he is doing to implement them, to the parliaments, the media, and the universities of different countries. In doing so, he does not seek to incite criticism of their governments' policies; his aim is to encourage a clearer and fairer view of matters affecting other countries, and sometimes the whole world. I have been assured by many governments that, far from creating difficulties for them, such action by the Secretary-General helps them to counteract the parochialism of their domestic opinion.

I should like to end on a personal note. The Secretary-General is constantly subjected to many and diverse pressures. But in the last analysis, his office is a lonely one. He cannot stand idle. Yet helplessness is often his lot. The idealism and hope of which the Charter is a luminous expression have to confront the narrow dictates of national policies. The Secretary-General's efforts must be based on reason but, behind many a government's allegedly logical position, there are myths and silent fears. The voice of the Charter is often drowned by clashes and conflicts between states. If the Secretary-General is to ride above these contradictions in international life, two qualities are essential.

One is faith that humanity can move—and indeed is moving—towards a less irrational, less violent, more compassionate, and more generous international order. However grim the past and present may seem, the Secretary-General has to remain firm in his belief that, although people are swayed by short-term interests and local preoccupations, the movement towards good has an enduring appeal, and that good will triumph in the end.

The other essential quality is to feel that he is a citizen of the world. This sounds a cliché, but the Secretary-General would not deserve his mandate if he did not develop a sense of belonging to every nation or culture, reaching out as best he can to the impulse for peace and good that exists in all of them. He is a world citizen because all world problems are *his* problems; the Charter is his home and his ideology, and its principles are his moral creed.

The Good Offices Function of the UN Secretary-General

THOMAS M. FRANCK

IT is particularly appropriate that it is under the auspices of
Oxford University that this book addresses the United Nations'
first forty years of survival and endurance. Oxford's loose but
enduring confederation signifies eloquently that a firm sense of
purpose and of common endeavour may unite and ennoble
diverse and autonomous constituencies in pursuit of a higher
vision. If that message—the example of a great university
composed of free and autonomous constituent colleges, of
'bonds lighter than air but stronger than steel'—could be translated to the world of sovereign states, the UN might yet come to
measure up to the vision embodied in its Charter.

Since modesty is becoming in those of high responsibility, the
UN Secretary-General, in his chapter in this book, is duly
modest in describing his own direct interventions in disputes
between states that undermine or threaten world peace. By the
same token, I am free to be quite immodest about the role, and
intend to indulge myself in that freedom which, in some part,
compensates for lack of present direct responsibility.

(a) The Office of Secretary-General

Nevertheless, I have worked for the UN and, at times, in some
proximity to the Secretary-General. The task of the unit which I
headed was to examine the strengths and weaknesses of the
organization, with a view to fashioning middle-range proposals
that would augment the former and ameliorate the latter.
During my several years at this task, I gradually concluded that
the greatest strength of the organization lay in the office of the
Secretary-General and its functional growth, case by case, over
these forty years. My purpose, in this chapter, is to chronicle

some of that growth, which, for the most part, is but little known or appreciated, and to make some brash proposals for building on existing strengths.

As for the weaknesses, since they reside particularly in the highly visible political organs of the organization—the General Assembly and the Security Council—these need little adumbration. Moreover, since the weaknesses of these organs inhere in their structures as forums for expression of the will of sovereign states, those weaknesses, at their root, can only be addressed by recourse to the political will and conscience of the member states. All that, happily, is beyond the scope of my assignment here.

In his chapter in this book, Secretary-General Pérez de Cuéllar concludes by stating:

> the Secretary-General would not deserve his mandate if he did not develop a sense of belonging to every nation or culture, reaching out as best he can to the impulse for peace and good that exists in all of them. He is a world citizen because all world problems are *his* problems; the Charter is his home and his ideology, and its principles are his moral creed.

While this vision of the office must permeate all of the activities of the Secretary-General, from the administration of the Secretariat to the servicing of various organs, nowhere is it more apposite than in the discharge of his 'good offices' function.

(b) Six Recent Examples of the 'Good Offices' Role

Let me begin by giving six recent illustrations of the role, then go on to outline its historical development and conclude with proposals for its strengthening.

1. *Cyprus*

In the more than twenty-year-old conflict between ethnic Turkish and Greek communities in Cyprus, the Secretary-General remains the only person currently engaged in active efforts to prevent a renewal of bloodshed. In addition, he has mediated between the parties in an effort to begin direct negotiations towards a constitutional formula that would resolve the communal crisis through an agreed-upon confederal structure of government. Early in 1986, after presenting a new set of proposals to the leaders of both communities, he appeared on the verge of success, at least to the extent that both parties' leaders accepted in principle the parameters for negotiating a confederal solution. That these were later repudiated by the second tier of the Greek Cypriot political establishment merely means that the effort will have to be resumed, for there is no alternative to a negotiated solution and no alternative to the Secretary-General as convener of such face-to-face negotiations.

2. *The* Rainbow Warrior *dispute*

Quite a different facet of the 'good offices' function is revealed by the role of the Secretary-General, in summer 1986, in resolving the *Rainbow Warrior* dispute between New Zealand and France. That conflict was occasioned by the role of French agents in the death of a Dutch citizen aboard the *Rainbow Warrior* and the demolition of that vessel as it was intending to make itself hostage to French Pacific nuclear tests in Mururoa Atoll. Two French agents were captured by New Zealand authorities and sentenced to ten-year prison terms. So acrimonious had the dispute become that it threatened to thwart European Common Market operations because of French retaliation against New Zealand agricultural products. New Zealand lambs' brains, for example, were being subject to extraordinary health checks by the French authorities. There were *sotto voce* threats to cut the New Zealand butter quota.

It was the Dutch government which proposed to the parties that they seek a solution on the 38th floor of the UN Secretariat. As a consequence, on 19 June 1986, the office of Secretary-General was inducted to arbitrate certain differences between the parties and, equally important, to legitimize the compromise that would terminate the dispute. In this instance, the Secretary-General acted as a quasi-arbitrator. The parties made a written submission in which they outlined the problem, the elements of a solution they had already negotiated, and indicated remaining aspects of the dispute which they had been unable to resolve. They also agreed, in advance, to treat the Secretary-General's decisions as binding. The Secretary-General then addressed written enquiries to the parties, and produced a written proposal which the parties, as agreed, have implemented.[1] It involved a formal apology by France to New Zealand, the payment of US$7 million in compensation, and the release of the two French agents to French custody on the understanding that they would serve three years 'on assignment' to a totally isolated post on the French island of Hao in Polynesia. France was also to undertake not to try to restrict New Zealand butter, mutton, and goat meat trade with the European Community.

This solution is not without critics in both countries, but it proved much more acceptable—precisely because of its unimpeachable source—than would have been the same, or any other, solution arrived at solely by the parties themselves. Neither government could now be accused by its internal critics of having yielded to the other. Thus, both arbitration and legitimization entered into the Secretary-General's role.

3. Western Sahara

Also in the summer of 1986, the Secretary-General illustrated the 'quiet diplomacy' aspect of his good offices function by his visit to King Hassan II of Morocco. They discussed the ultimate discharge of Morocco's obligation to give self-determination to the people of the Western Sahara in accordance with the Charter, an advisory opinion of the International Court of Justice, and resolutions of the General Assembly. The Secretary-General's principal advisers, who accompanied him on this mission, returned feeling considerable optimism about the degree of agreement on future steps to resolve a conflict which has not only divided Morocco and Algeria, but which has traumatized the Organization of African Unity and continues to engender considerable loss of life. With the OAU effectively out of action on the issue, the Secretary-General has stepped into the void to resume negotiations, being, once again, the 'only ballgame in town'.

4. Afghanistan

In a somewhat different kind of diplomatic enterprise, the Secretary-General has appointed one of his Under-Secretaries-General, Diego Cordovez, to serve as his personal repre-

---

[1] The text of the UN Secretary-General's ruling of 6 July 1986 on the *Rainbow Warrior* affair is published in *American Journal of International Law*, 81 (1987), p. 325.

sentative in negotiations between Pakistan, the Soviet Union, and Afghanistan on modalities for the removal of Soviet troops from Afghanistan. UN efforts towards a negotiated settlement have continued since 1980;[2] and by 1986 the resulting 'proximity talks' had drawn up an agreed framework for three of the projected four elements of a settlement. However, the time-table for Soviet troop withdrawal still needs to be worked out! The negotiations have been conducted by shuttling between the capitals of Afghanistan and Pakistan, and between separate rooms allotted to the parties, simultaneously, in the Geneva headquarters of the UN. They are hampered somewhat by the involuntary absence of the Afghan resistance leaders, although these leaders are consulted indirectly via Pakistan.

In the agreements envisaged to date, the Soviet Union and the United States would act as co-guarantors in accordance with an instrument on international guarantees which has been accepted by the parties subject to the conclusion of an agreed timetable of withdrawal.

In this connection, it should be noted that the agreements worked out so far are nothing without the successful completion of an agreed timetable, something which continues to elude the negotiators. It has even been suggested that the Soviet Union has been using the Secretary-General and the negotiations to create the illusion of movement to screen from world opinion the reality of Moscow's intransigence.[3] However, the Secretary-General is fully aware of the possibility of being used. On two occasions he has already privately told the parties that he would discontinue his efforts, only to be persuaded to reconsider by strenuous representations both from Washington and Moscow.[4]

In the Afghanistan, as in the Cyprus, negotiations, the Secretary-General's office has not merely facilitated dialogue between the parties but repeatedly floated proposals intended to effect convergence and agreement.

5. Chemical warfare in the Iran–Iraq war

Another role of the Secretary-General, as finder of fact, is illus-

---

[2] See GA Res. ES-6/2 of 14 Jan. 1980 (the first General Assembly resolution regarding the Afghanistan problem that asks for the Secretary-General's 'good offices').
[3] Sabah Kushkaki, 'Afghans Will Fight On', *New York Times*, 22 June 1983, p. A27.
[4] See e.g. *New York Times*, 24 Apr. 1983, p. 10 (statement by Andropov).

trated by several missions of experts sent at his instigation to examine evidence of the use of chemical warfare in the Iran–Iraq war.[5] On 8 November 1983 Iran asked the UN Security Council for an examination of the medical and military evidence of chemical weapons employed by the Iraqi forces. This was followed by a number of studies conducted under the authority of the Secretary-General which confirmed, from March 1984 onwards, that such weapons had been used.[6] In 1986 a UN group of experts who had visited Iran on 26 February–3 March reported on 14 March that Iraq had used chemical weapons against Iran: as a consequence of this report, the Security Council on 21 March 1986 for the first time explicitly condemned the use of chemical weapons by Iraqi forces.

6. Human Rights in Poland
Similarly, the Secretary-General has investigated, and reported on, human rights abuses in Poland, using, for the purpose, a senior member of the Secretariat.[7] There is reason to believe that this reportage, together with the Secretary-General's quiet diplomacy, was not only tolerated by the Polish authorities but has contributed to a degree of normalization in that country.

(c) Differences in Style and Content
These various exercises of the Secretary-General's 'good offices' function differ enormously in style and content. Indeed, since the 'good offices' function is nowhere mentioned in the UN Charter, but, as we shall see, grew up out of context and necessity, it is difficult to draw any sharp boundaries that would determine whether these disparate efforts all fit within the 'good offices' rubric. Such definitional concerns, however, are of little practical importance.

There are other differences, beyond the functional, which distinguish these various activities. The Secretary-General's role in Cyprus originates with a mandate extended by resolution of the Security Council.[8] The Secretary-General's role in

---

[5] See e.g. UN Daily Press Briefing (Mr Giuliani), 9 Mar. 1984. Summary for UN Secretariat.

[6] See the reports of the Secretary-General listed in n. 7 of Pérez de Cuéllar's chapter, p. 67 above.

[7] See UN doc. E/CN.4/1983/18 of 21 Feb. 1983, p. 1.

[8] See para. 6 of SC Res. 367 of 12 Mar. 1975.

connection with the Western Sahara dispute, by contrast, has its origins in resolutions of the General Assembly.[9] His investigation of conditions in Poland grows out of a mandate from the Commission on Human Rights.[10] Further, although provision for it is made in a General Assembly resolution,[11] the dispatch of experts to investigate chemical warfare between Iran and Iraq was undertaken by the Secretary-General on the basis of his own inherent authority.[12] The *Rainbow Warrior* exercise was undertaken at the request of the two parties concerned. Thus we see the Secretary-General carrying out 'good offices' functions at the request of parties to a dispute, and of various UN organs, as well as on his own authority.

Another difference is operational. In the Cyprus case, it is the Secretary-General himself who has met—very many times, indeed—with each of the parties, engaging in a form of shuttle diplomacy which is sometimes stationary, sometimes mobile. Because he has served in Cyprus, and knows the parties, this is an instance in which the 'good offices' function has been assumed by him personally. So, too, in the case of the *Rainbow Warrior*, in part because the arbitral function was assigned to him in his personal capacity and therefore could not be delegated. Such 'quiet diplomacy' activities as those on behalf of the Western Sahara are also often undertaken by the Secretary-General in person. Another example, not mentioned hitherto, is the Secretary-General's personal quest for modalities to accomplish the withdrawal of South Africa from Namibia, negotiations which he has carried on in his own official capacity, carefully distinguishing himself from the political organs of the UN.

This distinction, one might add parenthetically, becomes particularly important when the political organs, as in the case of Namibia, have taken a stridently adversarial position against the activities of the state with which the Secretary-General is negotiating. In those instances, it becomes necessary to demonstrate that the Secretary-General is uninstructed by the political

---

[9] GA Res. 3458A (XXX) of 10 Dec. 1975.

[10] Commission on Human Rights Res. 1983/30 of 8 Mar. 1983. This resolution was passed by a vote of 19 to 14, with 10 abstentions. Commission on Human Rights Report, 1983, p. 160.

[11] GA Res. 37/98D of 13 Dec. 1982.

[12] UN Daily Press Briefing (Mr Giuliani), 9 Mar. 1984. Summary for UN Secretariat.

organ and can be employed as a neutral intermediary between
the position of the state and that of the UN organ. To a
surprising degree, he has been able to achieve this delicate
balance.[12a]

In other instances, he has stayed in the background,
deploying trusted members of the Secretariat to exercise the
'good offices' functions on his behalf. The protracted, complicated, seemingly endless Afghanistan negotiations, cannot be
conducted by the Secretary-General without imperilling the
discharge of his many other functions. It is to Under-Secretary
Diego Cordovez that this task has been delegated, with the
Secretary-General only intervening very selectively. In the case
of the fact-finding mission to determine the status of human
rights in Poland, that task, too, was assigned to a subordinate,
Hugo Gobbi.[13] The experts sent to monitor the use of chemical
weapons were recruited from outside the UN system on the basis
of their professional ability to address a highly technical
matter.[14]

(d) Historical Perspective: Earlier Cases

I have tried to suggest the pattern of activity by reference to very
recent cases. However, it is equally important that current practice be understood in historical perspective, because each
Secretary-General is at least as interested in enhancing the historical, evolving role of the office as in solving a particular
dispute.

After forty years, there is a very substantial inventory of cases
in which the Secretary-General has been asked to use his 'good
offices' to mediate between members, either at the request of the
disputants or at the request of a UN organ. There is also a somewhat smaller, but perhaps more institutionally important,
group of instances when the Secretary-General has intervened
in a crisis entirely on his own authority.

The first of these categories is the better known. Less familiar,
and potentially more important, are the cases in which the
Secretary-General has acted not on the authorization of the

[12a] However, SC Res. 601 of 30 October 1987 authorized the S-G to arrange a cease-
fire between South Africa and SWAPO in order to emplace UNTAG in Namibia.

[13] GA Res. 38/10 of 11 Nov. 1983.

[14] See GA Res. 35/144C of 12 Dec. 1980 asking the S-G to appoint experts.

parties, or of the Security Council or General Assembly or Commission on Human Rights, but on his own authority. These are worth examining briefly, in order to facilitate consideration of their potential for future development.

As early as September 1946, when the Security Council was considering whether to send a commission of inquiry to investigate alleged infiltration across Greece's northern frontier, Secretary-General Trygve Lie announced that his office claimed an independent power of investigation separate from that of the Council. He said: 'I hope that the Council will understand that the Secretary-General must reserve his right to make such enquiries or investigations as he may think necessary, in order to determine whether or not he should consider bringing any aspect of this matter up to the attention of the Council under the provisions of the Charter.'[15] In October 1948 he again stepped forward with his own detailed solutions to the Berlin crisis,[16] proposals which were not accepted.[17] Undaunted, two years later he sought to negotiate with China's emissary, General Wu, to start talks on a settlement of the Korean War.[18]

Much more successful and celebrated was Hammarskjöld's initiative in obtaining the release in 1955 of American aircrew imprisoned by Peking. Although his initiative was specifically authorized by the Security Council,[19] Hammarskjöld, initiating what became known as the Peking Formula, dissociated himself from that resolution, in part because it was too judgemental and in part because he wished to assert clearly his independent powers of intervention, untethered to prescriptions devised by one of the political organs.[20] In 1956, after President Nasser's nationalization of the Suez Canal, Hammarskjöld, on his own authority, initiated private negotiations between the foreign ministers of Egypt, Britain, and France. Two years later, during the landing of American marines in Lebanon, Hammarskjöld acted on his own authority in the face of a deadlocked Security

[15] *SCOR*, 1st year, 70th mtg., 20 Sept. 1946, p. 404.
[16] Arthur W. Rovine, *The First Fifty Years: The Secretary-General in World Politics, 1920–1970* (Leyden, 1970), p. 227; Evan Luard, *A History of the United Nations*, vol. 1 (New York, 1982), p. 347.
[17] Rovine, *The First Fifty Years*, pp. 227–8.
[18] Ibid., pp. 244–5.
[19] GA Res. 906(IX) of 10 Dec. 1954.
[20] Brian Urquhart, *Hammarskjöld* (New York, 1972), p. 101.

Council to augment the UN Observer Group in Lebanon (UNOGIL) in order to make it strong enough to replace the American presence.[21] 'Were you to disapprove,' he said to the Security Council, 'I would, of course, accept the consequences of your judgment.'[22] In so formulating the limits on his authority, the Secretary-General indicated his belief that he could act in the interest of world peace when the political organs had fallen into desuetude, at least until such time as the political organs acted to rescind his claimed authority.

In the autumn of 1959, during the Laotian civil war, Hammarskjöld accepted an invitation from the government of that kingdom to go to investigate in order to give himself the 'opportunity to get, at first hand, as complete a picture as possible of conditions and developments in Laos of relevance from the point of view of the general responsibilities of the Secretary-General'.[23] This he justified on the basis of his 'general responsibilities . . . regarding developments which may threaten peace and security' and his administrative authority under the Charter.[24] The mission neither sought, nor received, approval from the deadlocked Security Council. When Thailand and Cambodia proposed taking a dispute to the Security Council, he quietly urged them to accept, instead, the mediation of his personal representative, Yohan Beck-Friis of Sweden. 'You can see how much more effective and smooth working such a technique is than the regular one,' he wrote, 'which involves all the meetings and debates, and so on.'[25]

In July 1961, during the French occupation of the city of Bizerta, Hammarskjöld flew to Tunisia at the request of the Tunisian government.[26] Two years later, the new Secretary-General, U Thant, took the initiative in working out an agreement between the parties to the Yemeni civil war. It called for UN observers to be posted along the demilitarized zone at the Yemen–Saudi border to prevent infiltration.[27] Without seeking

[21] SCOR, 13th year, 837th mtg., 22 July 1958, p. 4.
[22] Ibid.
[23] Urquhart, Hammarskjöld, p. 352 (quoting letter from Hammarskjöld to each member of the Security Council).
[24] Ibid.
[25] Wilder Foote (ed.), Dag Hammarskjöld—Servant of Peace: A Selection of His Speeches and Statements (New York, 1962), p. 264.
[26] Urquhart, Hammarskjöld, p. 533.
[27] UN doc. S/5298 of 29 Apr. 1963, pp. 1–3.

authorization, U Thant sent a team of 114 Yugoslavs borrowed from the UN Emergency Force in the Middle East, augmenting it with fifty personnel borrowed from the Royal Canadian Air Force. Although that initiative had the approval of the parties to the conflict, the Security Council did not meet to authorize that force until several days after it had already been put in place.[28] In October 1962, U Thant also took a series of personal initiatives in regard to the Cuban missile crisis, none of which had been authorized by other organs or by the parties.[29] When fighting erupted between India and Pakistan in August 1965, he took the lead in setting up a new observer group, the United Nations India–Pakistan Observation Mission (UNIPOM) to monitor the truce he had helped to negotiate. The funding for UNIPOM was drawn from an account for unforeseen peacekeeping contingencies, and US$2 million were expended without prior budgetary authorization.

In 1970, U Thant agreed to mediate the dispute over the future of Bahrain, on which Britain was about to bestow independence, but which was claimed by Iran. The actual negotiations were undertaken for him by Ralph Bunche and eventually led to an agreement which averted a crisis. Ambassador Vittorio Winspeare Guicciardi was sent to conduct a field inquiry which reported that the people of that territory desired independence rather than union with Iran, a finding accepted by both adversaries and ultimately endorsed by the Security Council.[30]

Perhaps most remarkable, if not successful, was U Thant's determined search for a negotiated peace in Vietnam during 1964–5, even though that conflict had never been brought before any UN organ, and despite considerable lack of enthusiasm for his efforts first by the United States[31] and later by North Vietnam.[32]

When Kurt Waldheim, on Christmas Eve 1977, brought about the release of eight French hostages being held by the

[28] SC Res. 179 of 11 June 1963.
[29] See UN Press Release SG/1357, 26 Oct. 1962, p. 1; UN Press Release SG/1358, 26 Oct. 1962, p. 2.
[30] SC Res. 278, 11 May 1970. See also Anthony Parsons' discussion of the Bahrain issue, pp. 54–5 above.
[31] *New York Times*, 7 Aug. 1964, p. 1.
[32] Ibid. 12 Apr. 1965, p. 1.

90   THOMAS M. FRANCK

Saharawi Liberation Movement (Polisario) and personally flew
them from Algiers to Paris, he, too, neither requested nor
received authorization from either the Security Council or the
Assembly.[33] On a much larger scale, he took personal initiatives
in convening a sixty-five-nation meeting on Vietnamese refugees and displaced persons in July 1979, at which he secured a
doubling of the number of resettlement places (to 260,000) and
elicited US$190 million in new funds for resettlement centres.
He also negotiated an agreement with Hanoi that resulted in
the introduction of orderly departure procedures.[34] This was
followed by a highly successful pledging conference on behalf of
Kampuchean refugees, a step taken entirely on the Secretary-
General's own authority.[35] Using Olof Palme of Sweden, he
attempted to mediate the conflict between Iran and Iraq.[36]

Secretary-General Pérez de Cuéllar has mediated in numerous conflicts, including a near-miss in the Falklands dispute in
1982. We have noted his efforts relating to Afghanistan, and to
the use of chemical weapons in the Iran–Iraq war. In 1987 he
visited Iran and Iraq to explore modalities for a cease-fire in
accord with Security Council resolution 598 of 20 July 1987.

Effectiveness is not always easy to measure. Some disputes
seem to simmer down by themselves when they are referred
to the Secretary-General. The Guyana–Venezuela boundary
dispute, one may hope, is an example of that. However, whether
effective or not in carrying out their independent functions in
particular instances, Secretaries-General have been completely

33 Kurt Waldheim, *The Challenge of Peace* (New York, 1980), pp. 1–2; see the *New York Times*, 13 Nov. 1977, p. A3; 16 Dec. 1977, p. A7; *The Times* (London), 21 Dec. 1977, p. 5; *New York Times*, 24 Dec. 1977, p. 2; UN Press Release SG/SM/2521/Rev. 1, 14 Dec. 1977, p. 1.

34 T.T.B. Koh, 'The United Nations: Perception and Reality', Speech to a meeting of Asian mass media, sponsored by the UN Department of Public Information, Manila, 12–14 May 1983, p. 14 (mimeo). *New York Times*, 22 July 1979, p. 1. See Memorandum of Understanding, 30 May 1979, between the Government of the Socialist Republic of Vietnam and the United Nations High Commissioner for Refugees (UNHCR) concerning the departure of persons from the Socialist Republic of Vietnam. UN doc. A/C.3/34/7 of 2 Nov. 1979, Annex; the announcement of the moratorium on expul-sions—two-thirds of which were of ethnic Chinese—by sea was made by Waldheim in a press conference at the end of the Geneva meeting, UN Press Release SG/REF/8, 23 July 1979, p. 1. In a dissonant note, officials of the UNHCR were quoted as dissociating themselves from the agreement and expressing distaste for its provisions limiting the right of Vietnamese to flee their country (ibid.).

35 See Koh, 'The United Nations', p. 1.

36 Annual Report of Secretary-General, Sept. 1981, pp. 3–4.

successful in drawing a line between their role and the role played by political organs at the behest of member states. Successive incumbents have created for themselves a role that is separate and often different from the expressed intent of some, or even most, members. Secretaries-General have felt justified, at times, in acting on their own to safeguard what they perceived to be minimum standards of world order.

By now, there can be little doubt that the only important winner in the intra-institutional power struggle has been the Secretary-General. The General Assembly can make more noise, and the Security Council can still act when there is unanimity among the Permanent Members; but to the limited extent the UN is now having any salutary effect on the real world beyond its own compound, it is primarily because of the functions being performed by the Secretary-General.

(e) Tackling the Constraints on the 'Good Offices' Function

It would be no exaggeration to say that the UN is well worth preserving if it serves no other purpose than to facilitate the fact-finding, mediating, and peacekeeping initiatives of the Secretary-General. There is strength, here, on which the future ought to build.

At present, the Secretary-General is limited to a few million dollars in discretionary funds, in order to discharge the growing array of functions coming under the 'good offices' rubric. This is too short a leash: the regular budget of the organization, as legislated by the General Assembly, ought to establish a regularly replenished trust fund in the order of US$40 million to underwrite the 'good offices' operations. This would permit the Secretary-General to start negotiations, deploy mediators, fact-finders, occasional truce observers, and even small contingents of peacekeepers in circumstances where the deployment has been requested, or even merely accepted, by the parties concerned. With the security of adequate fiscal resources, the Secretary-General would also be able to enter a crisis on his own initiative, at an earlier stage, remain involved for a longer period of time, and take more constructive risks.

Even more serious than the fiscal constraints on the 'good

offices' function of the Secretary-General are the informational constraints. As the Secretary-General himself indicates in his chapter in this book:

At present, the UN lacks independent sources of information: its means of obtaining up-to-date information are primitive by comparison with those of member states—and indeed of most transnational corporations. To judge whether a matter may threaten international peace and security, the Secretary-General needs more than news reports and analyses made by outside experts: he needs full and impartial data, and he needs to be able to monitor developments worldwide.

More than thirty-five years ago Trygve Lie proposed the stationing of UN ambassadors in the capitals of member states, primarily to act as listeners and fact-gatherers and to permit the Secretary-General to maintain a continuing presence in potentially troublesome situations. The proposal was renewed by Secretary-General Waldheim, but has not been taken seriously. It has been argued that the project is too expensive and that representatives of UN specialized agencies already fulfil the same function. These are not convincing answers. The UN need not maintain 'embassies' everywhere, but the stationing of personal representatives of the Secretary-General in twenty to thirty key countries, with regional responsibilities, would add immeasurably to that sensitivity which conduces to the successful discharge of the 'good offices' function. It would also add to the sensitivity of governments, heightening their awareness of the Secretary-General's availability, particularly at the stage of a dispute when perceptions and positions have not yet become set in concrete. The savings realized by averting a single significant crisis through such opportune intervention would more than equal the annual cost of a system of listening-posts.

Ultimately, however, the effectiveness of such a diplomatic network would depend on the ability of the Secretary-General to use it creatively. This suggests some significant restructuring of the office's functions and priorities, so as to release the incumbent from the tedium and meaninglessness of so many of his present—indeed, ever-present—ceremonial obligations. In a word, the UN may need a titular monarch to conduct the *pro forma* functions of the office, including the obligation to listen to set-piece speeches and to meet with dignitaries when no urgent business is to be transacted.

Beyond that, the office of the Secretary-General also needs help in better utilizing the flow of information: specifically, a small team highly skilled in assessment, data flow, and crisis management to receive and analyse reports from the field, filter them for consumption, and set out options.

One final note. In his remarkably candid chapter, the Secretary-General rightly emphasizes his need to be, and perceived to be, both impartial and accountable only to the UN Charter, the member states, and the peoples of the world that make up the foundation of the organization. 'Impartiality', he says, 'is thus the heart and soul of the office of the Secretary-General. His impartiality must remain untainted by any feeling of indebtedness to governments which may have supported his appointment.' This quality is the *sine qua non* of successful exercises in deploying his 'good offices'. It may not be enough, however, to pursue the reality of true neutrality entirely by appealing to the better nature of UN delegates and world leaders. One way to manifest the quality of impartiality of the Secretary-General would be by electing a candidate to a longer term than the present five years—say seven or eight years—and establishing the principle of non-re-electability. There is nothing in the Charter which specifies anything about these matters, one way or another. In practice, however, it is extraordinarily difficult for a Secretary-General to appear to be both decisive and impartial while seeming to want a second term. True, an incumbent may use the threat of refusing a second term, to obtain concessions that are important to the vitality of the organization. Pérez de Cuéllar did that in 1986, demanding action by the US government in connection with the debt crisis as a precondition to allowing himself to be drafted for a second term. On balance, however, the occasional leverage that may come from such tactical recalcitrance is probably outweighed by the leverage which, rightly or wrongly, powerful states are thought to exercise on an incumbent's prospects for renomination.

These are proposals which, as I said at the outset, I feel at liberty to make because I am no longer with the UN and no longer directly responsible for any part of it. As a citizen both of my nation and of the world, however, I feel, acutely, a personal stake in the survival and growth of the institution and, in particular, of the office of the Secretary-General. More than forty years after the UN's establishment, the remarkable thing is that the office of the Secretary-General—that is, the one part of the UN system which is separate from, and independent of, the member states—finds itself in much better health than could have been expected in 1945. It can reasonably be asked, and expected, to accomplish much more in the next forty years.

6

The UN and Human Rights: More than a Whimper, Less than a Roar

TOM J. FARER

(a) Human Rights in the Pre-Charter Era

UNTIL the Second World War, most legal scholars and governments affirmed the general proposition, albeit not in so many words, that international law did not impede the natural right of each equal sovereign to be monstrous to his or her subjects.[1] Summary execution, torture, arbitrary arrest, and detention: these were legally significant events beyond national frontiers only if the victims of such official eccentricities were citizens of another state. In that case international law treated them as the bearers not of personal rights but of rights belonging to their government and ultimately to the state for which it spoke. In effect, for the purposes of interstate relations, the individual was nothing more than a symbol and a capital asset. Assaults on his person carried out or acquiesced in by representatives of another state were deemed

[1] Richard Bilder, 'An Overview of Human Rights Law', in Hurst Hannum (ed.), *Guide to International Human Rights Practice* (Philadelphia, 1984), pp. 4–5. See also Hersch Lauterpacht, 'General Rules of the Law of Peace', in Elihu Lauterpacht (ed.), *International Law: Collected Papers of Hersch Lauterpacht*, vol. 1 (Cambridge, 1970): 'The predominant theory is clear and emphatic. International Law is a law of States only and exclusively. Individuals are only the objects of international law' (p. 279). But he goes on to demonstrate that, over the course of the twentieth century, the predominant theory has become riddled with exceptions to such a degree as to require a far more qualified and nuanced statement of it. 'It may now be submitted, by way of summary, that these examples show that there is nothing in the existing international system [i.e. post-World War II] which makes it impossible for individuals to be directly subjects of international duties [and correspondingly rights] imposed upon them as such . . . Secondly, reasons have been given why even in those cases in which States are formally made subjects of international duties, the actual centre of legal and moral responsibility is in the individual and not in the metaphysical personality of the State. Decisive reasons of progress in international law and morality seem to favour that construction' (p. 285). See also pp. 141–9.

assaults on the dignity and material interests of his state, requiring compensation.[2]

Guardians of the spiritual realm were episodically less permissive. Virtually from the start of that bloody enterprise known as the Spanish Empire in the New World, some priests struggled to moderate the awful cupidity and grotesque caprice of the *conquistadores*, their secular associates in Spain's civilizing mission.[3] In addition, Christian missionaries worked to alert decent opinion in Europe, such as it was, to the genocidal features of the trade in African slaves,[4] and thereafter to such abominations as the Belgian King Leopold's personal empire in the Congo.[5]

Even Europe's colonial powers thought, or at least found it convenient to appear to think, that the Congo's indigenous population required some guarantee of minimally decent treatment. And so, while negotiating the orderly division of Africa at the Congress of Berlin in 1884–5, they announced, and Leopold nominally accepted, arguably as a condition of his suzerainty over the Congo, an obligation to look after the well-being of its inhabitants.[6] Since the Congress provided no enforcement mechanism, relying rather on the good faith of the ineffable Leopold, the people of the Congo did not quickly hear of or

---

[2] See L. Oppenheim, *International Law: A Treatise*, vol. 1 (7th edn., ed. H. Lauterpacht, London, 1948), pp. 304–6, 310; on reparations see pp. 318–19.

[3] See e.g. Roger Merriman, *The Rise of the Spanish Empire*, vol. 2 (New York, 1962), pp. 656–63.

[4] See e.g. D.B. Davis, *Slavery and Human Progress* (New Haven, 1984), pp. 304–5. See also Paul Lovejoy, *Transformations in Slavery* (Cambridge, 1983), pp. 253–4: '[The missionaries] were firmly opposed to the slave trade and enslavement; indeed, the missions were intimately associated with the abolition of the trans-Atlantic slave trade.' But, he adds, 'on the other hand, they generally concluded that [in Africa] conversion to Christianity should precede the abolition of slavery. Slave holders, for example, were allowed to become Christians, slavery was to be tolerated temporarily, so that the Christian church could be established. Only when Christians were a majority of the population would it be safe to abolish slavery.' The struggle for abolition, particularly when it assumed the form of pressure by Great Britain on other states and the stopping and boarding of vessels on the high seas, was, of course, an augury of movement in the architectonic plates of moral and legal sentiment.

[5] See generally Neal Ascherson, *The King Incorporated* (London, 1963). See also E.C. Stowell, *Intervention in International Law* (Washington, DC, 1921), pp. 163–79.

[6] Lauterpacht, n. 1 above, vol. 2 (1975), p. 103. To be precise, pursuant to Article 6 of the Berlin Act, all the powers exercising rights in the Congo Basin undertook to care for the moral and material conditions of the natives. Similar provision in the Act concluding the Brussels Conference of 1890 was thought, Lauterpacht says, to require 'positive measures for the improvement of the natives' lot'.

experience the good news.[7] Nevertheless, the very recognition of limits on a fellow sovereign's discretion in the disposition of his human assets was significant.

The effort to inhibit Leopold was one among a number of events in the latter part of the nineteenth century and the first part of the twentieth expressing an epochal shift in moral sentiment which would ultimately find expression in law. Heralds of this shift had appeared a good deal earlier to trumpet its arrival. While historians will always dispute when the first faint notes could be distinguished, the American and French revolutionists, by invoking on their own behalf universal and inalienable rights, unmistakably declared the new age. The often vacillating but finally decisive Anglo-French intervention in the Greek War of Independence from Ottoman rule (1821–30),[8] justified in part by the allegedly peculiar cruelty of the Ottoman administration, reinforced the evangelical message of the French Revolution that, in the spirit of human solidarity, one state might choose to liberate the people of another from perceived oppression.

During the remainder of the nineteenth century, the Ottoman Empire continued to serve as a magnet for essays in 'humanitarian intervention' by great powers: the Russians, on behalf of Orthodox Christians, and the French, on behalf of Catholics.[9] There were also protests by Western powers against outbreaks of anti-Semitism in Russia. In addition to evidencing the power of transnational solidarities, these interventions demonstrated the possible incompatibility of such claims with harmony in the relations of states. The way in which the First World War broke out tragically underscored the potentially destructive impact on inter-state relations of claims for liberation and justice asserted by peoples against the political structures containing them. At the same time, however, because the Allies sought to marshal support by characterizing their exertions as a struggle to defend and promote freedom,[10] one consequence of the war was to

---

[7] Massacre, mutilation, and forced labour continued at least through the first decade of the twentieth century. Ascherson, *The King Incorporated*, pp. 241–60.

[8] See generally Douglas Dakin, *The Greek Struggle for Independence 1821–33* (London, 1973).

[9] See generally Stanford and Ezel Shaw, *History of the Ottoman Empire and Modern Turkey*, vol. 2 (Cambridge, 1977).

[10] 'We shall fight for the things which we have always carried nearest to our hearts, for

enhance the perceived legitimacy of individual and group claims
against the state.

The process of unpacking the individual from the state went
on with the inclusion in the post-war settlement of provisions
purporting to guarantee fair treatment for minorities, principally in the infant countries carved out of the Austro-
Hungarian Empire's corpse. Subsequent experience suggested
both the importance of such guarantees and the diffidence of
guarantors on those many occasions when compassion did not
coincide with more traditional state interests.

The minority provisions in the post-war treaties[11] created a
special regime for the protection of a limited cluster of interests
of carefully circumscribed peoples. In this respect they were not
unique, having been preceded by the capitulations[12] coerced
from the Ottoman Sultan, the Chinese Emperor, and other non-
European dignitaries by Western governments determined to
insulate their citizens, primarily traders, from local jurisdiction.
But the capitulations were simply a discriminatory expansion of
each state's acknowledged right to fair treatment for its own
subjects when they were abroad, a right equally operative in
relations among the great powers.

Even in making the treatment of the subjects of one sovereign
a matter of legitimate concern to other sovereigns, the minority-
protection clauses did not open entirely new ground. Under
duress, the Sublime Porte had conceded rights of protection over
the Empire's Orthodox and Catholic populations to the
Russians and the French respectively.[13]

In the final stages of the Second World War, the victorious
allies decided to prosecute Nazi leaders not only for waging
aggressive war and massacring people in occupied territories,
but also for the slaughter of German citizens. In pressing this last
matter, under the heading of 'crimes against humanity',[14] they
were opening new territory. German nationals did not enjoy the

democracy, for the right of those who submit to authority to have a voice in their own
governments . . .' Woodrow Wilson, speech to Congress, 2 Apr. 1917, quoted in
Frederick Calhoun, *Power and Principle* (Kent State, 1986).

[11] See Lauterpacht, n. 1 above, vol. 2, pp. 49, 147 and 506.

[12] Lord Kinross, *The Ottoman Centuries* (London, 1977), pp. 427 and 479; see also
Shaw and Shaw, n. 9 above, pp. 131, 300, and 367.

[13] See Kinross, *The Ottoman Centuries*, and Shaw and Shaw, *History of the Ottoman
Empire*.

[14] Lauterpacht, n. 1 above, vol. 1, pp. 470–1.

protection of any special treaty regime. So if they had uncon-
ditional rights subject to violation by the Third Reich, these had
to be rights under customary international law or under general
principles of law to be found in every civilized society. Thus the
judgment of the International Military Tribunal at Nuremberg,
and the General Assembly Declaration affirming the legitimacy
of the principles supporting that judgment,[15] implied a core of
obligations applicable to all sovereigns concerning the treatment
of their citizens. In this way the realm of human rights became
available for general occupation.

In the ensuing decades, both through formal agreements and
declarations evidencing the consensus necessary for customary
law,[16] states have bound themselves not to torture or summarily
execute or enslave their citizens;[17] not to convict them without
due process of law; not to dissolve their trade unions; not to dis-
criminate among them on the basis of race or religion; and not to
do various other things which are the authors of despair. Many
nations, going beyond declarations of self-restraint, have rallied
with varying degrees of commitment behind the claim that the
state has an affirmative obligation to protect its citizens from
economic, social, and cultural impoverishment.

(b) Building a Normative Framework

1. The UN Charter

At its inception, the United Nations seemed destined to be the
engine of human rights. Article 1 (3) of the Charter announces
the UN's purposes to include 'promoting and encouraging
respect for human rights and . . . fundamental freedoms for all
without distinction as to race, sex, language, or religion'. Article
13 mandates the General Assembly to 'initiate studies and make
recommendations for the purpose of . . . assisting in the realization of human rights'. Article 56, combined with Article 55,
pledges all UN members 'to take joint and separate action in

---

[15] GA Res. 95(I) of 11 Dec. 1946.

[16] See generally Anthony D'Amato, *The Concept of Custom in International Law* (Ithaca, 1971).

[17] Some of these matters, including slavery, had been the subject of agreements well before the UN era. Note, for example, the 1926 Slavery Convention and the 1930 ILO Convention Concerning Forced or Compulsory Labour.

cooperation with the Organization for the achievement of . . . universal respect for, and observance of, human rights'. Article 68 requires the Economic and Social Council to 'set up commissions . . . for the promotion of human rights'.[18]

To be sure, these provisions did not spring from a fierce, collective will to shatter the wall of national sovereignty wherever it sheltered some variety of oppression. John P. Humphrey, the first Director of the Division of Human Rights at the UN, reports that but for the efforts of a few deeply committed delegates, and the representatives of some forty-two private organizations brought in as consultants by the United States, human rights would have received 'only a passing reference'.[19] While in the end they obviously did much better than that, their subordination in the organization's hierarchy of purposes is evident, above all in the fact that the Charter authorizes UN enforcement action only in cases where it is required to prevent or terminate armed conflict between states.[20]

Not only did the founders thereby appear to deny human rights the prospect of collective armed intervention on their behalf—an impression heightened by the Charter's broad prohibition[21] of forceful action by states except in self-defence—but in addition they incorporated language which could be construed as ruling out every sort of collective action against violations of human rights. Article 2(7) says: 'Nothing contained in the present Charter shall authorize the United Nations to intervene in matters which are essentially within the domestic jurisdiction of any state or shall require the Members to submit such matters to settlement under the present Charter . . .' In succeeding decades, every rogue regime would seek shelter behind that formula.

---

[18] See also the direct reference to human rights in the UN Charter Preamble and in Articles 62(2), 68, and 76(c).

[19] John P. Humphrey, 'The UN Charter and the Universal Declaration of Human Rights', in Evan Luard (ed.), *The International Protection of Human Rights* (New York, 1967), p. 39.

[20] Chapter VII, Articles 39–51.

[21] Article 2(4): 'All Members shall refrain in their international relations from the threat or use of force against the territorial integrity or political independence of any state, or in any other manner inconsistent with the Purposes of the United Nations.' Article 51: 'Nothing in the present Charter shall impair the inherent right of individual or collective self-defence if an armed attack occurs against a Member of the United Nations . . .'

Events surrounding the adoption of the Charter and the UN's early life suggest that there was widespread ambivalence, if not towards human rights *per se*, then certainly to the prospect of their enforcement through the UN. The Soviet bloc quickly established the position to which it would thereafter cling, namely that UN activity should be confined to promulgating rights; enforcement, on the other hand, was a matter of purely domestic concern.[22] But it was hardly alone in wishing to keep the UN out of the enforcement business. The colonial powers were hardly more enthusiastic at the prospect of UN 'meddling' in their respective preserves.[23]

It is, therefore, not surprising that a joint initiative by Panama and Chile to include in the Charter articles guaranteeing specific human rights, and also a Panamanian proposal for a separate Bill of Rights, were rejected as too controversial.[24] Nor is it grounds for astonishment that at its very first session the Commission on Human Rights determined that 'it had no power to take any action in regard to any complaints concerning human rights'.[25] Its immediate superior in the UN hierarchy, the Economic and Social Council, not only confirmed the Commission's noble act of self-denial, but rubbed salt in the self-inflicted wound by deciding that Commission members should not even review the original text of specific complaints by individuals lest, one supposes, the horrors recounted therein should inspire second thoughts about the virtues of self-restraint.[26]

---

[22] Farrokh Jhabvala, 'The Soviet Bloc's View of the Implementation of Human Rights Accords', *Human Rights Quarterly*, 7 (1985), p. 466.

[23] 'General Romulo of the Philippines urged the Commission to conduct itself like a court of appeal, guaranteeing immunity to plaintiffs from any nation. Mrs Roosevelt reasoned that the Commission had power to make recommendations to ECOSOC, but not to conduct an inquiry. Australia, the United Kingdom, and the USSR opposed Commission review of individual petitions.' Howard Tolley, jun., 'The Concealed Crack in the Citadel: The United Nations Commission on Human Rights' Response to Confidential Communications', *Human Rights Quarterly*, 6 (1984), p. 422. The UK also proposed successfully that the right of petition, including petition to the UN, be removed from the final draft of the 1948 Universal Declaration of Human Rights. Ibid., p. 423.

[24] Peter Meyer, 'The International Bill: A Brief History', in Paul Williams (ed.), *The International Bill of Human Rights* (Glen Ellen, 1981), p. xxiv.

[25] Report of the first session, E/259 (1947), paras. 21 and 22.

[26] ECOSOC Res. 75(V) of 5 Aug. 1947. In a consolidated resolution on communications concerning human rights which the Council adopted in 1959, it reiterated its approval. Res. 728 F (XXVIII) of 30 July 1959.

2. The International Bill of Rights

While some auguries for the future of the normative fledgling
were ominous, others trembled with the promise of achievement. Aside from their considerable prominence in the Charter
itself, human rights got an early boost from President Harry S.
Truman when he addressed the closing session of the founding
conference. 'We have good reason', he told the delegates, 'to
expect the framing of an international bill of rights . . . that . . .
will be as much a part of international life as our own Bill of
Rights is a part of our Constitution' (which, he might have
added, also began life without one).[27] As if inspired by the
American President's vision, the Economic and Social Council
(ECOSOC), having in early 1946 carried out its mandate to
establish a Commission on Human Rights, made the drafting of
an international bill of rights the Commission's first priority.

Led by Eleanor Roosevelt in her role as chairperson, the
Commission went to work at a speed remarkable in comparison
to the gait it would assume in later years when controversial
issues of human rights begged for resolution. That the drafting
task was destined for controversy quickly became apparent. As
one could have predicted from the jousting over the Charter, the
central point of conflict was whether, or to what extent, international concern for human rights should be allowed to breach
the wall of national sovereignty. No state seemed more determined to keep the wall intact than the organization's most
powerful enthusiast for transnational liberation movements, the
USSR. When the first drafting stage culminated in the presentation to the General Assembly of the Universal Declaration of
Human Rights, the Soviet delegate declared it defective
primarily because 'a number of articles completely ignore the
sovereign rights of democratic governments. . . . [T]he
question of national sovereignty', he maintained, 'is a matter of
the greatest importance.'[28]

Delegates also tended to polarize over the relative emphasis
between individual rights and community interests. If the
proposed Bill 'did not stipulate the existence of the individual
and his need for protection in his struggle against the State',

---

[27] Cited in A. H. Robertson, *Human Rights in the World* (Manchester, 1972), p. 25.
[28] *GAOR*, 3rd session, part I, plenary meetings, 10 Dec. 1948, pp. 923–4.

declared the distinguished philosopher, Charles Malik, representing Lebanon, 'the Commission would never achieve its
intended purpose'.[29] The Yugoslav representative insisted that,
on the contrary, the 'new conditions of modern times [make the]
common interest . . . more important than the individual
interest'.[30]

In late 1947, facing the danger of impasse over political and
ideological differences, the Commission on Human Rights
agreed to divide the Bill of Rights into three parts: a declaration
of principles which the General Assembly could adopt; a
Covenant rhetorically tied to the Declaration under which ratifying states would become subject to explicit legal obligations;
and a separate agreement detailing enforcement machinery. As
Peter Meyer notes in his 'Brief History' of the International Bill
of Rights, the eight-person drafting committee appointed by
the Commission rapidly completed a draft of the Declaration.
Thereafter it 'wound its way through the full Commission, the
Economic and Social Council . . . and eighty-one meetings and
168 proposed amendments of the General Assembly's Third
Committee [before ending up] in almost the same form as that
first proposed by the committee.'[31]

Rejecting a Soviet proposal to postpone consideration until
the following year,[32] on 10 December 1948 the General
Assembly adopted the Universal Declaration by a vote of forty-
eight to none, with eight abstentions: South Africa, the Soviet
Union, the Ukraine, Byelorussia, Czechoslovakia, Poland,
Yugoslavia, and Saudi Arabia.[33] When the vote was announced,
Eleanor Roosevelt expressed the hope that the Declaration
would be 'the Magna Carta of all mankind'.[34]

Since, under the Charter, most General Assembly action has
a non-binding character, initially most scholars took the view
that the Declaration expressed moral values rather than legally
binding norms. However, in part because it had passed without
a negative vote, in larger part because many of its provisions
subsequently found their way into formal international agreements or were incorporated in national constitutions, it has

29 UN *Weekly Bulletin*, 25 Feb. 1947, pp. 170–1.   30 Ibid.
31 Meyer, n. 24 above, p. xxx.   32 *GAOR*, n. 28 above, p. 929.
33 GA Res. 217 (III) A of 10 Dec. 1948.
34 Cited in Robertson, n. 27 above, p. 27.

acquired a legal aura, the appearance of stating, if not having by its existence created, binding norms of state behaviour.[35]

The Declaration, as Meyer notes, was only the first step of the International Bill—a quickstep compared with the eighteen-year trudge which followed.[36] Only through a further decoupling of the originally envisioned elements of the Bill were the disputants finally able to resolve their often rancorous differences. The old polarities—human rights versus national sovereignty, individual liberty versus communal needs—continued to discourage consensus. The former was concretized by the issue of international enforcement. The latter led to dispute primarily over two questions. One was whether economic, social, and cultural interests should be accorded the status of rights on a par with the traditional liberal values of free speech, religion, press, association, and so on. Despite Franklin Delano Roosevelt's inclusion in 1941 of 'freedom from want' among the 'four freedoms' for whose attainment the US would face the risk of war, the Western allies as a group were inclined to answer 'no'. The Eastern bloc, increasingly supplemented by newly independent states from the Third World, said 'yes'. The question of whether the covenant should include a right to property created a similar grouping of antagonists.

The drafters finally broke free from their impasse by agreeing as follows. First, there would be two covenants, one dealing with political and civil rights, the other with economic, social, and cultural rights. Both these covenants were eventually concluded in 1966, and entered into force in 1976. Second, in so far as implementing machinery was concerned, states could ratify either or both conventions, without thereby assuming any more onerous obligation than provision of a periodic report.

The 1966 International Covenant on Civil and Political Rights requires states to submit reports 'on the measures they have adopted which give effect to the rights recognized [therein] and on the progress made in the enjoyment of those rights'. These reports are to be transmitted through the Secretary-General to an elected eighteen-person committee of experts

[35] Egon Schwelb and Philip Alston, 'The Principal Institutions and Other Bodies Founded under the Charter', in Karel Vasak (ed.), *The International Dimensions of Human Rights*, vol. 1 (Westport and Paris, 1982) p. 245.
[36] Meyer, n. 24 above, p. xxxi.

authorized to study and thereafter transmit reports to the states parties and ECOSOC together with 'such general comments as it may consider appropriate' (Article 40).

Reports under the 1966 International Covenant on Economic, Social, and Cultural Rights cover 'the measures . . . adopted and the progress made in achieving the observance of the rights recognized [therein]' (Article 16). These reports must be submitted to ECOSOC 'for consideration in accordance with the provisions of the . . . Covenant', and it in turn transmits them to the Human Rights Commission 'for study and general recommendation' (Article 19).

Parties ratifying the Civil and Political Covenant have the option under Article 41 of recognizing the jurisdiction of the Covenant's Human Rights Committee to hear complaints from other states that have also accepted this procedure. The Committee may hold hearings and promote friendly settlement. What it apparently cannot do is form an independent judgement about the merits of the complaint.

That power is reserved for cases, if any, arising under the so-called 'Optional Protocol' to the Civil and Political Covenant. States adhering to it recognize the Committee's authority to hear petitions from individual citizens alleging violations of their rights under the Covenant. After considering the petition 'in the light of all written evidence made available to it by the individual and by the State Party concerned . . . The Committee shall forward its views to [them]' (Article 5). And then? The Protocol says only that 'The Committee shall include in its annual report . . . a summary of its activities under the . . . Protocol' (Article 6).

When these powers are compared to those exercised even by the UN Human Rights Commission, much less the European and particularly the Inter-American Commission on Human Rights, one is inclined to feel that the drafters of the Covenants managed to produce something not readily distinguishable from a mouse. In light of the little accomplished to date, perhaps the most generous thing that could be said is that while this mouse does not exactly roar, it has on occasion managed more than a squeak.[37] These weak and for the most part optional instruments

[37] For a very concise but acute appraisal, see 'Draft Interim Report on Monitoring States of Emergency', presented to the Committee on the Enforcement of Human

of compliance mollified the opposition of those numerous governments hostile to external assessment of their domestic behaviour. Also, the form in which substantive norms are stated is anxiety-easing, since states are given a considerable margin of discretion. Many of the rights guaranteed in the Civil and Political Covenant, for instance, are subject to suspension 'in time of public emergency which threatens the life of the nation', albeit only 'to the extent strictly required by the exigencies of the situation' (Article 4). The rights to life and protection from torture are not derogable; but governments can, among other things, detain citizens for substantial periods of time on the basis of evidence normally insufficient for arrest and without expeditious charge and trial.

A margin of state discretion is, moreover, incorporated in the very statement of certain rights. In the Civil and Political Covenant, for instance, the right to freedom of expression 'may . . . be subject to certain restrictions . . . provided by law and . . . necessary . . . for the protection of national security or of public order (*ordre public*), or of public health or morals' (Article 19). Article 20 actually requires the prohibition of 'any propaganda for war'. And Article 21, while recognizing the right of peaceful assembly, makes it subject to restrictions 'which are necessary in a democratic society in the interests of national security or public safety, public order, the protection of public health or morals or the protection of the rights and freedoms of others'.

Some flexibility in the interpretation and enforcement of most rights is, of course, essential, if for no reason other than to assure their availability to all groups in society and to maintain that degree of public order without which no right is secure. Everyone cannot exercise the right of assembly in the same place at the same time. If the government cannot referee, private power will be imperious and freedom correspondingly reduced. Governments must, therefore, have a margin of discretion: but

Rights Law of the International Law Association by its Rapporteur, Professor Joan F. Hartman, at its 1986 conference in Seoul, pp. 11–16. See also Farrokh Jhabvala, 'The Practice of the Covenant's Human Rights Committee, 1976–82: Review of State Reports', *Human Rights Quarterly*, 6 (1984), p. 81.

if the exercise of that discretion is essentially unmonitored, a limited discretion readily deteriorates into licence.

The economic, social, and cultural realms are even less susceptible to categorical directives. Governments have a legitimate interest, for instance, in promoting a common culture which will help to harmonize the relations between diverse social groups. That interest must be balanced against the equally appealing claim for freedom to maintain cultural identity within the framework of a multi-cultural state. Governments must also balance an interest in minimizing poverty for the current generation against the claims of the next for a higher standard of living; the latter requires among other things some postponement of consumption in favour of investment. Decisions concerning the language of public business and instruction, the organization of the economy, the allocation of wealth, the forms of taxation, and the model of economic and social development, have traditionally been thought of as falling exclusively within the range of national discretion.

The 1966 International Covenant on Economic, Social and Cultural Rights is by the very nature of its subject-matter an intrusion into once inviolate national territory, an intrusion effected without any corresponding dilution of national sovereignty as the international system's principal ordering concept. As a result, the flexibility of its normative and procedural provisions is a precondition of their by no means universal acceptability to states. The opening statement of a ratifying state's obligations (Article 2) implicitly confirms retention of a broad discretion:

Each State Party to the present Covenant undertakes to take steps, individually and through international assistance and cooperation, especially economic and technical, to the maximum of its available resources, with a view to achieving progressively the full realization of the rights recognized in the present Covenant . . .

In the articles requiring the submission of reports, the Covenant re-emphasizes the extent to which compliance under it is a question of time and degree by assuring the states parties that 'Reports may indicate factors and difficulties affecting the degree of fulfilment of obligations under the present Covenant' (Article 17).

108   TOM J. FARER

It was only in 1966, after twenty years of struggle, that the two
covenants and the separate protocol were finally laid before the
General Assembly. The Covenant on Civil and Political Rights
received 106 votes in favour, none against; its sibling received
105 votes with none against. Despite the fact that a state's
favourable vote did not commit it to subsequent ratification, the
Optional Protocol managed to attract only sixty-six affirmative
votes; there were two negatives and thirty-eight abstentions.[38]
Another ten years passed before the respective covenants
received the thirty-five, and the protocol the ten, ratifications
required for their entry into force.

(c) The Human Rights Machinery: Form

While enthusiasts for the International Bill of Rights were
suffering through its prolonged gestation, the UN member
states, rather than invoking that process as an excuse for
avoiding initiatives certain to attract the same conflicts of
interest and ideology as those delaying the Bill's delivery, moved
forward (gingerly, to be sure) under the authority of the Charter
and the banner of the Universal Declaration. The UN's relevant
activities over the years fall into three distinct categories:
defining and clarifying the rights of individuals (standard
setting); studying particular human rights, or human rights in
particular places; and recommending measures for their fuller
realization (subdivided by some writers into 'promotional' and
'protective' functions); and providing assistance directly to
victims of human rights delinquencies (the humanitarian
function).

1. Humanitarian assistance

This is the activity which, in our time, has had without doubt the
most tangible and far-ranging impact on human rights; yet it is
the least controversial. Indeed, it often skips the minds of people
when they talk about human rights activities of the United
Nations (or disparage the absence thereof). The two most indis-

[38] International Covenant on Economic, Social and Cultural Rights, adopted by GA
Res. 2200 (XXI) of 16 Dec. 1966, *GAOR*, 21st session, supplement no. 16 (A/6316),
pp. 49–52; International Covenant on Civil and Political Rights, ibid., pp. 52–8;
Optional Protocol to the International Covenant on Civil and Political Rights, ibid.,
pp. 59–60.

putably effective and important instruments of direct assistance have been the UN International Children's Emergency
Fund (UNICEF) and the UN High Commissioner for
Refugees (UNHCR). Unlike many other economic and technical assistance organizations, such as the World Bank (International Bank for Reconstruction and Development) and the
US Agency for International Development, UNICEF has
concentrated its resources first on enabling the most desperate
and vulnerable sectors of Third World populations to survive,
and then on helping them to acquire the skills necessary for self-
maintenance.

The office of the UNHCR has been less successful in
avoiding controversy because its mission, protecting those who
flee their native lands for fear of persecution, necessarily
embroils it in the hot spots of international politics. The very act
of extending protection to individuals is often itself a harsh
commentary on the behaviour of the public authorities in the
country from which they have fled. The High Commissioner
may also find himself treated as a nuisance if not an outright
adversary by the host government, for the refugees may
complicate its relations with their home country. They may,
moreover, cause difficulties locally by attempting to enter
domestic labour markets or squatting on undeveloped land.
Although the UNHCR's original mandate contemplated a
short-term protective mission for rather limited numbers of
people pending negotiation of conditions for their safe return to
the country of origin, the vast numbers actually displaced by
civil war and persecution, and the often indefinite prolongation
of exile, have required the High Commissioner and his staff to
marshal resources for maintaining and in some cases integrating
their clients into new lands.

Observers of the operations of UNICEF and the UNHCR
are impressed by their leanness, and by the energy and commitment of those who administer them. Their achievements alone
would support the claim that, with all its institutional
constraints, the United Nations has managed to play an important role in the defence of human rights.

2. Standard-setting, promotion and protection

A lush variety of organs work to carry out the UN's other

DIAGRAM: UN BODIES WITH RESPONSIBILITIES

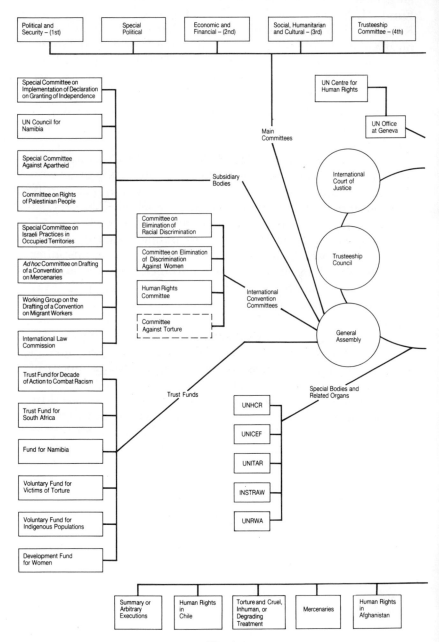

Fig 6.1

IN THE HUMAN RIGHTS AREA

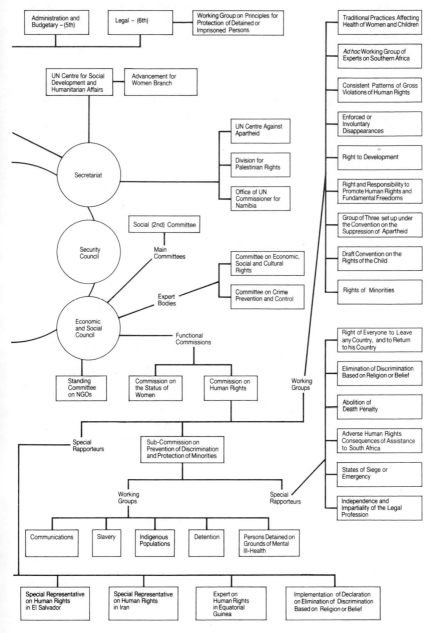

Fig 6 1

tasks in the field of human rights. A diagram of the relevant bodies[39] (see pp. 110–11) unfocuses the eye with its complex mix of boxes, circles, and lines representing and connecting councils, commissions, sub-commissions, committees, special committees, working groups, divisions, centres, offices, and special rapporteurs. A full account of this structure is beyond the scope of this chapter. But some brief summary is necessary for understanding how the UN operates in this field, and for assessing in a preliminary way its present or at least potential efficacy.

The General Assembly reigns, of course, at the apex of the institutional pyramid. It has plenary authority to create subsidiary bodies for any purpose enumerated or implied in the Charter—a power which was used, for example, to establish the Office of the UNHCR in 1951 and the successive committees on apartheid beginning with the Special Committee of 1962. The General Assembly is free to act either through those subsidiaries or directly on any human rights issue that engages the concern of its members. Within the institutional framework created by the Charter, the Economic and Social Council (ECOSOC) serves, subject to the ultimate authority of the Assembly, as the principal organ of the UN concerned with human rights.

Articles 62–6 of the UN Charter authorize ECOSOC to 'make recommendations for the purpose of promoting respect for, and observance of, human rights and fundamental freedoms for all', to 'prepare draft conventions for submission to the General Assembly', to call international conferences, to coordinate the activities of the specialized agencies, to obtain reports both from them and from member states 'on the steps taken to give effect to its own recommendations and to recommendations on matters falling within its competence made by the General Assembly' and to perform 'such other functions . . . as may be assigned to it by the General Assembly'. ECOSOC is a quintessentially political body, its fifty-four members, elected by the General Assembly on the basis of so-called 'equitable geographical distribution', being formal representatives of UN member states.

[39] This diagram is an amended version of one which originally appeared in *Human Rights Internet Reporter*, 11 (Dec. 1985), pp. 21–2; permission to use it here is gratefully acknowledged. It has been revised with assistance from Dr Gudmundur Alfredsson and Benedict Kingsbury. It shows the position at 1 January 1987.

Equally political in its form as in its functions is the Commission on Human Rights established by ECOSOC in 1946[40] to serve as the UN's principal locus for human rights activity, of whatever kind it might be. Politicization of the Commission seems to have been a second thought, albeit one which came quickly after the first. At its first session in 1946, ECOSOC appointed in their individual capacity nine members to serve as the nucleus of a larger body. The 'Nuclear Commission,' as it was called, quickly issued a report recommending that 'all members of the Commission on Human Rights should serve as non-governmental representatives'. Meeting later in 1946, ECOSOC rejected this proposal, deciding instead that the Commission should consist of one representative from each of eighteen member states of the UN selected by the Council.[41]

The Human Rights Commission has since grown to forty-three state representatives, elected, as has become customary in most parts of the UN, pursuant to precise understandings about the appropriate representation of each regional and ideological bloc. Under the present disposition, Africa has eleven of the forty-three representatives (up from one out of eighteen in 1952, and none out of twenty-one in 1962); Asia (minus Japan) has nine, Latin America eight, Eastern Europe five, and Western Europe together with Japan, the US, and the White Commonwealth countries have ten.[42]

In the performance of its several functions, to be discussed below, the Human Rights Commission has frequently employed working groups and special rapporteurs. As of January 1987, eight of the former were conducting studies on

[40] ECOSOC Res. 5(I), first session, Feb. 1946 (establishing the Nuclear Commission); and Res. 9(II), second session, June 1946 (laying down the basic structure and guide-lines in light of, but not consistent with, key elements in the Nuclear Commission's Report).

[41] Schwelb and Alston (n. 35 above, pp. 243–4) comment: 'To those who wanted the Commission to consist of persons serving as individuals and not as representatives of governments, a small concession was made by providing that 'with a view to securing a balanced representation in the various fields covered by the Commission, the Secretary-General shall consult with the governments so selected before the representatives are finally nominated by these governments and confirmed by the Council.' In the 34 years following the enactment of this provision no case of the Secretary-General objecting to the qualification of a representative, or of the Council refusing to confirm him, has become known.' (The Nuclear Commission's report was UN Doc. E/38/Rev. 1.)

[42] Howard Tolley, jun., 'Decision-Making at the United Nations Commission on Human Rights, 1979–82', *Human Rights Quarterly*, 5 (1983), p. 29.

topics as diverse as human rights in South Africa, enforced or involuntary disappearances, the right to development, and rights of the child. Meanwhile a clutch of special rapporteurs were working to enlighten the Commission on such issues as torture, summary or arbitrary executions, and such oxymorons as human rights in El Salvador, Iran, Chile, and Afghanistan.

An additional flock of working groups and rapporteurs indirectly service the Human Rights Commission through its principal subsidiary, the Sub-Commission on the Prevention of Discrimination and the Protection of Minorities. In theory the twenty-six members of the Sub-Commission are elected as independent experts. However, partly because they must be nominated by states (in practice almost invariably their own state), many are no less instruments of their respective governments than their counterparts on the parent body.[43] But at least until very recently, enough members have actually satisfied the formal requisites of independence and expertise to make this child considerably more adventurous and scrupulous than its parent.[44] In 1987 it had working groups on communications concerning consistent patterns of gross violations of human rights, on slavery, and on indigenous populations; and it has special rapporteurs on such topics as states of siege, the death penalty, and the right to leave and return to one's own country.

Twenty years ago, a sketch of UN institutions concerned with human rights which did not include the Special Committee on the Situation with regard to the Implementation of the Declaration on the Granting of Independence to Colonial Countries and Peoples (the 'Committee of 24') would have seemed conspicuously incomplete, if for no other reason than that its name could, more easily than that of any other organ, form the substance of a mantra. Having been established essentially as a prod to decolonization by encouraging and defending indigenous political entrepreneurs and publicizing whatever it deemed to be foot-dragging on the part of the colonial powers, its writ finds few places to run now that the list of colonial territories

---

[43] Hartman, Draft Report, n. 37 above, pp. 36–8.

[44] Ibid. See also Tom Gardeniers, Hurst Hannum, and Janice Kruger, 'The UN Sub-Commission on Prevention of Discrimination and Protection of Minorities: Recent Developments', *Human Rights Quarterly*, 4 (1982), pp. 353–70; and Peter Haver, 'The United Nations Sub-Commission on the Prevention of Discrimination and the Protection of Minorities', *Columbia Journal of Transnational Law*, 21 (1982), pp. 103–34.

has shrunk to comprise mainly a few microscopic atolls and rocks. But even as it sinks towards desuetude, it leaves behind two not trivial legacies. One is a precedent for vigorous investigation and exposure in detail of official acts violating international norms. The second is the procedure, adopted by the Human Rights Commission in 1970, for the consideration of individual communications relating to gross violations of human rights. The Special Committee played a catalytic role in the process leading to the adoption of this procedure.[45]

Unlike the Special Committee on Decolonization, the Commission on the Status of Women has a future as well as a past. Or, in light of occasional proposals to abolish it, one can at least say that it does not face a rapidly disappearing sphere of action. Originally established as a subsidiary of the Human Rights Commission, it was granted full Commission status by ECOSOC during the Council's second session in 1946.[46] Its mandate was (a) to prepare recommendations and reports to ECOSOC on promoting women's rights in political, economic, civil, social, and educational fields, and (b) to make recommendations to the Council on urgent problems requiring immediate attention in the field of women's rights with the object of implementing the principle that men and women shall have equal rights, and to develop proposals to give effect to such recommendations.[47]

The Commission on the Status of Women has functioned primarily to raise consciousness (through reports and conferences) about the distinctive obstacles women face in attempting to enjoy the human rights theoretically guaranteed to all without distinction, and to articulate detailed standards for guiding and measuring the efforts of states to reduce those obstacles. Among its achievements are the Declaration on the Elimination of Discrimination against Women, adopted by the General Assembly in 1967, and the associated Convention approved by the Assembly in 1979.[48] Other important Conventions prepared by the Commission and adopted by the Assembly

[45] Tolley, n. 23 above, pp. 424–9.

[46] See ECOSOC Res. 5(I) and 11(II), both in 1946.

[47] For a summary of its work, and UN action in the women's rights field in general, see Schwelb and Alston, n. 35 above, pp. 254–60.

[48] Respectively, GA Res. 2263 (XXII) of 7 Nov. 1967, and GA Res. 34/180 of 18 Dec. 1979.

are one on the Political Rights of Women, and another on the Nationality of Married Women.[49]

Article 28 of the Covenant on Civil and Political Rights provides for the establishment of an eighteen-member Human Rights Committee composed of nationals of states parties to the Covenant and elected by the parties from a list of nominees presented by them to the Secretary-General. The Committee's role is limited so far as most states are concerned. It is to consider the reports which the parties are required to submit concerning the measures they have taken to give effect to the rights enumerated in the Covenant. The same Committee has the power to hear complaints between states that have expressed acceptance of Committee jurisdiction in such cases under Article 41 of the Covenant. However, no complaints of this kind have in fact been received. The Committee also hears complaints by individuals against states which are parties to the Optional Protocol: well over 200 such complaints have come before it.

The Human Rights Committee has been functioning since 1977. Under the Civil and Political Covenant, the Committee has a legal basis independent of the UN Charter. However, the Covenant makes the UN Secretary-General an integral part both of election and reporting procedures, and the Committee is dependent on the UN for logistical support: so it is regarded as a body functioning within the general framework of the UN system.

(d) The Human Rights Machinery: Praxis

It is a commonplace of scholarship to discern three phases in UN human rights activities during which the main focus was, in turn, standard-setting (conventions and declarations); promotion (advisory services, broad studies, and an incipient reporting system); and protection (establishment of procedures for assessing information received from private persons and groups concerning possible gross violations and reporting thereon to the general membership, fact-finding in certain cases where member states allege grave violations, and efforts to mitigate or

[49] Respectively, GA Res. 640 (VII) of 20 Dec. 1952, and GA Res. 1040 (XI) of 29 Jan. 1957.

terminate violations in particular cases). 'Since 1977', according to two scholars who seem to endorse this temporal ordering of UN activity, 'a fourth stage has . . . emerged, which emphasizes the structural and economic aspects of human rights issues.'[50]

Like all scholarly efforts to order the confused scrum of life, these phases correspond only roughly to actual events within the UN system. For instance, the fact that the so-called fourth stage (also referred to commonly as the recognition of 'third generation rights') manifests itself to a large extent in proposed declarations and similar efforts at norm generation[51] nicely illustrates the overlapping, indeed cumulative, character of these phases.

The phases themselves are not the expression of an ineluctable logic of sequence. One can argue, for instance, that standards spelt out in the first phase had in fact already been set even before the main human rights conventions were drawn up.

---

[50] Schwelb and Alston, n. 35 above, pp. 250–1.

[51] For a biting and persuasive critique of efforts to transform every sort of interest, but particularly those frequently included in lists of 'third generation rights', into a human right, see Philip Alston, 'Conjuring Up New Human Rights: A Proposal for Quality Control', *American Journal of International Law*, 78 (1984), p. 607. He argues, therein, that the General Assembly's role as the authoritative definer of human rights is in serious danger of being undermined. The problem, as he sees it, is as follows: 'First, the General Assembly has, on several occasions in recent years, proclaimed new rights (i.e., rights which do not find explicit recognition in the Universal Declaration of Human Rights or the two International Human Rights Covenants) without explicitly acknowledging its intention of doing so and without insisting that the claims in question should satisfy any particular criteria before qualifying as human rights. Second, there has been a growing tendency on the part of a range of United Nations and other international bodies, including in particular the UN Commission on Human Rights, to proceed to the proclamation of new human rights without reference to the Assembly. Third, the ease with which such innovation has been accomplished in these bodies has in turn encouraged or provoked the nomination of additional candidates, ranging from the right to tourism to the right to disarmament, at such a rate that the integrity of the entire process of recognizing human rights is threatened.' Alston has been consistent and consistently persuasive in his scepticism. In an article published two years earlier he wrote: 'In many respects the concept of third generation rights smacks rather too strongly of a tactical endeavour to bring together, under the rubric of human rights, many of the most pressing concerns on the international agenda and to construct an artificial international consensus in favour of human rights by appealing to the 'favourite' concerns of each of the main geopolitical blocs . . . In sum, the concept of third generation solidarity rights would seem to contribute more obfuscation than clarification in an area which can ill afford to be made less accessible to the masses than it already is.' 'A Third Generation of Solidarity Rights: Progressive Development or Obfuscation of International Human Rights Law?', *Netherlands International Law Review*, 29 (1982), p. 322.

Implicit in the Nuremberg indictments in 1945 was the proposition that at least with respect to the right to life and freedom from torture, there already were clear norms. As for other rights essential to even the slimmest conception of human dignity, surely they were stated with sufficient clarity in the 1948 Universal Declaration to allow their immediate use for assessing the behaviour of member states.

One can also argue that the long years of the second phase, of advisory services and broad studies, were far from an essential precondition of the third phase, concerned with protection. Violations of those rights (like the right to life) the centrality of which is universally admitted—as evidenced, for example, by provisions in the principal covenants and conventions making them non-derogable—have long been readily identifiable in any and every context. Governments have not been in doubt about the content of their obligations. The UN's protective activity, such as it has been, came last and late because a large proportion of governments, while not insisting on a plenary discretion in the choice of means for their various ends, were reluctant to subject themselves to the risk of exposure. Viewed only as an institution engaged in standard-setting, the UN looks impressive. By very large majorities, sometimes approaching unanimity, the General Assembly has approved declarations and conventions broadly elaborating the core rights of human dignity. Its subordinate body, ECOSOC, has also set significant standards. It has, for instance, gone beyond condemning slavery to identifying and prohibiting slavery-like practices such as debt bondage which are not unknown in the contemporary world.[52] And in spelling out the rights of women, the General Assembly itself has cut right across the grain of custom in more than a few member states. When, however, one views, as I now will, its efforts to protect the actual exercise of enumerated rights, something less engaging meets the eye.

---

[52] Supplementary Convention on the Abolition of Slavery, the Slave Trade, and Institutions and Practices Similar to Slavery, adopted by Conference of Plenipotentiaries convened by ECOSOC Res. 608, 21 UN ESCOR supp. no. 1 at p. 7, UN doc. E/2889 (1956) and done at Geneva on 7 Sept. 1956; entered into force 30 Apr. 1957. For a balanced and hence somewhat mordant review of UN activity with respect to the problem of slavery, see Kathryn Zoglin, 'United Nations Action Against Slavery: A Critical Evaluation', *Human Rights Quarterly*, 8 (1986), pp. 306–39.

1. The Problematics of Protection

One can get a picture of the UN's present capacity for protective activity by examining the actions and omissions of the Human Rights Commission and the Sub-Commission, and their inter-actions with ECOSOC and the General Assembly over the course of four decades: and also by looking at the work of the Human Rights Committee under the Civil Covenant. Attributing any capacity at all to the UN requires a certain leap of faith in the efficacy of exposure by a credible fact-finder. For except in the unusual case where human rights violations produce a threat to or breach of the peace, thus providing the jurisdictional conditions for mandatory sanctions under Chapter VII of the Charter, exposure is the principal weapon in the UN armoury.

Because the Inter-American Commission on Human Rights has been in the forefront of intergovernmental bodies employing this weapon and may well have plumbed its limits, its powers, procedures, and activities provide a useful bench-mark for assessing the behaviour and the potential of the UN's roughly comparable organs.[53] Founded in 1959, the Inter-American Commission consists of seven persons elected in their individual capacity by the members of the Organization of American States (OAS) from a slate of government-nominated candidates.[54] Commission members are supposed to be strictly independent

[53] A very useful collection of inter-American norms, and Commission rules, activities, and doctrine, including summaries of reports on the general condition of human rights in various countries, is Inter-American Commission on Human Rights, *Ten Years of Activities: 1971–81* (OAS, Washington DC, 1982). For an effort to locate the work of the Commission in relation to inter-American politics and social systems, see Tom J. Farer, *The Grand Strategy of the United States in Latin America* (New Brunswick, 1987).

[54] Fifth Meeting of Consultation of Ministers of Foreign Affairs (Santiago 1959), Resolution on Human Rights, Final Act, OAS Official Records, OEA/Series C/II.5, pp. 10–11. The Second Special Inter-American Conference (Rio de Janeiro 1965) enlarged the Commission's powers so that it could review individual petitions, request pertinent information concerning the petitions from member states, and make recommendations to said states. Final Act, Official Documents, OEA/Ser.E/XIII.1 (1965), pp. 45–6. The Protocol of Buenos Aires (adopted 1967, entered into force 1970), amending the Charter of the OAS, made the Commission a 'Principal Organ', thus giving it a normative base in the Charter itself as distinguished from mere resolutions which could be altered by a simple majority of the annual General Assembly, to defend the norms set out in the American Declaration on the Rights and Duties of Man, which had been adopted by the Ninth International Conference of American States, Bogota, 1948, OEA/Ser. L./V/I.4 Rev. (1965).

and distinguished in the field of human rights. They are supported in their work by a permanent staff of lawyers and investigators headquartered in Washington and forming a part of the OAS secretariat.

The Inter-American Commission is authorized by the Charter of the OAS and resolutions of its political organs, and by the American Convention on Human Rights,[55] to investigate allegations of human rights violations made by individuals or non-governmental organizations such as Amnesty International. Where it concludes that a violation has occurred and the delinquent government thereafter fails to take satisfactory remedial action, the Commission is empowered to include its findings and recommendations in its Annual Report.[56] The Commission also has a plenary discretion to inquire into the general situation of human rights in any OAS member state, and to publish detailed reports containing its conclusions and recommendations.

To facilitate its inquiries, the Inter-American Commission invariably requests permission from concerned governments to make on-site inspections (the *observation in loco*) to be carried out under rules it adopted in 1977 which allow it to collect information by all means it deems appropriate, including visits to detention centres and private interviews with detainees. In granting permission to enter (the *anuencia*), governments coincidentally undertake to facilitate the Commission's work in every reasonable way including public reassurance to citizens that they are free to contact the Commission without fear of reprisal. In all cases, governments have an opportunity to comment on draft reports, and the Commission takes those comments, proposed corrections, offers of remedial action, and so on into account as it proceeds to a final report for publication and presentation to the General Assembly. Since 1975, Commission Presidents have been invited to present and defend its reports,

[55] Signed 22 Nov. 1969, entered into force 18 July 1978. *OAS Treaty Series* no. 36, at 1, OAS Off. Rec. OEA/Ser.L/V/II.23 doc. Rev 2.

[56] As late as 1973, the Inter-American Commission was receiving only a few dozen cases a year. As a consequence of the violent overthrow of Chile's democratic system, the case-load leaped into the thousands, where it remained throughout the decade as cases poured first out of Uruguay, and then, like a tidal wave, out of Argentina when, in 1976, the Argentine armed forces launched their campaign of extermination against urban guerrillas and their support structures.

including the Annual Report, before the OAS General Assembly, where concerned governments have often exercised their right to respond. Frequently—indeed invariably from 1977–80, when Jimmy Carter was President of the United States—the Assembly adopted resolutions calling on governments that had been the subjects of reports to implement Commission recommendations.

From its inception, the Inter-American Commission has in general construed its mandate and exercised its powers to the end of bringing maximum pressure to bear on governments violating human rights, on the whole without reference to their professed ideology, their political influence, or any other extraneous consideration. Both influential and politically inconsequential states, regimes of the right as well as the left, have been subjects of harshly critical Commission reports.[57]

The organs of the UN concerned with human rights, above all the Commission on Human Rights and its institutional superior ECOSOC, have evinced neither a comparable enthusiasm for the protective mission nor a comparable capacity for impartial judgement. As early as January 1947, when the members of the UN Commission on Human Rights gathered for their first regular session, the UN had already received a large number of letters containing allegations of human rights violations.[58] In effect, the Commission was being petitioned for assistance in obtaining the redress of grievances against member states. As

---

[57] One or more reports on each of the following countries have been published as of January 1987: Argentina, Bolivia, Chile, Colombia, Cuba, El Salvador, Guatemala, Haiti, Nicaragua, Panama, Paraguay, and Uruguay. The first report on Nicaragua described conditions under the regime of Anastasio Somoza during the civil war which culminated in his flight and the establishment of a new government. In response to an invitation from the revolutionary government, the Commission revisited the country approximately a year after the revolution and prepared a report, published in 1981. In 1982, a third visit was conducted by a special committee of the Commission charged with inquiring into conditions on the Atlantic coast affecting its indigenous populations. Since the 1962 suspension of Cuba's right to participate in OAS activities, the government of Fidel Castro has refused to recognize the jurisdiction of the Commission, or any other OAS organ. However, in light of the fact that Cuba was suspended, not expelled, and the fact that Cuba has never formally exercised its right to withdraw from the OAS, the Commission has consistently concluded that it does have jurisdiction, and it has periodically reported on conditions in that country. The Commission's report on the situation of human rights in Argentina from 1976 to 1979 (the period of mass 'disappearance') served as the base point for the trials of former military leaders which were initiated by the democratically elected government of Raul Alfonsín.

[58] Schwelb and Alston, n. 35 above, p. 270.

pointed out earlier, it responded to this initial opportunity to define some protective role by concluding that it had none.[59] In the words of the report of that first session summarizing the Commission's reaction to individual communications: 'The Commission recognizes that it has no power to take any action in regard to any complaints concerning human rights.'[60] In what seemed an effort to avoid even inadvertent pressure on governments accused of human rights violations, it also decided that communications containing such allegations would not be circulated to the individual members even on a confidential basis. Rather they would receive, but only in private meetings, a confidential list containing only a brief, presumably sanitized indication of the substance of these dangerous if not positively offensive epistles.

To one of the legal paladins of that day, the Cambridge don Hersch Lauterpacht, the Human Rights Commission's crippling act of self-denial was wholly unjustified,[61] a view the Economic and Social Council was unable to share. At the first opportunity it explicitly endorsed the Commission's position[62] while coincidentally rejecting a request from the Commission on the Status of Women for a clear mandate to make recommendations to the Council on urgent problems requiring immediate attention in defence of women's rights.[63]

Scholars and spokesmen for women's rights were not the only persons unimpressed by ECOSOC's and the Human Rights Commission's marvellous self-restraint. As Schwelb and Alston note:

The two Sub-Commissions, whose members were persons serving in their individual capacity and not as government representatives, recommended amendments of [the Council's] resolution . . . which would make it possible to take action in certain cases. In regard to the recommendations of the Sub-Commission on Discrimination and Minorities, the Commission on Human Rights decided not to sanction any change in the procedure. As far as the recommendations of the Freedom of Information Sub-Commission were concerned, the

[59] See above, nn. 25 and 26.
[60] E/259 (1947), paras. 21 and 22.
[61] H. Lauterpacht, *International Law and Human Rights* (New York, 1950, reprinted 1968), pp. 223–62.
[62] See above, n. 26.
[63] ECOSOC Res. 76 (V) of 5 Aug. 1947.

Economic and Social Council approved the proposal for the compilation twice a year of a list of communications on freedom of information, but expressly decided that this was not to apply to communications which contained criticism or complaints against Governments in the field of freedom of information (Council resolution 240 C(IX) of 28 July 1949).[64]

For more than twenty years thereafter the UN Commission on Human Rights remained an instrument of non-protection lounging under the protective wing of ECOSOC. As proof of its existence, it summoned the energy to draft soaring standards and issue occasional reports of a comfortably general character. Yet, despite its fierce commitment to inoffensiveness, the Commission could not always manage to match ECOSOC's reticence. In 1950 it requested establishment of a system of annual human rights reports by member states. The Council responded by returning the proposal for further study.[65] And there it might have remained had not the United States taken up the matter in 1953, apparently as a counterweight to its concurrent declaration that it would not become a party to any human rights treaty.[66] United States' support produced a prodding resolution addressed by the General Assembly to ECOSOC.[67] The latter body, moving with all its deliberate speed, managed in only three years to adopt an operative resolution.[68] This left the very making of a report to the discretion of states, so the reporting process was not calculated to upset any of the world's chancelleries. And with one exception it did not.

That exception stemmed from a 1965 modification of the reporting system. In what may be taken to have been a fit of inattention, ECOSOC instructed the Sub-Commission on Prevention of Discrimination and Protection of Minorities to study such information as was provided by states under the reporting procedures and to forward resulting comments and

[64] Schwelb and Alston, n. 35 above, p. 271.

[65] ECOSOC Res. 303 E(XI) (1950).

[66] Statement by Secretary of State John Foster Dulles before the US Senate Judiciary Committee, 6 Apr. 1953, reproduced in 'Review of the United Nations Charter, A Collection of Documents, 83rd Congress, 2nd session', Senate doc. no. 87, 1954, pp. 295-6.

[67] GA Res. 739 (VIII) of 28 Nov. 1953.

[68] ECOSOC Res. 624 B (XXII) (1956).

recommendations to the Human Rights Commission. In 1967 the Sub-Commission, with a zeal its majority would subsequently regret, appointed a Special Rapporteur to prepare a survey of salient current developments in human rights, presumably in light of reports under the ECOSOC procedures. The work he subsequently submitted to the Sub-Commission included an Annex containing observations on human rights matters submitted by non-governmental organizations (which had been looking for UN fora willing to receive information about the real world of human rights), and comments by governments touched by those observations. Responding swiftly, a Sub-Commission member moved that the dangerous Annex should be destroyed. By a vote of eight to six, with four abstentions, the Sub-Commission decided to withdraw it. This act of rectification for its negligence in appointing a Rapporteur so uninitiated in Council and Commission ritual apparently did not satisfy the demanding standards of ECOSOC: it proceeded to relieve the Sub-Commission of further responsibility for reviewing reports.[69]

While this little contretemps, seen in isolation, seemed to confirm the continued supremacy of the doctrine of impotence, in retrospect it has the look of a death spasm. For 1967, the doctrine's twentieth anniversary, was also the year when the Human Rights Commission and ECOSOC collaborated both to annul it and to concede the legitimacy and value of communications from the unofficial world of victims and their non-governmental champions. The doctrine's fortifications collapsed under the weight of African voting power which by the mid-1960s was becoming a decisive factor at the UN. In balancing their own vulnerability to charges of delinquency against their goal of ending colonial and racist rule in southern Africa, the African states came down in favour of risking the former to advance the latter.

The beginning of the end of the doctrine of impotence was signalled in 1965 when the Committee of Twenty-Four summoned ECOSOC's attention to information concerning violation of human rights in southern Africa submitted by petitioners to the Committee.[70] As if awakened thereby from a long

[69] ECOSOC Res. 1230 (XLII) (1967).
[70] Richard Lillich and Frank Newman, *International Human Rights* (Boston, 1979), p. 271.

dream of sleep, ECOSOC responded immediately by inviting the Human Rights Commission to consider as a matter of importance and urgency the question of the violation of human rights, including policies of racial discrimination and segregation and of apartheid in all countries, with particular reference to colonial and other dependent countries and territories, and to submit its recommendations on measures to halt those violations.[71]

In their valuable survey of human rights institutions under the Charter, Schwelb and Alston summarize the successive actions of the General Assembly, ECOSOC, the Human Rights Commission, and the Sub-Commission on Discrimination and Minorities. During the period 1966–71 these bodies fashioned the machinery for human rights protection which has continued to operate without fundamental change.[72] The principal components of its normative framework are Commission resolution 8 (XXIII) of 1967 and ECOSOC resolutions 1235 of 1967 and 1503 of 1970. In resolution 8 the Commission added an agenda item on the 'Question of Violations' and, in a marked expansion of Sub-Commission jurisdiction beyond the problems of minorities, directed it to bring to the attention of the Commission 'any situation which it has reasonable cause to believe reveals a consistent pattern of violations . . . [and] to prepare . . . a report containing information on violations of human rights and fundamental freedoms from all available sources'. Under its resolution the Commission could choose to initiate 'a thorough study' of the described situations which it said were exemplified by apartheid in South Africa and racial discrimination in Southern Rhodesia.

In resolution 1235, adopted on 6 June 1967, ECOSOC welcomed the Commission's decision, and declared the Commission's and the Sub-Commission's right 'to examine information relevant to gross violations of fundamental rights and fundamental freedoms' contained in the individual communications which, under ECOSOC's successive edicts, had been screened from Commission review since 1947.

These steps left in their wake uncertainty about the way in which communications would be handled and employed; and

[71] ECOSOC Res. 1102 (XL) (1966).
[72] Schwelb and Alston, n. 35 above, pp. 272–3.

about the willingness of Sub-Commission, Commission, and
ECOSOC actually to study, much less publicize, human rights
violations occurring outside southern Africa. Sensitivity on the
latter point surfaced during the debate preceding the adoption of
resolution 1235, expressed in the form of objections (from representatives of the United Kingdom, the Philippines, and
Tanzania) to the very idea of studies being made without the
target state's consent,[73] and in the successful amendment
pressed by the Soviet Union and Afro-Asian states making racial
discrimination the primary point of concern.[74] Continued sensitivity about publicizing the contents of private communications
became apparent when some governments objected to use by
Sub-Commission experts of such communications as evidence
in reports under resolution 1235 describing human rights
violations by named states.[75]

While efforts by the Eastern bloc and most Afro-Asian states
to impose a narrow focus as a matter of principle continued to be
defeated by narrow margins, in practice the Human Rights
Commission advanced only with studied caution beyond
southern Africa and the territories occupied by Israel during
the 1967 Middle East war. Moreover, the procedures finally
adopted for handling private communications eased the concerns animating advocates of the narrow focus. Authorized by
ECOSOC resolution 1503 (XLVIII) of 1970 ('Procedure for
dealing with communications relating to violations of human
rights and fundamental freedoms'), and elaborated by the Sub-
Commission on Discrimination and Minorities in 1971, they
operate in the following manner.[76]

Personnel of the UN Centre for Human Rights (formerly the
Human Rights Division) prepare summaries of the thousands of
communications received annually alleging violations of human
rights, and forward them to a five-member Working Group of
the Sub-Commission on Discrimination and Minorities. The
Working Group convenes for two weeks each summer, just prior
to the annual four-week meeting of the Sub-Commission, and

[73] UN doc. E/AC.7/SR.567, E/AC.7/SR.569 (1967).
[74] Tolley, n. 23 above, p. 428.
[75] Ibid., p. 429.
[76] There is a concise description in Tolley at pp. 429–53. Lillich and Newman, n. 70
above, pp. 318–87, provide a well-documented and annotated case study (Greece under
military rule) of the UN's 1503 procedures.

decides whether communications concerning a particular government, considered in light of that government's response, if any, 'appear to reveal a consistent pattern of gross and reliably attested violations of human rights and fundamental freedoms'. All communications satisfying that criterion, in the opinion of a majority of the working group (which must have the usual geographic balance), are placed on the Sub-Commission's agenda. The Working Group's meetings are closed and its decisions confidential.

Since neither the Secretariat nor the Working Group inform correspondents that their letters or petitions are being considered, the latter, if they are to supplement their original communication at all, must do so blindly—that is without any knowledge either of the Working Group's initial reaction or of the contents of a government's response. The Working Group could, but apparently does not, alleviate this difficulty—indeed, one could argue, this fundamental unfairness in its pro-cedures—by exercising its discretion to seek additional infor-mation. Exclusion of correspondents and petitioners continues through all stages of the 1503 procedure.

Nothing in the resolution establishing the Working Group, or in the practice of the Sub-Commission on Discrimination and Minorities, suggests that the Working Group has discre-tion not to forward communications which meet the criterion. The Sub-Commission, however, has acted as if it bears no comparable obligation to the Commission. For reasons known only to it, since *its* review of resolution 1503 communications also is confidential, it has postponed forwarding cases despite access to evidence of gross violations that would have satisfied fact-finders afflicted with even the slightest degree of impartiality.[77]

Resolution 1503 explicitly authorizes the Sub-Commission to take into account not only the communications brought before it by the Working Group and the replies of governments but also 'other relevant information'. Perhaps taking a cue from its parent, the Working Group is reliably reported to have behaved

---

[77] Most notoriously in 1972 when it decided to send the Greece, Iran, and Portugal cases back to its Working Group, ostensibly to provide the governments with yet addi-tional time to respond. Since that inauspicious beginning, the Sub-Commission on Discrimination and Minorities has been considerably less inhibited.

in at least one case as if it too had a plenary discretion to decide what situations should move on through the process.[78]

Cases forwarded by the Sub-Commission on Discrimination and Minorities must then pass successfully through the Human Rights Commission's own five-member Working Group before arriving at last on the Commission's agenda. The Commission is empowered under resolution 1503 to respond in a variety of ways. It may, in effect, dismiss the case (technically it terminates consideration) either by finding that a consistent pattern of gross violations has not been established, or, apparently, for any other reason it deems satisfactory. Or it may keep the case on its agenda for further consideration at a later session (a minimum delay of one year). Or it may decide to initiate a 'thorough study' of the situation, with or without the consent of the concerned government. Or, with the consent of the relevant government, it may investigate the situation through the medium of an *ad hoc* committee of 'independent persons whose competence and impartiality is beyond question'.

As an alternative, however, the Human Rights Commission could break out of the constraints of the resolution 1503 procedure. Drawing on its authority under resolution 1235, it can appoint an *ad hoc* working group or a special rapporteur to study the situation, prepare a report and draft recommendations which the Commission can then debate publicly, adopt, and forward to ECOSOC.[79] Governments facing indictments have made strenuous efforts to bar public debate (and, *a fortiori*, action) concerning situations being considered under 1503— efforts which have, unfortunately, succeeded in some cases.[80]

---

[78] Tolley, n. 23 above, p. 440. The original report surfaced in an article in *Le Monde*. Its credibility was enhanced when the Soviet representative to the Sub-Commission introduced a resolution asking the Secretary-General to investigate the source of the leak.

[79] For an overview of the interaction between 1235 and 1503 procedures, see Tolley, n. 23 above, pp. 449–53. One example of the movement from confidential to public procedures is the case of Afghanistan. Monitoring under 1503 was discontinued in 1984 when the Human Rights Commission appointed a Special Rapporteur to prepare a report. Paraguay has been subject to both procedures simultaneously; each one focused, however, on a different aspect of the situation in that country: alleged massacre and enslavement of Indian tribes was the subject of a 1503 procedure while a public resolution under 1235 addressed the country's prolonged state of siege. In 1982 Iran's treatment of the Bahais was the subject of both a public resolution and a confidential referral. Sub-Commission Res. 1982/25, UN doc. E/CN.4/183/4.

[80] Tolley (n. 23 above, p. 457) concludes acerbically: 'To the extent that an oppressive government feigns cooperation with the Commission's confidential scrutiny, it can

2. 'Action' under resolutions 1235 and 1503

At the time of its adoption, resolution 1503 was widely seen by scholars and activists as a step beyond resolution 1235 in the development of protective machinery. This perception probably stemmed from the fact that, while initiatives under 1235 lie entirely in the hands of member states and hence are inevitably governed by political criteria, 1503 gave the power of initiative for the first time to individuals and non-governmental organizations. Under it, they could trigger action, even if only the action of confronting unpleasant facts of international life. To many, this seemed an enormously valuable precedent, a breach in the citadel of the mutual protection society, one that could be progressively enlarged. Perhaps in the long run it will turn out that the optimists were right. But to this point, 1235 has shown greater promise. What can nevertheless be said for resolution 1503 proceedings is that at least they have ceased to be a bottomless receptacle for petitions of the desperate.

UN action during the first years of the process was enough to depress Dr Pangloss. The case of Greece under military rule, 1967–74, was an early and well-documented fiasco.[81] It began

escape public inquiry and political shame under the Resolution 1235 procedure.' He cites, as a case in point, the Human Rights Commission's failure to place on its agenda the situation in Argentina during the era of the disappeared. In contrast, the Argentine regime's effort to avert an Inter-American Commission report by a show of formal cooperation (e.g. rapid response to inquiries about disappeared persons; but in almost every case the substance of the response was a denial that the person had been detained by the security forces) was not successful. In 1977 a majority of the Commission invoked the confidential procedures while blocking a public inquiry into the situation in Idi Amin's Uganda. See statement of Mr Kooijmans of the Netherlands in UN doc. E/CN.4/1985/SR.45. Commission practice with respect to presentations by non-governmental organizations has been erratic. See Menno Kamminga and Nigel Rodley, 'Direct Intervention at the UN: NGO Participation in the Commission on Human Rights and Its Sub-Commission', in Hannum, n. 1 above, pp. 195–6: 'In 1978, an informal agreement was reached among members of the Commission that no public reference to situations which had already been considered behind closed doors under the 1503 procedure should be allowed. Several NGO representatives were interrupted during their oral statements and asked to identify the countries to which they were referring. If it was a country that had already been considered under the 1503 procedure, the NGO was prohibited from continuing its statement. The agreement applied only to that session, however, and in 1980 the Commission resorted to its earlier practice of scheduling the public discussion of country situations before the 1503 procedure, thus avoiding the problem.' They go on to point out that in 1981 the Chair ruled, in effect, that NGO reference to particular countries was all right so long as a statement did not refer to decisions made or materials submitted under the confidential procedures.

81 See Lillich and Newman, n. 70 above, pp. 318–87.

with an extremely detailed and well-prepared communication sent by Professor Frank Newman of the University of California, on behalf of various private human rights organizations, well in advance of the first meeting of the Working Group of the Sub-Commission on Discrimination and Minorities. (Greece had previously been a subject of incipient concern by the Sub-Commission in 1968, but the Human Rights Commission itself had refused to consider the situation under 1235.) Unofficial reports of its subsequent phases have never been disputed. It appears that the Working Group reviewed the case and forwarded it, along with those of Iran and Portugal, to the Sub-Commission. Despite the fact that the governments had not chosen to formulate responses in the ample time available before the Working Group meeting, the Sub-Commission chose to send the cases back to the Working Group, ostensibly to give the governments another opportunity to state their positions. Thus, at a blow, a year was lost in cases alleging systematic ongoing torture and other grave violations.

In the midst of the next session of the Sub-Commission on Discrimination and Minorities with Greece once more on the agenda, the dictatorial regime of General Papadopoulos officially ended martial law and declared a general amnesty for political prisoners. The Sub-Commission thereupon decided to remove Greece from the agenda although the institutional structure of repression was unaltered. Some two months later the Papadopoulos regime was overthrown in another military coup and violations of human rights intensified. But since the Sub-Commission had not then, as it has not now, any procedures for emergency action between meetings, its experts could not refer confidential communications concerning Greece to the Human Rights Commission in time for its annual winter meeting. By the time the Sub-Commission had reconvened in August 1974, events triggered by the military government's intervention in Cyprus had culminated in the restoration of civilian rule. Greece was again dropped from the agenda.

Idi Amin's Uganda was another case to pass vagrantly through the maze established by resolution 1503. Communications concerning this regime of mass murder did reach the Human Rights Commission, apparently having been referred there in 1974 and again in 1976 and 1977.[82] Not until 1978, on the eve of Amin's flight following defeat by the Tanzanian armed forces aided by Ugandan insurgents, did the Commission take any action at all. That action assumed the form of a request to the Secretary-General to appoint a Special Representative to Uganda. In UN practice, such representatives function only to plead for more genteel behaviour, that is to say, they talk softly and carry a twig.

Although, as I have already suggested, the Sub-Commission on Discrimination and Minorities can hardly be accused of carrying out its tasks with reckless zeal, since 1973 it has forwarded for Human Rights Commission consideration a substantial number of cases. They have included regimes aligned with both the US and the USSR, as well as some more or less unaligned in global politics. Howard Tolley, a leading authority on the Commission and Sub-Commission, estimates a referral rate of six to eight cases a year. From 1978, when the Commission began naming countries that had been the subject of 'decisions' (without indicating the nature of the decision), to 1984, twenty-eight countries were so identified.[83] But in no case to date has the Commission exercised its power to undertake a thorough study or to seek the consent of a delinquent state for the creation of an investigating committee. The closest it has come is in the case of Equatorial Guinea, another of the great abattoirs of our time.[84] Despite a record of atrocities dating back to the dictator Macias's accession to power in 1968, the case bobbed about in the great sea of 1503 until 1979. Then, in the face of Macias's rejection even of secret contacts with a personal representative of the Secretary-General, the Commission authorized disclosure of the 1503 materials. When, shortly thereafter, Macias was overthrown, the Commission invoked not 1503 but 1235 to justify appointing a Special Rapporteur who thereafter

[82] Tolley, n. 23 above, p. 442.
[83] Ibid., p. 446, lists the twenty-eight governments subject to Commission decisions under resolution 1503 from 1978 to 1984. They were as follows: Seven in *Africa*: Benin, Central African Republic, Equatorial Guinea, Ethiopia, Malawi, Mozambique, Uganda. Nine in *Asia*: Afghanistan, Burma, Indonesia, Iran, Japan, Republic of Korea, Malaysia, Pakistan, Philippines. Nine in *Latin America*: Argentina, Bolivia, Chile, El Salvador, Guatemala, Haiti, Paraguay, Uruguay, Venezuela. Two in *Eastern Europe*: Albania, German Democratic Republic. One in *Western Europe and Other*: Turkey.
[84] Thomas Franck, *Nation Against Nation* (Oxford, 1985), pp. 234–5.

compiled what amounted to a mere historical account of the regime's crimes.

While the Human Rights Commission has done little to vitalize the resolution 1503 procedure, it has not entirely abjured a protective function. But, as already suggested, it has acted, either expressly or implicitly, pursuant to the grant of authority under resolution 1235 and/or *ad hoc* requests for action from the General Assembly or ECOSOC. The brutal overthrow of the democratically elected government of Salvador Allende in Chile in 1973 stimulated the first serious rights-protecting initiative of the Commission—and, indeed, of the UN system as a whole—which was not related to conditions in colonial territories, Israeli-occupied territories, and South Africa. Thomas Franck, in his useful and provocative study of the UN, *Nation Against Nation*, describes the system's variegated response:

On March 1, 1974, the Commission . . . [authorized] its chairman to address a cable to the Chilean military authorities expressing the members' concern for the protection of the lives of political prisoners and calling for strict observance of the principles of the United Nations Charter and the International Covenants on Human Rights. ECOSOC, by consensus, quickly seconded that demand. Next, the Sub-Commission . . . called for a 'study' of Chilean human rights violations, and the General Assembly—charging the Chilean junta with 'gross and massive violations,' including 'the practice of torture' and operating 'concentration camps'—demanded the immediate release of all political prisoners and safe conduct out of the country for those who desired it.

In the spring of 1975 the Human Rights Commission set up a working group of five members to inquire into these charges. Although the working group was refused admission to Chile, it was able to report to the 1975 Assembly, which, in turn, expressed '*its profound distress* at the constant flagrant violations of human rights, including the institutionalized practice of torture, cruel, inhuman or degrading treatment or punishment, arbitrary arrest, detention and exile.' . . . The vote on this resolution was 95 to 11, with 23 abstentions. The United States, Canada, and all of Western Europe voted for its adoption.[85]

Since then the Human Rights Commission has exercised the right to investigate on its own motion notorious cases of gross violations, and to consider such cases in public proceedings.

[85] Franck, n. 84 above, pp. 238–9.

Investigations have been carried out by *ad hoc* working groups or individual rapporteurs. (In the Bolivian case, he was called a 'special envoy'.) The subjects of such procedures have included Bolivia, El Salvador, Guatemala, Poland, Afghanistan, and Iran. The Commission has even been moved to criticize a state's human rights record without benefit of an extensive prior investigation. In a 1983 resolution on the situation in Kampuchea—following, paradoxically, Vietnam's overthrow of Pol Pot's genocidal regime—the Commission condemned 'the persistent occurrence of gross and flagrant violations of human rights' in that country.[86] Presumably most members were more inflamed by Vietnam's invasion of a fellow Third World state than by the suffering inflicted on the Cambodian people by Pol Pot. However, in most cases public criticism of a regime by the Commission came only after inconclusive confidential processing under resolution 1503. Examples are El Salvador, Guatemala, Bolivia, Afghanistan, and Iran.

The Sub-Commission on Discrimination and Minorities has also asserted the authority to make public recommendations for action even in cases being simultaneously considered under resolution 1503. Tolley records five cases where the confidentiality requirement was thereby avoided: Uganda, Bolivia, Paraguay, Afghanistan, and Iran.[87]

(e) The Future of UN Enforcement Activities

The United Nations is now a participant, however ambivalent, in the defence of human rights. That is indisputable. Equally indisputable is its highly selective attitude towards enforcement, and its refusal in all cases other than Rhodesia and South Africa to recommend sanctions.

There is not much sympathy among UN members for unauthorized humanitarian intervention.[88] Being weak and vulnerable states, most members see themselves only as objects of intervention. Moreover, being former colonies or *de facto* dependencies of powerful states, most recall the many occasions

---

[86] Human Rights Commission Res. 1983/5 (1983).

[87] Tolley, n. 23 above, p. 442.

[88] See Tom J. Farer, 'The Regulation of Foreign Intervention in Civil Armed Conflict', *Recueil des Cours*, 142(1974), pp. 344–9 and 387–402.

in the past when the words 'humanitarian intervention' served as a fig-leaf for the crass thrust of imperial interests. Anxious to build walls of precedent behind which to shelter, they have condemned intervention even by other Third World states against irredeemably barbarous regimes. In 1971, for instance, when India attacked the armed forces of West Pakistan (as it then was) who were busily engaged in a campaign of extermination against Hindus and educated Bengali Muslims in East Pakistan, the General Assembly, by a vote of 104 in favour to 11 against (with 10 abstentions) called for an immediate cease-fire and, in effect, for the withdrawal of Indian troops, despite the predictable consequences (had it been implemented) for the population of East Pakistan.[89]

The trajectory of political and social developments within and among nations will determine the form and vigour of UN-sponsored activity. Predicting that trajectory is work more for the seer than the analyst. One thing can be said with confidence: human rights enforcement will remain highly politicized and, therefore, intensely controversial.

How could it be otherwise? As Stanley Hoffmann noted shortly after the inauguration of Jimmy Carter: 'The issue of human rights, by definition, breeds confrontation. Raising the issue touches on the very foundations of a regime, on its sources and exercise of power, on its links to its citizens or subjects. It is a dangerous issue . . .'[90] But the history of the last forty years suggests that, absent a nuclear holocaust, it will remain an unavoidable one.

It certainly seems to be fixed on the United States' agenda for superpower diplomacy. Reluctantly planted there by Nixon and Kissinger, it has now survived through the Ford, Carter, and Reagan Administrations. Its durability was confirmed by its easy transition from Carter to Reagan, presidents otherwise so different in ideology and style. Events have also confirmed its capacity to complicate negotiations over issues central to humanity's future.

In his address to the Russian people following the summit meeting in Iceland in October 1986, General Secretary Gorbachev described US insistence on discussing human rights issues

---

[89] Res. 2793 (XXVI) of 7 Dec. 1971.
[90] Stanley Hoffmann, 'The Hell of Good Intentions', *Foreign Policy*, 29 (1977–8), p. 8.

as an effort to insinuate intractable ideological differences into the discussion of nuclear arms control and disarmament. While the General Secretary congratulated himself for, as he saw it, warding off this diversion, President Reagan's spokesmen celebrated the President's success in forcing reference to the issue.

Communist leaders are by no means alone in seeing efforts to enforce primarily political and civil rights as a form of ideological assault by the advanced capitalist democracies rather than as the promotion of universally shared values. The sight of so many Third World regimes, spread right across the ideological spectrum, reacting at best ambivalently and often with outright hostility to Carter's initiatives (despite his readiness, at least rhetorically, to treat freedom from want on a par with political and civil freedoms),[91] did persuade more than a few observers that human rights were just a provincial product of the Western liberal tradition with poor prospects in the global market of ideas. The outlook is particularly bleak, they argue, in those many parts of the world where, unlike Latin America and possibly India, indigenous concepts of political legitimacy survived the era of Western imperial domination.

Let us assume that the assumptions and values of liberalism have contributed enormously, perhaps were preconditions, to the idea of human rights, and have determined much of its content. And let us concede that liberalism is a product of Western origin. For that matter, so are socialism and nationalism, and they certainly have found good markets throughout the world. The appetite for various Western ideologies may have spread in part because victory lends prestige to the ideas as well as to the bayonets of the victors, in part because an impulse to expand and exert influence has animated all Western institutions, including those organized to transmit culture

---

[91] In a 1977 speech at the University of Georgia, published in *Dept. State Bulletin*, 76 (1977), p. 505, clearly intended and subsequently treated as an official statement of the Carter Administration's human rights policy, Secretary of State Cyrus Vance defined 'what we mean by "human rights" ' as follows: *'First, there is the right to be free from governmental violation of the integrity of the person . . . Second, there is the right to the fulfillment of such vital needs as food, shelter, health care and education.* We recognize that the fulfillment of this right will depend, in part, upon the stage of a nation's economic development. But we also know that this right can be violated by a Government's action or inaction—for example, through corrupt official processes which divert resources to an elite at the expense of the needy, or through indifference to the plight of the poor. *Third, there is the right to enjoy civil and political liberties . . .* Our policy is to promote all these rights.'

and belief as well as those of a military, political, and economic character.

But surely cultural products spread for much the same reason as material ones—because they serve the consumer's needs. Nationalism helped to mobilize indigenous resistance to colonial rule and to stabilize the post-independence ethnic and tribal mix. Socialism, or at least its harsh communist deviation, has helped to justify concentration of power in the new political élites and to explain economic failure when it occurs.

Liberalism had its problems for non-Western consumers, yet also a certain utility, initially as a means for eroding the moral basis of Western hegemony. Now, in the post-imperial era, for the burgeoning middle classes of the Third World it has the same appeal it had originally for their Western counterparts who had invoked its name and its reasons as they fought to break loose from the suffocating grip of absolute monarchies and narrow aristocracies. Liberalism remains a powerful weapon in the struggle to move from ascriptive to meritocratic criteria for the acquisition of wealth and power.[92]

The idea of human rights—today, in fact, a not always comfortable coalition of liberal and socialist ideologies—may have been born in the West, but it has made its venue global. Its champions these days are not invariably the high-tech capitalist democracies. When, in 1982, the UN Secretary-General signalled his intention not to reappoint Theo van Boven as Director of the UN Human Rights Centre, not a voice was raised among the leaders of the Western bloc, although, as a man with courage, commitment, and ability, he was almost unrivalled in the higher echelons of the UN bureaucracy. Perhaps one should substitute 'because' for 'although'.

Except during the Carter years, not one of the large Western democracies (as opposed to the Dutch and the Swedes) has been a leader in the UN or regional fora either in efforts to strengthen the machinery of human rights protection or to marshal pressure

---

[92] Demands in Jan. 1987 for democratic reform of the Chinese political system—articulated principally by students and finding a certain resonance even among some Party members—underline the appeal of liberal values in the context of any contemporary polity with a rapidly expanding economy and middle class. However, the Party's immediate response to the demands was a campaign against 'bourgeois liberalism'; the resignation on 16 Jan. 1987 of Hu Yaobang as General Secretary was widely construed by China experts as evidence of powerful resistance within the Party to democratic reforms.

against non-communist villains. France, for example, was among the last members of the Council of Europe to adhere to the treaty provisions granting individuals the right to petition for enforcement of their rights under the European Human Rights Convention. Throughout the history of the United Nations, the British government has looked with little sympathy on efforts to strengthen the enforcement machinery.[93] And the United States, during the Reagan era, has often stood virtually alone in opposing condemnation of Chile, South Africa, and other delinquents with whom it shares, among other things, secret intelligence.[94]

By contrast, a small number of Third World states have some-times been in the vanguard of human rights defence. In the OAS, for example, Barbados, Mexico, and Venezuela were prominent among those members attempting, after the coming of Reagan, to maintain the institutional momentum achieved during the Carter years. At the UN, one of the better special rapporteurs was the Chief Justice of the Senegalese Supreme Court, while one of the poorest pieces of reportage was the work of a British Lord.[95]

Despite all the horror that surrounds us, I believe that we are in a new era. At its outset, we had the Word, the Universal Declaration. In the past four decades it has acquired a little flesh. Within its means, means so conspicuously limited by the fact that material sanctions and incentives remain at the discretionary disposition of powerful states, the UN has helped.

---

[93] See e.g. n. 23 above. Recall, moreover, that when ECOSOC was debating adoption of resolution 1235, it was the representative of the United Kingdom, along with those of the Philippines and Tanzania, who claimed that the Commission could not undertake studies of the situation of human rights in any country without that country's consent. UN doc. E/AC.7/SR.567, E/AC.7/SR.569 (1967). In the course of a debate among members of the Human Rights Committee established under the Covenant on Civil and Political Rights, Sir Vincent Evans, the *de facto* UK member of the Committee, was among those members who took an extremely restrictive view of the Committee's authority to assess the justifications adduced by states party to the Covenant for emergency measures suspending various rights. UN doc. CCPR/C/SR.351 para. 31 (1982).

[94] See Lawyers' Committee for Human Rights and the Watch Committees, *The Reagan Administration's Record on Human Rights in 1985*, (New York, 1986), pp. 43–4.

[95] The first Special Rapporteur for Chile was Judge Abdoulaye Dieye. Viscount Colville has served as Special Rapporteur for the Guatemalan case. For an assessment of his performance, see the Watch Committees, *Four Failures: A Report on the UN Special Rapporteurs on Human Rights in Chile, Guatemala, Iran and Poland* (New York, 1986). The Chilean failure referred to in the title is that of Judge Dieye's ultimate successor as Special Rapporteur in the case of Chile, Mr Fernando Volio of Costa Rica.

Historical perspective eases the pull of cynicism. Having won a revolution in the name of man's inalienable rights, the Founding Fathers of the United States incorporated slavery into the new nation's constitutional foundations. Seventy-six years passed before formal emancipation. And another century passed before blacks in America could enjoy the full rights of citizenship.

The distance the UN has come in four decades is one ground for optimism about where it will go in the next four. Another is the effort so many governments have made to restrain its forward progress and to evade its primitive machinery of enforcement. By their acts they have recognized the influence the idea of human rights has acquired over the minds of their subjects. Hypocrisy continues to offer credible evidence of the possibility of virtue.[96]

[96] While it is nice to end on a sunny note, to do justice to the uncertainties which haunt the whole human rights endeavour and the ambivalence of UN members, I should mention that, as a consequence of the organization's severe budgetary problems, arising primarily from the decision of the US to withhold a substantial proportion of its assessed contribution, the 1986 meeting of the Sub-Commission on Discrimination and Minorities was cancelled. Although human rights activities have not been singled out by the Secretary-General for budget cuts, neither has he felt the need to extend to them any special dispensation. Nor should the UN's recent performance in connection with Iran's barbarous treatment of the Bahais go unremarked. Since 1984, when the General Assembly directed the Human Rights Commission to study charges of gross violations (which may be of such dimension as to justify claims of incipient genocide) committed by Iran, two successive Special Rapporteurs have enjoyed absolutely no cooperation from the Iranian government. The first brief report went no further than to find that allegations against Iran could not be dismissed as groundless. The second, equally marked by a failure to collect information available despite the government's intransigence (from refugees, for example) contains not a critical word, to the extent it contains anything at all. While a Special Rapporteur's conclusions should not be and often are not predictable, the energy with which he or she carries out the Commission's assignment usually is. In other words, the failure of a Special Rapporteur is fairly imputable to the Commission.

The United Nations and the Problem of Economic Development

KENNETH DADZIE

THE first part of this chapter is devoted to a brief survey of the main phases and essential features of the UN's involvement with economic development. In the second part I offer some personal reflections on the issues and challenges of the future.

By conventional measures, such as growth of *per capita* national income and improvement in various other social and economic indicators, an unprecedented degree of development has taken place since the founding of the United Nations. Much of that development has been very uneven across and within countries and, of course, it is often not a direct product of UN-related activities. At the same time, poverty, disease, hunger, inadequate housing, unemployment, and other deprivations now exist on a much vaster absolute scale and continue to grow ever larger. What the various measures of economic performance suggest about the extent of development attained should accordingly be tempered by an appreciation of the limited scope of any actual reduction in human misery.

(a) Three Phases of UN Involvement in Development

1. The first phase: 1945–1963

I see three broad phases in the evolution of the UN's involvement with economic development since 1945. The first phase stretches from 1945 to 1963. In this post-war, colonial period systematic thinking on economic development—at least in so far as it concerned what were then called underdeveloped countries—was still in its infancy. The intellectual landmark of this period was a report prepared in 1950 by a group of five experts, entitled 'Measures for the Economic Development of Underdeveloped Countries'.[1] It is interesting to recall that this report followed upon an earlier one devoted to developed countries, entitled 'National and International Measures for Full Employment'.[2] In fact, the former group had been asked to prepare a report on 'unemployment and underemployment in underdeveloped countries, and the national and international measures required to reduce such unemployment and underemployment'. The group, however, decided to address the more general question of economic development, this being, in their view, the means by which unemployment in the underdeveloped world could be overcome. With hindsight, one may well remark that despite the economic progress achieved, unemployment has grown progressively larger.

This 1950 report set the stage for United Nations development activity—thus it is important to appreciate its central characteristics. An immediately striking feature is that no attempt was made to discuss what is meant by economic development, or, as it was otherwise called, economic progress. At that time, the meaning of these notions seems to have been considered self-evident. Again, with hindsight, one might question the wisdom of such an assumption. The main message of the report was that underdeveloped countries should promote 'progressive attitudes and organizations', 'receptiveness to progressive technology', increased domestic capital formation, and reduced growth of population. Thus development was essentially, indeed almost exclusively, a matter for 'measures requiring domestic action'. The report did, however, represent a departure from what was called 'colonial economics', in that it addressed the issue of society- and institution-building under the broad rubric of the preconditions for economic development, in which were included the removal of relevant structural impediments through, for instance, land reform. The report pointed to the administrative and legal actions, both in the public and private sectors, that were considered necessary for 'economic progress'. It also recognized a somewhat expanded role for government in the promotion of economic development,

---

[1] United Nations, *Measures for the Economic Development of Under-developed Countries* (New York, 1950).
[2] United Nations, *National and International Measures for Full Employment* (New York, 1949).

going beyond the simple provision of physical infrastructure, social services, and administration.

These ideas bear a noticeable resemblance, in their essentials, to those advanced by Professor Arthur Lewis, who was actually a member of the expert group, in his book *The Theory of Economic Growth*, published a few years after the UN report.[3] Ironically, domestic measures and policies have resurfaced in the 1980s, in some circles, as the new hallmark of development wisdom. Measures by developed countries in support of development were limited to a show of self-restraint in refraining from subsidizing certain products competing with the exports of underdeveloped countries. International action was restricted to increasing World Bank lending, and organizing technical assistance through an international development authority.

The impact on UN development activity was to be seen in the spread of 'development planning', the techniques and priorities of which were spelled out in the expert group's report; in the sectorializing of international assistance, and the related development of technical programmes; and in the targeting of development resource transfers from developed countries. The UN First Development Decade, which was actually proclaimed in 1962, was in effect an operationalized version of basic ideas contained in the original expert group's report.

This first phase of the UN's involvement with economic development was also characterized by the absence of a collective presence on the part of the developing countries; by the implicit assertion of a wholly convergent process of world development; and by the assumption of an essentially benign external policy environment, and hence of the irrelevance of negotiated policy reform.

2. The second phase: 1963–1982

The second phase in the evolution of the UN's involvement with economic development extends from 1963 to about 1982. The impulses for new orientations in this period were many. They included the decolonization process, the radical transformation this effected in the UN's membership, and the interest of many of the new nations in socialist doctrines. As the period progressed there was a clearer perception of the reality that political

[3] W. Arthur Lewis, *The Theory of Economic Growth* (London, 1955).

independence did not by itself bring economic autonomy and development. This perception, together with the more blatant abuses by transnational enterprises and the dramatic demonstration of OPEC's power, contributed to the evolution of a new outlook on relations between the developed and developing countries.

By the mid-1960s the UN was ripe for a major revision of its development philosophy. This time the intellectual underpinning was provided by the developing countries themselves, in the form of the doctrines of Raúl Prebisch and his collaborators at the Economic Commission for Latin America. Although these ideas were being shaped from the latter part of the 1940s onward,[4] they did not emerge in the form of specific propositions for North–South, or, as it was then called, centre–periphery, cooperation until the first United Nations Conference on Trade and Development (UNCTAD) was held in 1964, with Prebisch as its Secretary-General.[5]

The notions that informed the new approach to development theory and practice were radically different from those of the 1950s and of the First Development Decade. The new approach asserted the existence of a process of inequalizing exchange between the North and South, as the latter's terms of trade of primary commodities exports for manufactured imports persistently deteriorated as economic surplus was transferred from the South to the North through transnational enterprises, as mercantilist policies restricted access to technology, and as international capital limited structural change and the potential for growth. A distinguishing feature of these new theories was their preclusion of the possibility that spontaneous self-correcting forces might operate. Persistent divergence between North and South was seen as the natural order. If these tendencies were to be corrected, deliberate policy actions would have to be taken, and thus international policy negotiations would become a special and continuing responsibility of the United Nations. There was accordingly a concentration on improving the international economic environment to promote development

[4] CEPAL, *Estudio económico de América Latina y algunos de sus principales problemas* (Santiago, 1950); Hans Singer, 'The Distribution of Gains between Investing and Borrowing Countries', *American Economic Review*, May 1950.
[5] UNCTAD, *Towards a New Trade Policy for Development* (Geneva, 1964).

across a broad front. This was an attempt to rectify the gaps and shortcomings of the post-war system (encompassing IMF, IBRD, and GATT) which had given insufficient weight to the development issue. In this sense, the original, virtually exclusive, preoccupation with 'measures requiring domestic action' as the critical determinant of development was relegated to a less important place in the UN approach to economic development.

During this period therefore the focus of attention in the UN, and especially in UNCTAD, turned to the negotiation of international policies and principles, organized on the basis of four country groupings—the Group of 77 (developing countries), the developed market-economy countries, the socialist countries of Eastern Europe, and China. The main areas of negotiation were commodity prices, trade in manufactures, the international monetary system, the transfer of technology, transnational corporations, restrictive business practices, international shipping, and, at a more general level, the economic rights and duties of states. Many of these negotiations led to agreements, codes, and resolutions, some with greater legal significance than others.[6]

At the same time, it must be said, a different path was being pursued by the International Monetary Fund and the World Bank where, increasingly, access to their resources was being made conditional on the adoption of domestic measures and policies recommended by them. During this period too there was an impressive growth in technical and financial assistance to the various sectors of economic activity in developing countries, intended to enhance these countries' domestic capabilities. In the field of technical cooperation there was a considerable expansion in the range and volume of activity by the United Nations Development Programme (UNDP) which was formed in 1965 by a merger of the UN Expanded Programme of Technical Assistance and the UN Special Fund. This expansion was itself to give rise to continuing questions about the UNDP's priorities, coherence, and cost-effectiveness.

---

[6] e.g. International Commodity Agreements, the Agreement establishing the Common Fund for Commodities, the Code of Conduct on Liner Conferences, the Set of Principles and Rules on Restrictive Business Practices, the Generalized System of Preferences, the resolution on debt relief for the least developed countries, and the Charter on Economic Rights and Duties of States. Negotiations on proposals for Codes of Conduct on the Transfer of Technology, and on Transnational Corporations, have not been completed.

The action taken by OPEC in 1973 naturally gave a strong new impetus to the 'policy negotiation' approach to international development cooperation. It lent credence to the possibility of fundamental change, and to the aspiration that a world of economic equity and justice, as envisaged by the developing countries, might actually be created. The 1974 Declaration on the Establishment of a New International Economic Order (NIEO) and its accompanying Programme of Action convey this new message of strength and purpose.[7] These impulses for change, deriving from a new sense of commodity power, were so strong that the period from 1973 might well be considered a distinct sub-phase, or even a new phase altogether. Essentially, they underscored the developing countries' conviction that change was needed in the operation of the international economic system, and that that change could be effected through a process of global negotiation, in a context of strengthened bargaining power on the part of the developing countries and of the concrete demonstration by OPEC of world interdependence. It is worth noting, for example, that the NIEO was ostensibly proclaimed to reassert and strengthen the 'spirit, purposes and principles of the Charter of the United Nations'.

I view these events as part of the phase beginning in 1963 since despite the language and the ambitiousness of the programme of international economic reform, as well as the more explicitly confrontational approach of the post-1973 period, the essential notions, and the measures envisaged for their realization, were not greatly different from those that inspired and engaged the attention of the international community in the 1960s. However, in practical terms the new consciousness of and stress on 'permanent sovereignty over natural resources' gained in influence, while the notion of interdependence emerged more explicitly and with greater clarity as a rationale for international economic *management*. These notions, together with the basic ideas associated with the founding of and developments in UNCTAD, merged with the older development currents of the 1950s to influence the shape and content of the International Development Strategy as proclaimed for the second and third UN Development Decades (which began respectively in 1971 and 1981).[8]

[7] GA Res. 3201 (S-VI) of 1 May 1974.
[8] GA Res. 2626 (XXV) of 24 Oct. 1970, and 35/56 of 5 Dec. 1980.

3. The third phase: since 1982

The third and final phase dates from the early 1980s. The new strength and hopes inspired by OPEC and the NIEO were to be relatively short-lived. By about 1982 the servicing of the massive petrodollar borrowing of developing countries ran into severe difficulty as self-induced recession in the North, under the impact of anti-inflationary monetary and fiscal policies, cur- tailed the export earnings of developing countries.[9] Besides this, a number of other influences have had a modifying effect on the UN's development philosophy. There has been much dis- appointment over the failure to negotiate and implement important aspects of the international agenda—international commodity agreements, the Common Fund for Commodities, the Code of Conduct for the Transfer of Technology, the NIEO. The weakening of OPEC and of commodity power generally has diminished the Third World's bargaining power. And the revival of the arms race and persisting East–West ten- sions have put the North–South dialogue lower on the agenda of international concerns.

We are witnessing now a return, primarily at the insistence of the developed market economy countries, to a preoccupation with national measures and policies of developing countries, similar to that of the 1950s. In major Western economies, the ascendancy of neo-classical economics with its faith in market forces, together with the trend towards deregulation, has gone hand-in-hand with a reduced interest and investment in forms of international management. Both of these tendencies seem to imply a diminished concern with negotiated international policies in the design of development cooperation. They also seem to point to a greater role for the private enterprise sector in the promotion of international cooperation and development.

Some of these tendencies are potentially of positive value. There is much to be gained by a better complementarity between international policy and domestic action, and between the public and private sectors, in both developing and developed countries. The exchange of assessments on different develop- ment experiences is also worth while. The danger, however, is of moving from one extreme to the other, of replacing choice and

---

[9] UNCTAD, *Trade and Development Report 1986* (Geneva, 1986).

freedom by dogmatism and pressure. It is to be hoped that we are moving into a new, more mature phase of international development cooperation, one that blends creatively the good features of the older and newer philosophies on economic development.

(b) Issues and Challenges of the Future

1. Criticisms of the UN's development performance

Well-publicized criticisms have recently been voiced of the UN's performance in regard to its economic development mission. Most of these criticisms are not new and they are probably no more or less severe than those raised in the national debates on economic and financial management in many countries. However, on the world scale that the United Nations represents, well-considered judgements are often constrained by the lack of exposure to the relevant facts or to legitimate differences of opinion. As a result, assessments are made, sometimes by professional experts, on the basis of incorrect information (frequently of the more newsworthy type) or of incomplete evidence and analysis. It is thus all the more important that those efforts that are undertaken in the name of objectivity, scholarship, and reform, particularly under the sponsorship of influential governments, should be informed by a sense of the responsibility involved, and that they shall be careful in the collection and analysis of information as well as in the interpretation of conclusions. Authoritative observers have pointed out that there have been many instances in which the scholarship displayed in these analyses is not wholly beyond reproach, prestigious as the works and institutions concerned may be.

The revival of criticisms of the UN at the present time may well be more closely related to the protracted world economic recession, and to abrupt changes of stance among several of the major Western industrial countries in regard to the role of government, than to any perceived substantial new deterioration in the capability and performance of the UN. These new national stances have inevitably led to a diminished political and financial commitment on the part of those governments to multilateral cooperation for economic development.

The traditional lines of criticism, especially in official circles in the developed countries, are clear enough. They have recently been restated by Maurice Bertrand with great intellectual incisiveness.[10] According to these views, the UN, in seeking to execute the duty undertaken by its members to 'achieve international cooperation' for economic and social development, operates a system that is not well adapted to the execution of development assistance programmes. In specific terms, its individual sector programmes are viewed as conceptually disparate and out of harmony with the development *problématique*, fragmented, doctrinally incoherent, and operated by remote control. As such, they seem to lack analytical and functional integration and to be devoid of a sense of priority; they are prone to waste through duplication of effort and an unproductive division of responsibility. On top of these operational defects—perhaps to some extent a cause of them—is an unmanageable intergovernmental negotiating and decision-making apparatus; one, moreover, that lacks systematic resource allocation procedures and effective accountability mechanisms.

These are indeed very serious and substantial criticisms. They cannot and should not be treated lightly. It is not difficult to discover instances of most of these defects in the UN institutions devoted to economic development. To the extent that these and other defects exist and can be corrected with generally beneficial results, appropriate reforms ought to be implemented. Naturally, as in all human institutions, efficiency efforts, at least in financial accounting terms, are likely to fall far short of perfection in the absence of continuing vigilance and rigorous reform.

However productive efficiency reforms may be, I do not feel convinced that the defects at which they are aimed lie at the root of the dissatisfaction with the UN's role and performance in regard to development. I am thus sceptical that the correction of essentially mechanical flaws is all that is required for a decisive, qualitative improvement in international development cooperation. I should therefore now like to take this discussion to a different plane, where the questions are concerned with the quality of the international commitment to world development and with

---

[10] Maurice Bertrand, *Some Reflections on Reform of the United Nations* (JIU Report 85/9; UN doc. A/40/1988 of 6 Dec. 1985). See also his chapter in this volume.

the political dimensions of international economic policy. The
focus has therefore to be widened beyond the UN.

2. Broadening the scope of analysis

The 'purposes and principles' inscribed in the UN Charter are
self-imposed guidelines set by states to direct their overall international conduct; they are not duties to be honoured merely in
so far as nations participate in and finance certain common
activities executed through the agency of the UN. If there is to
be a balanced or even a comprehensible assessment of the UN's
role and performance in regard to economic development, we
must take a broader view of the issue. This view cannot be
limited to the UN, but must encompass the whole complex of
international economic organizations and economic relations
among states.

In such a perspective, while the efforts and resources of the
UN are relatively small, international policy assumes a much
greater salience. In this perspective too, there may be a better
appreciation of the exogenous limits to the effectiveness of the
UN's efforts and of the reasons why operational reforms of the
UN, whilst valuable, cannot themselves put right what is wrong
with international development cooperation. I feel therefore
that current critiques of the UN's role in economic development
need to be complemented by reflections of a more fundamental
nature on the foundations, practice, and future of a broader
conception of international development cooperation.

Any such reflections would probably begin with some
hesitation about the strength of the UN's commitment to
development. Some certainly doubt the credibility of this
commitment.[11] Compared with the purposeful and direct
language used in the UN Charter in regard to peace—'to save
succeeding generations from the scourge of war', 'to maintain
international peace and security and . . . to take effective collective measures for the prevention and removal of threats to the
peace'—that used in respect of development has been viewed as
fragile and ambiguous. The words are 'to employ international
machinery for the promotion of the economic and social
advancement of all peoples', and 'to achieve international co-

---

11 United Nations, *Is Universality in Jeopardy?* (Geneva, 1987), a collection of papers
prepared for a Symposium organized on the occasion of the UN's fortieth anniversary.

operation in solving international problems of an economic . . . character'.[12]

Over the past forty years a number of concepts have been invoked to underpin the UN's commitment to development—from self-help and fair opportunity in the 1950s to reason and generosity in the 1960s; from partnership and mutual interest in the 1970s to interdependence and collective security in the 1980s. None of these notions, however, has succeeded in inspiring durable foundations for a dynamic and predictable system of international cooperation for development. It would seem that cooperation on this scale is not a spontaneous habit or a self-catalysing impulse. On the contrary, defection from organized, systemic cooperation increasingly appears an attractive option. There are thus, from the start, challenging, indeed critical, questions to be faced. Is there a credible, compelling rationale for global development cooperation? Or, do we now need more penetrating insights into the actual evolution of co-operative forms in human society as a basis for organizing more realistic models for facilitating social change? Would such models of international cooperation be more or less anthropo-graphical, integrated, planned, evolutionary . . .?

Such a formulation of the issue goes much beyond questions about the appropriate structure for North–South economic negotiations, such as the Economic Security Council proposed by Maurice Bertrand. Economic issues probably do need a higher profile in UN affairs: greater coherence in the policies and activities of the various international economic institutions would certainly be beneficial, as would improvements to the negotiating machinery. Nevertheless, as indicated above, I am not convinced that organic restructuring is a sufficient answer to more fundamental issues about the quality of the UN's commitment to world development and to shared management of the international economic system.

3. Dogmatism and single models of development

It seems unlikely that in the near future there could be in a world of over 160 extremely heterogeneous nations a common, universal understanding of the meaning of development or of the measures and policies by which the development objectives of

---

[12] The quotations are from the UN Charter, Preamble and Article 1.

states may be attained. Whilst there are some areas of convergence, there remain wide differences of outlook and method as between developing countries and the donors of development assistance. These differences are frequently at the heart of questions about the role and performance of development cooperation. They have become crystallized in the frictions between the developing countries on the one hand and the IMF and the World Bank on the other. The latter are often viewed as dispensing more or less uniform prescriptions for a wide variety of economic ailments and circumstances, and thus as being insufficiently sensitive to the peculiar features and potential of each developing country, and to the goals that these countries have or would like to set for themselves. Access to the resources of these institutions and, through their seal of approval, to the private capital market, is usually conditional upon acceptance and monitored implementation of their recommendations. In most cases there are no alternatives open to developing countries, short of autarky.

Two basic concerns are common to most of the criticisms that are made in respect of this area of development cooperation. First, there is some uneasiness about the precision and dogmatism which characterizes the prevailing underlying theory of development, based, as it is argued, virtually exclusively on the role of prices—the prices of product, capital, labour, and foreign exchange—and on the overriding importance of 'getting these prices right'. In response, a substantial volume of carefully researched criticism has accumulated over the years.[13] Questions have been raised about World Bank financing principles that led to uneconomic investments in, for example, primary commodities and infrastructure, to the neglect of domestic agriculture; and also led to structural adjustment lending programmes that were simply unrealistic and unworkable. Similarly, there has been substantial empirical research critical of the theory underlying the IMF's approach to the balance-of-payments adjustment process, especially its application to the developing countries.[14] In particular, the results of its general-

[13] Useful summary material and further references may be found in Commonwealth Secretariat, *Towards a New Bretton Woods: Challenges for the World Financial and Trading System* (London, 1983); and Edmar L. Bacha and Richard E. Feinberg, 'The World Bank and Structural Adjustment in Latin America', *World Development*, 14, no. 3, 1986.
[14] Tony Killick, *Balance of Payments Adjustment and Developing Countries* (Overseas

ized recommendations for devaluation and demand compression have certainly prompted several well-researched economic critiques.

A second concern stems from doubts that a single model of development can be recommended as a universal norm in a world in which the circumstances, possibilities, socio-economic preferences, and political values of developing countries are so varied. The countries of South East Asia are sometimes singled out as 'success stories'. Strong reservations have been raised about the standards employed in identifying and determining this 'success'. More than that, these portrayals of economic success, drawn solely and explicitly in terms of the dominance of private enterprise systems and openness to foreign investment and trade—outward orientation, as it is called—have been countered, even in respect of these countries, by more cautious and perhaps more revealing interpretations.[15]

Assessments of this kind have become perturbingly stylized. Thus some World Bank reports not only calculate so-called price 'distortion' in individual developing countries (judged against market norms), but claim that such distortion is inversely correlated with economic growth.[16] It is reassuring to note that there is still room for legitimate criticism of such methods in official circles in countries that are major contributors to development assistance. One example is worth quoting:

In the end, market forces and policies matter; import substitution and export promotion occur simultaneously and in a more supportive relationship than is generally supposed. But, in the name of even-handedness, it is not a helpful circumstance to have our premier international financial institutions wedded to a single model of what constitutes a successful development policy or to a narrow definition of what constitutes an effective stabilization programme. It seriously undermines the role of the Fund and the Bank in the world economy by restricting their scope and their effectiveness. It politicizes them by having them represent . . . an ideology, when their role is to be responsive to a variety of types of governments and economic systems.[17]

Development Institute, London, 1985). See also R. Cassen (ed.), *Does Aid Work?* (Oxford, 1986).

[15] John P. Lewis and Valeriana Kallab (eds.), *Development Strategies Reconsidered* (Overseas Development Council, Washington DC, 1986).

[16] World Bank, *World Development Report, 1983* (Washington DC, 1983).

[17] Testimony of Colin I. Bradford jun., Associate Director, Yale Center for

152 KENNETH DADZIE

The point developed in that testimony represents an extremely difficult challenge for the future. How can international resources for development be liberated from the confines of a predetermined political ideology and a fixed norm of economic development? By what means can the international financial institutions be made more open and responsive to the views of developing countries and alert to a more eclectic scholarship?

4. The importance of the international economic policy environment

The prospects for development also depend on the external policy environment, as distinct from external development assistance. External policy is ultimately a good deal more important than resource transfers because to a large extent it determines the capacity of developing countries to earn their own resources for development. Development assistance can only be a supplement to domestic efforts. It is not surprising therefore that international economic policy should be an arena of intense conflict between developing and developed countries.

For this reason, any evaluation of the UN's role and effort in support of development would not be complete without attention being given to the external policy aspect. It is thus a matter of some regret that such disproportionate attention should now be devoted to the efficiency of the administration of the relatively small share of development resources that the UN accounts for, to the exclusion not only of the much greater share managed by the complex of international economic institutions other than the UN and by national governments, but especially also to the neglect of international economic policy as one of the important determinants of development performance internationally.

As indicated earlier, UNCTAD is an institution in which international economic policy as it affects the developing countries is debated and reforms and innovations negotiated at the levels both of principle and of practice. These efforts have in the main been directed to securing a more liberal and fair international trading system for the exports of developing countries, more stable conditions for trade in primary commodities, and a

International and Area Studies, before the US House of Representatives Sub-Committee on International Development Institutions and Finance, 25 July 1985.

more predictable and supportive international monetary and financial system. Concern with these aspects of international economic policy has become more urgent over the last few years, as higher and new protectionist barriers have been imposed, as real commodity prices have sunk to the levels of 1890, as debt burdens have escalated at a time of much diminished capacity to service them, and as disorder has become an enduring feature of the international monetary system. While there have been considerable achievements over the twenty or more years of UNCTAD's existence, it must be said frankly that, on the whole, the record has fallen short of the possibilities and expectations.

The critical issue has been the unwillingness of the great industrial powers to match their recognition of the reality of world economic interdependence with a preparedness to share with their developing country partners the management of the global economic commons that the world's trading, monetary, and financial systems represent. The basic facts on these matters are clear enough. Whatever improvements may be needed to the quality of research, to the analysis of developing countries' domestic policies, and to the logistics of negotiating procedures, there remains much scepticism that, in the final analysis, these are the decisive impediments to the reform of international economic policy. It is regrettable that many evaluations of the UN's involvement with development cooperation should, because of their limited focus on development assistance, fail to envision much scope for shared international economic management as an instrument of international development cooperation.

The challenges of the future are no less daunting in regard to these international policy issues. By what means can the governments of the major industrial countries be induced to upgrade the level of consensus in regard to the need for shared management of the international economic system, in their own longer-range interest? If this proves to be an impossible task, will the integration of the South into a hegemonic North be a politically feasible and durable proposition? Or will parallel North–South antagonistic systems emerge? If the only approach open to the UN is, as some feel, to pursue with tenacity any advances—however marginal—towards the distant goal of international society, is there not some risk that such advances may be overwhelmed eventually by the consequences of contradictions inherent in North–South relations?

5. *The coherence and effectiveness of bilateral development assistance*

Finally, development cooperation at the bilateral level must be brought into the picture. The importance of this component of international cooperation for development, at least in terms of resources, is underlined by the fact that it accounts for 75 per cent of official development assistance (ODA), i.e. resource transfers on concessional terms. By comparison, the World Bank and other international financial institutions administer about 15 per cent of ODA and the UN institutions administer 6 per cent. This distribution needs to be borne in mind not only in considering the UN's role and performance, but also in assessing the scope of, and limitations inherent in, UN efficiency reforms which can touch only a very minor part of the development problem.

Many and possibly most of the shortcomings that have been identified in the UN's administration of development resources are in fact features of bilateral ODA as well, and thus are liable to be magnified many times over. There is, of course, some justification for lighter allocation and accountability procedures in respect of development assistance being imposed by national parliaments. But what is gained in these respects could be lost in large measure when, as is often the case, such national procedures widen divergency in development objectives and priorities, both among donor governments, and between them and their development partners. The potential for positive or negative results at the level of individual recipients is well illustrated by the fact that since the 1960s ODA has accounted consistently for over 5 per cent of the GNP of some fifty developing countries; in other words, for well over 30 per cent of the national savings of most of these countries.

The criticisms usually directed at bilateral development cooperation mostly concern the objectives of the donors; the distribution of aid among developing countries; its coherence in relation to the development objectives of the recipient countries; and its effectiveness in terms of development. With respect to the objectives of donors and the distribution of aid, there have been some encouraging signs in the increasing proportion of resources allocated to the least-developed countries. At the same time, it has been noted that middle-income developing countries still receive well over 40 per cent of ODA. Moreover, the pattern of assistance of the three largest donors, the United States, France, and Japan, has aroused scepticism in some quarters about the weight they actually assign to purely develop-ment criteria in their calculations: nearly 70 per cent of US development assistance goes to the Middle East and Central America; 95 per cent of France's assistance goes to French-speaking countries in Africa and the Pacific; and over 90 per cent of Japan's aid is allocated to neighbouring countries. ,

The lack of coherence in bilateral development assistance has been a cause of no less concern. The Development Assistance Committee of the OECD might speak for itself:

The assumption was that the recipient would organize his request in accordance with his own priorities and would retain responsibility for bringing coherence to the whole. It soon emerged that this assumption was unsustainable. Few recipients had the capacity to maintain control over the complex flow of resources that had become available, and their task was rendered more difficult by differences in the priorities and preferences of individual donors. Country programming evolved as a means of clarifying the relationship of a recipient country's plans, policies and resources with the proposed uses of aid. . . . The depth and detail of the analysis on which (donor) country programmes rest varies considerably from donor to donor but there is a tendency to rely largely on the World Bank and the IMF for the necessary macro-economic analysis . . . The scope and context of the programmes vary as well. Programmes range from the identification of activities suitable for financial support to the elaboration of detailed plans for specific sectors, sub-sectors and individual projects.[18]

What emerges here is a picture of incoherence and fragmenta-tion, drawn by a multiplicity of donors, acting independently, with very different priorities, methodologies, and time-frames, and in which the recipients themselves appear, perhaps by default, as background figures.

As regards effectiveness of aid, the crucial but complex question that remains to be answered is whether development assistance having the characteristics discussed above is rather

[18] OECD, *Twenty-Five Years of Development Co-operation: A Review* (Paris, 1985).

supplementing or undermining the drive and desire for self-sustaining development. So far this question has been inadequately researched, and such answers as are forthcoming, even from sources close to the donors, leave an impression of vagueness and doubt. Such tentative or 'ambiguous' assessments would, in other contexts, seem intolerable for expenditures amounting to US $36 billion a year.

(c) Conclusion

Some of the questions for a future agenda might be: What can be done to improve the capacity of the developing countries themselves to formulate their own development objectives in the form of coherent, long-range programmes? And what mechanisms might be introduced, beyond the coordinating techniques currently employed in the OECD's Development Assistance Committee, to induce greater consistency, complementarity, and efficiency of effort among donor countries to promote development?

Whatever be the answers to the question raised earlier as to whether there is a compelling rationale for, an obligation to provide, development assistance, it is beyond doubt that an increase in that assistance and improvements in its quality could help to accelerate the pace of economic development in the South. In these respects, a basic issue that eventually needs to be tackled is whether sources of development assistance on an increasing scale could be found which are wholly or partially independent of government appropriations. Related to this issue must be the question as to how the disbursement of development assistance could be made more rational from a development standpoint. For example, would such an aim be encouraged by relating ODA targets to the recipient countries' efforts and objectives as distinct from, and in addition to, relating them to a proportion of the donor countries' GNP's?

I have raised in this chapter a number of basic, challenging questions concerning international cooperation for development. In doing so, I have tried to place the involvement of the UN in the broader context of the purposes and principles subscribed to by governments independently of the organization they have established. It seems to me that this is the context intended by the words and spirit of the UN Charter. I have no special wisdom to offer on these questions and challenges, other than what is hinted at in their formulation. Though of the greatest importance to the ultimate success of our task, they are regarded as somewhat removed from the detailed preoccupations of the day. Nevertheless, every opportunity must be seized to air and reflect on these concerns and to generate constructive insights with a view to improving our common understanding.

The United Nations and the Development of International Law

NAGENDRA SINGH

THIS survey of the UN's role in the development of international law will examine the contribution of the Charter, of various UN organs, and of the specialized agencies. It will then look at some examples of the new legal concepts which these contributions have pioneered. Finally, a brief conclusion will refer to some continuing gaps and ambiguities in contemporary international law, and to the important problem of implementation of the law.

International law is ordinarily defined as the body of legal rules which applies between sovereign states *inter se* and to other entities possessing international personality. A subject of international law, according to the advisory opinion of the International Court of Justice in the *Reparation for Injuries* case, is an entity 'capable of possessing international rights and duties, and . . . [which] has capacity to maintain its rights by bringing international claims'.[1]

The sources of international law are numerous, and include all those listed in Article 38 of the Statute of the International Court of Justice.[2] Not all sources and developments can be covered here. In this chapter I will concentrate on the threefold contribution of the UN. to intl law →

---

[1] *ICJ Reports*, 1949, p. 179.

[2] Article 38(1) of the 1945 Statute of the International Court of Justice states:

The Court, whose function is to decide in accordance with international law such disputes as are submitted to it, shall apply:

(*a*) international conventions, whether general or particular, establishing rules expressly recognized by the contesting states;

(*b*) international custom, as evidence of a general practice accepted as law;

(*c*) the general principles of law recognized by civilized nations;

(*d*) subject to the provisions of Article 59, judicial decisions and the teachings of the most highly qualified publicists of the various nations, as subsidiary means for the determination of rules of law.

First, apart from establishing a mechanism to promote new laws and to revise old ones, the UN Charter itself enunciates new principles of international law. This aspect requires examination at the very outset because some of these new principles, such as the principle of decolonization and that of self-determination, have significantly transformed the international community. *Many*

Second, a number of UN bodies with the specific task of developing international law have contributed much over four decades to the progressive development of international law. These UN bodies include the General Assembly, many resolutions of which have a progressive forward thrust; the International Law Commission, which has worked on the codification and progressive development of international law; and the International Court of Justice.

Third, the numerous specialized agencies of the UN have been active in developing different spheres of international law. These specialized agencies include the International Civil Aviation Organization (ICAO); the International Maritime Organization (IMO); the International Telecommunication Union (ITU); and the International Labour Organization (ILO).

Each of these three is discussed in turn below.

(a) The UN Charter: New Principles of International Law

1. *The League Covenant and UN Charter compared*

The League of Nations Covenant (1919) opens with these words:

The High Contracting Parties,
In order to promote international cooperation and to achieve international peace and security by the acceptance of obligations not to resort to war . . .

However, there was no assumption that non-resort to war was an established rule: it was simply the object of a possible voluntary commitment. Thus the French text speaks merely of 'certain' obligations not to resort to war.

The Covenant contained several provisions concerning collective security in the face of aggression, and concerning disarmament. However, there is one phrase in Article 12 that speaks volumes. Referring to the arbitration or judicial decision of disputes, it provides that the members of the League 'agree in no case to resort to war until three months after the award by the arbitrators or the report by the Council'. Such a weak restraint would be unthinkable in any international agreement today. Contrast Article 2, paragraph 4, of the UN Charter:

All Members shall refrain in their international relations from the threat or use of force against the territorial integrity or political independence of any state, or in any other manner inconsistent with the Purposes of the United Nations.

The League Covenant went on to speak of international relations founded upon justice and honour, but I do not observe any reference to honour in the UN Charter. Yet what is wrong with honour? Is it not an admirable concern? Well, its exclusion from the Charter is not in fact such a backward step as might appear. For it was 'honour' which the militaristic powers had most regularly invoked to justify war in the days when that word still retained its aura of glory.

Furthermore, the preamble of the Covenant enjoins 'scrupulous respect for all treaty obligations in the dealings of organized peoples with one another'. What did this mean? Who were then the *disorganized* peoples with whom the High Contracting Parties might conclude treaties which it was pardonable to disrespect? Doubtless some anarchistic tribal groupings who were there only to be hoodwinked. One recalls the noted nineteenth-century author of a code of international law who allowed the use of machine-guns but condemned 'savages' for such unfair practices as the dipping of their arrowheads in poison.[3] The Covenant, in other words, still contained remnants of a class system among peoples, attended by legal disqualifications for the lower classes.

In apparent contrast, the UN Charter contains many provisions devoted to the emergence of subject peoples from colonialism to independence and full membership of the international community. But the seeds had been sown in the 'sacred trust'

---

[3] Johann C. Bluntschli, *Das moderne Völkerrecht der civilisierten Staaten* (Nördlingen, 1878), p. 314. To be fair, it must be added that this author inveighed against genocide and emphasized the humane 'education' of the 'uncivilized'.

provisions of the Covenant which underlay the mandates system, and which the Charter transformed into the trusteeship regime.

The reference in the Statute of the International Court of Justice, which is annexed to the UN Charter and forms part of it, to 'the general principles of law recognized by civilized nations' has also been attacked for being discriminatory. This text dates back in fact to the early 1920s, for the Statute of the Court is virtually the same as that of its predecessor, the Permanent Court of International Justice. But I am not so sure that this particular expression is inept. Should we not rather draw the converse conclusion, namely that only nations which recognize general principles of law may be regarded as civilized?

Finally, the preamble to the Covenant of the League of Nations speaks of 'the firm establishment of the understandings of international law as the actual rule of conduct among Governments'. Now this is a very curious word, a very hesitant word: 'understandings'. It is as if the parties cannot bring themselves quite to admit the existence of norms, let alone rules of international law. Yet the French text uses a far stronger word: 'prescriptions'. The French text also implies, as the English does not, that *all* the prescriptions of international law are now or henceforth recognized as actually governing the conduct of states. These are significant differences. They show that the Covenant was situated on the brink of a transition from cautious approval of international law to its wholehearted acceptance. Why the English text is on one side of the brink and the French on the other is a matter I must leave to the specialists of *travaux préparatoires*. But these differences show the immensity of the transformation that has been completed since. They point to the contribution of the UN both to the development of international law and to the firming up of the concept of international law as a regulatory force and not as a mere collection of indications of inter-state understandings.

What in fact happened in 1945 with the foundation of the United Nations was the culmination of a process that had been going on for some three hundred years but, in the last hundred, had gathered momentum in response to ever more frightful wars. This process, in a nutshell, was the transformation of the law of nations into international law. One might almost say that it was also the transformation of the law of war into the law of peace.

For what had been the law of nations? The term itself was simply a translation of the Latin *jus gentium*, an extremely broad expression of which the possible connotations range from 'the code of conduct of patrician families' to 'the rights of peoples'. The one thing it does not suggest is the modern state. In practice, the law of nations, two or three hundred years ago, had not advanced very far from simply constituting the rules governing the relations of princes: diplomatic practice, in short. Since the main criterion of those relations was whether the princes were at war with each other or at peace, the law of nations was conceived as a diptych—one panel bearing the table of the rules of war, the other displaying the rules of peace. Those general rules were not written down in instruments bearing the princes' signatures, but were left to be made explicit by scholars such as Gentili, Grotius, and Vattel, who by recording and systematizing practice in a sober and not Utopian manner earned respect and began in essence the modern work of codifying custom.

Meanwhile the nations continued in the main to subsist side by side in a relationship either of armed benevolence or of outright hostility, and the customary law of nations was in practice reduced to the observance of the different etiquettes which either situation required. It had a split personality, and as a result much intellectual effort went into defining the conditions and rules of belligerency and neutrality, when in fact the outlawing of war was the only worthy goal.

Gradually, however, the realization emerged that only one panel of the diptych was worthy of development as law in the sense of a perennial expression of what was right and just. To be sure, if there had to be war, it was best that it should not be totally lawless, for to abandon all rules would be to withdraw protection from the helpless and condone the infliction of needless suffering. The war-rules panel of the now outmoded diptych had therefore to be preserved in some form, and this has eventually been achieved in international humanitarian law, otherwise called the laws of war, a corner of international law which throws an essential bridge between human rights and the conduct of states during hostilities. Apart from humanitarian obligations, proportionate self-defence is the only aspect of warfare which still constitutes a universally accepted component of international legality. The question of the right of legitimate national liberation movements to use force in their struggles, and of third states to assist them, continues to be controversial.

The prohibition of war is all to the good—or almost all to the good. Nobody, least of all myself, would question the outlawing of aggressive war. But by placing aggressors beyond the pale, we have also risked putting them beyond our grasp. This is a real dilemma. Only the untrammelled operation of the Red Cross and Red Crescent can ensure that the implementation of the 1949 Geneva Conventions and related agreements is monitored. It is fortunate that those magnificent organizations were created in time to alleviate so much of the sufferings of war that this century has known. But there are disquieting signs. New efforts will have to be made to ensure that international standards can be enforced even within situations of international illegality.

2. New principles in the UN Charter

The Charter introduces a new chapter in the development of international law, not only by crystallizing the still evolving and emerging rules, but also by enunciating new principles. At least in theory, these new principles of the Charter promote international peace, although they may lack the sanction and vigour necessary for their enforcement or due observance. It is sometimes said that the League of Nations had fostered the spirit of peace more effectively than does the UN. This observation would appear to be somewhat superficial. After World War I there was a great enthusiasm for promoting peace and the rule of law. This spirit was symbolized by two multilateral treaties of 1928: the General Act for Pacific Settlement of International Disputes, and the General Treaty for the Renunciation of War (the Kellogg–Briand Pact). There was an inclination among nations to respect the law and to avoid conflicts which could cause great destruction of both life and property. The same feeling did manifest itself after World War II, but perhaps not with the same intensity. In any case, my impression is that the lessons of the two world wars are gradually being forgotten, and that resort to force is becoming increasingly frequent in international relations. This may be the result of structural weaknesses in the UN, or of its defective functioning. But no fault lies with the enunciation of the new principles embodied in the Charter itself. Any survey of the development of international law must therefore give a prominent place to these principles of the Charter which, I believe, continue to indicate the path to peace. Some of them are listed below.

(i) The principle of non-use of force in international relations, and the consequent illegality of right of conquest as a mode of acquiring territory, has its origin in Articles 2(3) and 2(4) of the Charter. This has reversed the centuries-old recognition of the right of conquest as a means of acquiring territory.

(ii) The principles of the independence and the sovereign equality of states, and the concept of decolonization, are equally significant. They have led to a restructuring of the international community by more than doubling the number of its members.

(iii) The principle of equal rights and self-determination of peoples is stressed in Article 1(2) of the Charter. Article 55 further elaborates it by asserting that it would be a function of the UN to foster respect for 'the principle of equal rights and self-determination of peoples'. This principle has been linked to that of decolonization to establish the right to independence and sovereignty of the erstwhile colonies and dependencies.

(iv) The principles of non-interference in the domestic or internal affairs of states is spelt out in Article 2(7) of the Charter, which reads as follows:

Nothing contained in the present Charter shall authorize the United Nations to intervene in matters which are essentially within the domestic jurisdiction of any state or shall require the Members to submit such matters to settlement under the present Charter . . .

(v) The principle of non-discrimination which is codified in Article 1(3), Article 13(b), and Article 55(c) of the Charter. In all these articles the Charter enjoins the promotion of universal respect for human rights and fundamental freedoms without distinction as to race, sex, language, or religion.

(vi) The principle of interdependence and international cooperation is enunciated in Article 13(b). This Article requires the General Assembly to make recommendations for '(a) Promoting international cooperation in the political field and encouraging the progressive development of international law and its codification; (b) promoting international cooperation in the economic, social, cultural, educational, and health fields, and assisting in the realization of human rights and fundamental freedoms for all without distinction as to race, sex, language, or religion.'

(vii) The principle of good neighbourliness and friendly relations is recited in several different parts of the Charter, including Article 1(2), Article 55, and Article 74. The General Assembly has further developed this and other principles in its 1970 Declaration on Principles of International Law concerning Friendly Relations and Cooperation among States in accordance with the Charter of the United Nations.

(viii) The Charter espouses principles of human rights in various articles. Article 1(3) states that the purposes of the UN include 'promoting and encouraging respect for human rights', and Article 13(1) talks of 'assisting in the realization of human rights'. Article 55(c) pledges the UN to promote 'universal respect for, and observance of, human rights', and Article 62(2) empowers ECOSOC to make recommendations to this end. Under Article 76(c) an objective of the trusteeship system was 'to encourage respect for human rights'.

(ix) The principle of obligatory registration of treaties is enunciated in Article 102(1), which also provides for the Secretariat to publish all registered treaties. Unregistered treaties may not be invoked before any UN body. This system is helpful in listing and publishing the treaties which the members of the UN have to respect. Unfortunately publication of the *United Nations Treaty Series* is at present lagging several years behind, due to the failure of the UN budgetary organs to allocate sufficient funds to it. It is to be hoped that this important work will soon take higher priority.

Although many of these principles predate the UN Charter, they now enjoy a precise formulation and a distinct legal status by being incorporated in a multilateral treaty of exceptional standing. This represents a significant development in the field of international law which is clearly attributable to the UN.

(b) UN Organs for the Development of International Law

UN bodies with the specific task of developing international law include:

1. The UN General Assembly and its committees;
2. Conferences convened by the UN;
3. The International Law Commission;
4. The International Court of Justice.

These are examined in turn below:

1. *The UN General Assembly and its committees*

The General Assembly influences the developments of international law in many ways. First, it adopts general legal conventions, or convenes *ad hoc* global international conferences, almost the size of the General Assembly's Committee of the Whole, to give birth to new international conventions. Second, the General Assembly has been busy formulating resolutions by consensus, without vote, or by a majority vote. Third, it considers the reports of such organs as the International Law Commission, as well as working through committees, such as the Sixth Committee and the Committee on Outer Space, to tackle problems of inter-state relations and in the process to develop international law. An attempt will now be made to summarize some of these activities of the General Assembly.

(i) *The Genocide Convention.* A very early instance of the UN's involvement in the development of international law is to be seen in the 1948 Genocide Convention, adopted during the third session of the General Assembly.[4] The revulsion and horror inspired by the Nazi holocaust was of course the catalyst for this instrument. The Genocide Convention is a prime example of the swiftness with which international law can leap forward in modern circumstances, given the kind of forum which only the UN and its kindred agencies can provide. The scene for the elaboration and adoption of this convention was set by a request by Cuba, India, and Panama to include an item on genocide in the agenda of the General Assembly's first session, in 1946. This session adopted a unanimous resolution affirming genocide to be a crime under international law.

The Convention on the Prevention and Punishment of the

---

[4] The very word 'genocide' was still a neologism—or at least had enjoyed general currency only for the briefest of periods. All too unhappily, the phenomenon itself was far from new. Discussion of the international criminality of genocide prompted the Assembly to request the new International Law Commission to study the possibility of establishing a criminal chamber of the International Court of Justice—an idea which was to prove technically too difficult of attainment.

Crime of Genocide was adopted on 9 December 1948, after a mere two years of preparatory work. Such alacrity would have been inconceivable without the UN.

The final text of this Convention is markedly different from the initial draft prepared by the Legal Section of the UN Secretariat.[5] The initial draft had presented a far wider definition of genocide than eventually prevailed. Massacre was not its sole theme, for it had subsumed under 'genocide' such acts as destroying the specific characteristics of groups by the desecration of their shrines, the confiscation of their property, the deprivation of their means of livelihood, the prohibition of their language, the destruction of their books; in a word, the annihilation of their culture. In the final text, genocide is confined to killing, maiming, deliberate starvation, sterilization, and the forcible dispersal of the children of a group.

Of course, the one word 'genocide' could not have borne the full load of the original draft, and possibly the international civil servants, in the first flush of enthusiasm, had exceeded their responsibilities and trespassed on the field of legal development. It was very significant that the text (albeit in its revised form) was adopted by the fifty or so independent states of 1948, some of whom could not yet be exonerated of the charge of repressing ethnic groups by the pursuit of colonial policies. We see in that zealous Secretariat draft not only the definite link between the liberation of Europe and the liberation of Africa and Asia, a link which those who saw to the draft's later abridgement must have been quick to disapprove, but also—astoundingly—the implied requirement of a complete programme for the protection of human rights, family values, religious beliefs, the rights to work, to art, and to cultural heritage.

The Genocide Convention is in a somewhat Janus-like position. Although widely seen as a progressive development of international law, it also had an element of codification of existing law. Even before the Convention, no one except possibly the warped-minded perpetrators of the hideous acts it defines seriously believed in the lawfulness of such acts. In a way, the Convention simply stated accepted principles of law and thus could be regarded as a codification, especially as it was

[5] 'Draft Convention on the Crime of Genocide', UN doc. E/447 (1947).

concluded so quickly that nobody could claim that the law had actually developed between its initial proposal and its adoption.

Nevertheless, the Convention was a seminal development. Many of the ethnic or cultural groups who had been victims of genocide had actually been citizens of the perpetrating states. Yet action directed against a state's own citizens was now declared an offence against *international* law! This early initiative of the General Assembly thus placed a fateful gloss upon the principle of non-intervention in domestic affairs, a key safeguard which, as noted above, had been written into the Charter as Article 2(7).

(ii) *Other human rights conventions.* Later human rights instruments influenced by the Genocide Convention precedent include the 1966 International Convention on the Elimination of All Forms of Racial Discrimination, the 1973 International Convention on the Suppression and Punishment of the Crime of Apartheid, and the 1979 Convention on the Elimination of All Forms of Discrimination Against Women.

In my view, these and similar treaties (including the two 1966 international human rights covenants) show that the efforts of the representatives of states gathered together in the legal councils of the UN have not all been selfishly directed to building an invulnerable carapace around the national leviathan, but have made a serious contribution to piercing through the leviathan's tough hide in order to soothe and succour the victims in his maw.

These conventions, like several hundred other treaties, include a clause conferring jurisdiction upon the International Court of Justice in the event of a dispute as to their application or interpretation.[6] One of that Court's earliest tasks was to give its opinion on the effects of reservations made to the Genocide Convention.[7]

(iii) *General Assembly resolutions.* Many resolutions of the General Assembly have contributed significantly to the

---

[6] The number of treaties with compromissory clauses providing specifically for disputes arising under them to be referred to the International Court of Justice has risen from five in 1946 to at least 242 in 1980. It may now be as many as 400.

[7] *Reservations to the Genocide Convention, ICJ Reports,* 1951, p. 15. The Court's decision of principle in this case, making the compatibility of any reservation with the object and purpose of the convention a test of the validity of the reservation, was eventually reflected in the 1969 Vienna Convention on the Law of Treaties, Articles 19–23.

development of international law. When a General Assembly resolution on a basic tenet of law is not merely passed by a majority but is unanimous, it represents not just the *opinio juris* of many individual states but the *opinio juris communis*: the common opinion of states as to the law, which joins hands with custom and practice to become a rule from which no state may depart without positive proof of its having withheld consent.

There has always been much confusion and heated argument about the binding character of such General Assembly resolutions as general international law. It is often argued that the Assembly can legislate *vis-à-vis* the members of the UN in their capacity as such. But whether it can lay down norms of law, or whether its resolutions purporting to determine legal situations can or cannot be challenged by its members, are questions fiercely debated. Owing to the dominance of the Group of 77 in the General Assembly and the continuing predominance of the veto system in the Security Council, the normative importance of General Assembly resolutions is naturally emphasized by this group of states. Many of these states argue that General Assembly resolutions have the character of international legislation, but other groups of states have not accepted this view.[8]

To blunt the edge of the problem it is often said that some of its resolutions are 'normative', which is a way of avoiding the statement that they are law-making. However, the important question is not whether they would stand up to legal challenge, but whether they actually *are* challenged. If they are not, the application of the simple—or simple-seeming—doctrine of acquiescence will in the course of time create at least a rebuttable presumption that what those resolutions proclaim is law as between the member states. And since the membership of the UN verges on the universal, and since no non-member state seems to hold a particularly eccentric view of international law, we can properly assume—remembering yet again that international law is the emanation of states—that the general norms of conduct proclaimed by UN resolutions, if adopted in full

[8] On this question, see generally J. Castaneda, *Legal Effects of United Nations Resolutions* (New York, 1969); and R.P. Anand, 'Sovereign Equality of States in International Law', in the Hague Academy of International Law's *Recueil des Cours*, 197 (1986), pp. 9–228.

plenary unanimously or by an overwhelming majority, do become part and parcel of general international law. However, not all resolutions of the General Assembly can be so classified.

The General Assembly passes a wide assortment of resolutions every year. They include decisions as well as declarations. Their sum total each year could be in the vicinity of one hundred, but they are not all law-making. For example, the General Assembly's resolution adopting the Declaration on the Right of Peoples to Peace merely approves a text which is annexed to the resolution and requests the Secretary-General 'to ensure the widest dissemination of the Declaration to States, intergovernmental and non-governmental organizations'.[9] This declaration thus received UN approval and has a recommendatory force, but cannot be said to be legally binding. Again, the General Assembly passes resolutions on certain specific events or incidents which involve a member state of the UN. For example, the General Assembly passed a resolution on 15 November 1984 on 'The situation in Afghanistan and its implications for international peace and security'.[10] This resolution recognizes the right of the Afghan people to determine their own form of government, and calls for the immediate withdrawal of the foreign troops from Afghanistan. It requests the Secretary-General to keep member states informed of progress towards the implementation of the resolution and decides to include that item in the agenda of its next session. Such resolutions concerning specific cases have their own impact in the political field. They are certainly not law-making but they do apply the law to the facts of a particular case and draw their own conclusion. This is really the working of the General Assembly in the discharge of its obligations to maintain international peace. Such resolutions do not make law as such.

Certain resolutions of the General Assembly have been specifically declared to be law-making by the International Court of Justice. Such findings by the International Court of Justice are important in authoritatively recognizing these

[9] GA Res. 39/11 of 12 Nov. 1984, *GAOR*, 39th session, supplement no. 51 (UN doc. A/39/51).

[10] GA Res. 39/13 of 15 Nov. 1984, *GAOR*, 39th session, supplement no. 51 (UN doc. A/39/51). Similar resolutions have been passed every year since USSR troops entered Afghanistan in Dec. 1979.

resolutions as legally binding. The resolutions in this category include:

• General Assembly resolution 1514 (XV), the 'Declaration on the Granting of Independence to Colonial Countries and Peoples' was cited by the Court with approval in the *Namibia* advisory opinion in 1971.[11] This observation represents an important stage in the development of international law in regard to non-self-governing territories. Again, in the *Western Sahara* advisory opinion in 1975 the Court referred to the resolution in enunciating the principle of self-determination as a right of peoples.[12]

• General Assembly resolution 1541 (XV), 'Principles which Should Guide Members in Determining Whether or Not an Obligation Exists to Transmit the Information Called for under Article 73 of the Charter' was also cited in the *Western Sahara* advisory opinion.[13]

• General Assembly resolution 2131 (XX) entitled 'Declaration on the Inadmissibility of Intervention in the Domestic Affairs of States and the Protection of their Independence and Sovereignty' was quoted with approval by the Court in the *Nicaragua* v. *USA (Merits)* case. The Court observed:

The principle has since been reflected in numerous declarations adopted by international organizations and conferences in which the United States and Nicaragua have participated, e.g. General Assembly resolution 2131 (XX), the Declaration on the Inadmissibility of Intervention in the Domestic Affairs of States and the Protection of their Independence and Sovereignty. It is true that the United States, while it voted in favour of General Assembly resolution 2131 (XX), also declared at the time of its adoption in the First Committee that it considered the declaration in that resolution to be 'only a statement of political intention and not a formulation of law' (Official Records of the General Assembly, Twentieth Session, First Committee, A/C.1/SR.1423, p. 436). However, the essentials of resolution 2131 (XX) are repeated in the Declaration approved by resolution 2625 (XXV), which set out principles which the General Assembly declared to be 'basic principles' of international law, and on the adoption of which no analogous statement was made by the United States representative.[14]

---

[11] *ICJ Reports*, 1971, p. 31. [12] *ICJ Reports*, 1975, pp. 31–2.
[13] Ibid., pp. 32–3. [14] *ICJ Reports*, 1986, p. 107.

The Court thus took into consideration the question of consent by states to General Assembly resolutions.

• General Assembly resolution 2625 (XXV), the 'Declaration of Principles of International Law concerning Friendly Relations and Co-operation among States in accordance with the Charter of the United Nations' was endorsed in the advisory opinion on *Western Sahara*.[15] Furthermore, in *Nicaragua* v. *USA* the Court observed apropos the same resolution: 'The adoption by States of this text affords an indication of their *opinio juris* as to customary international law on the question.'[16]

• General Assembly resolution 3314 (XXIX), the 'Definition of Aggression', has been accepted by the Court as one that could be 'taken to reflect customary international law'.[17]

It must be emphasized that reference here is to resolutions enshrining general norms of conduct, not to positive rules of specific application. There is thus no contradiction between the view that the requirements of treaty law compel caution in general use of a convention until its universality is formally provable, and the view that these requirements can be softened in testing resolutions for their normative effect. To be committed to a principle under a resolution is not quite the same as to be bound by a rule under a convention, even if the element of voluntary consent is present in each case.

Among the most important UN General Assembly resolutions are those approving key declarations and treaties, including the 1948 Universal Declaration of Human Rights; the two 1966 Covenants, on Civil and Political Rights, and on Economic, Social, and Cultural Rights; the 1974 Charter of Economic Rights and Duties of States; and the 1970 Declaration on Principles of International Law concerning Friendly Relations and Co-operation among States.

Such resolutions and declarations as these are truly normative, in the sense of laying down norms and standards of international or even domestic conduct. As solemn proclamations of principle freely adopted, they amount to undertakings entered into by the principal subjects of international law, that is to say, the community of states. They form, in my view, contracts partaking of treaty law although they do not possess

---

[15] *ICJ Reports*, 1975, p. 33.   [16] *ICJ Reports*, 1986, pp. 100–1.   [17] Ibid., p. 103.

the formality of treaties. Formality is, however, a declining requirement for the validity of international commitments, as the jurisprudence of the International Court of Justice (to be surveyed below) has on more than one occasion made plain.

(iv) *General Assembly committees*. The General Assembly functions through Main Committees which are assigned specific roles. For example, the Sixth Committee is the legal committee comprising the legal advisers of the member states. It examines the report of the International Law Commission and makes concrete recommendations on legal problems or trends which concern the international community. The General Assembly also establishes special committees to examine specific legal matters. This is a regular procedural feature which helps to develop the law on the subject. For example, a special committee worked for many years on the question of defining aggression. Other special committees include the Committee on the Peaceful Uses of Outer Space, the Special Committee against Apartheid, and the Special Committee on Decolonization.

Several human rights conventions establish committees with supervisory or quasi-judicial powers. These committees all report to the General Assembly. In this category are the Committee on the Elimination of Racial Discrimination, established by the 1965 Convention on the Elimination of All Forms of Racial Discrimination; and the Human Rights Committee established by the 1966 International Covenant on Civil and Political Rights.

2. *Conferences convened by the UN*

(i) *Vienna conventions on diplomatic relations and on treaties*. Another example of the negotiation of important multilateral conventions by *ad hoc* conferences is furnished by the Vienna diplomatic conference of 1960, which laid the groundwork for the 1961 Vienna Convention on Diplomatic Relations and the 1963 Vienna Convention on Consular Relations. The 1969 Vienna Convention on the Law of Treaties was similarly adopted by an *ad hoc* conference convened at the instance of the UN. Each of these conferences had the benefit of draft texts prepared by the International Law Commission at the instance of the UN General Assembly.

In the case of the law of treaties it was realized that, with the tremendous proliferation of international agreements, it was for the good of the entire world community that certain choices should be made, and henceforth adhered to, as between different doctrines of treaty interpretation. It was understandable that with wide variations in domestic theories of contract, there should on the one hand have been those who favoured adherence to the plain meaning of treaties, and on the other hand those who felt it permissible to look behind the text to the intentions of the parties as revealed in the preparatory work. There were those who would only permit the placing of a literal construction on a treaty provision, while others wanted the spirit of a treaty to prevail. There were different schools of thought as to whether and how treaties could die a natural death, and as to whether their object and purpose could alter with changing circumstances. In a polyglot world, these doctrinal quarrels were dangerous sources of tension, but by imposing uniform rules of interpretation, freely agreed upon by the world community, the Vienna Convention (which came into force in 1980) has laid them largely to rest. The late and deeply missed Sir Humphrey Waldock was in no small degree responsible for this great work and, dare I say, for swinging its general emphasis towards the common-sense—by which I mean common law—interpretation of agreements. This was a sensible as well as an amazing achievement, because when faced with a welter of texts in several official languages, it is obvious that only a flexible, though methodical, approach could produce consistent results in treaty interpretation.

(ii) *Law of the sea conventions*. Codification of the law of the sea has been the object of three major UN conferences. The first, in 1958, led to the adoption of four conventions which are still in force. The second conference, in 1960, was unable to reach agreement on several divisive issues. Many of these issues were resolved by the monumental Third United Nations Conference on the Law of the Sea (1973–82). This conference adopted the comprehensive 1982 UN Convention on the Law of the Sea. The Convention will not enter into force until after sixty states have ratified or acceded to it.

3. *The International Law Commission*

Article 13 of the UN Charter provides: 'The General Assembly shall initiate studies and make recommendations for the purpose of . . . encouraging the progressive development of international law and its codification.' Responding to this requirement, the General Assembly established the International Law Commission by a resolution adopted on 21 November 1947.

Considering that international law is an emanation of states, whose opinion as to what the law is—*opinio juris*—is fundamental not only to its concretization but to its acceptance, it would not prima facie be entirely unreasonable if the members of the Commission were government appointees. But the majority view did not support this suggestion. Bearing in mind the scholarly nature of the work and the demands of objectivity, detachment, and continuity, it was decided to define its members simply as 'persons of recognized competence in international law'. The candidates can, however, be nominated by governments, and to ensure fair and balanced representation no two members can hold the same nationality. The official representatives of states play a formal role only when a conference is held to consider a draft code or convention prepared by the Commission.

Many initial drafts prepared by the Commission were eventually turned into multilateral conventions by special conferences convened by the UN, including the four 1958 conventions on the law of the sea, the 1961 and 1963 conventions on diplomatic and consular relations, the 1969 convention on special missions, the 1969 convention codifying the law of treaties, and the 1970 convention on the succession of states in respect of treaties.

The Commission has worked to develop new texts on, *inter alia*, the international responsibility of states, the status of the diplomatic courier and pouch, the relations between states and international organizations, the liability of states for transboundary damage (including pollution), and the law of international rivers. It has also prepared a declaration on the rights and duties of states; a code of offences against the peace and security of mankind; model rules of arbitral procedure; and articles on most favoured nation clauses.

The basic nature of a treaty is to be binding on the parties—but only on the parties. A convention may therefore proclaim, as it were, until it is blue in the face that it is laying down universal rules for the conduct of states in a particular domain, but it will never be self-fulfilling. Only as more and more states accede to its provisions will it have a chance of making good its claim to universality of application as treaty law. I emphasize, as treaty law, because there are numerous recent examples of courts, tribunals, and the legal officers of governments looking even to draft conventions, or conventions yet to come into force, for serious indications of the trend, if not the current state, of international law.

In pursuance of the General Assembly's Charter obligation to encourage the *codification* of international law, a Codification Division was set up in the Legal Department of the UN—a division which incidentally provides the International Law Commission with an excellent secretariat. But no division was set up corresponding to the other, associated obligation of the Assembly under Article 13, namely to encourage the *progressive development* of international law. This was no accidental omission. It illustrates the fact that, as in any national system, while it is a proper task for civil servants to assist in the recording and classification of existing law, i.e. codification, the development of the law is not a matter for civil servants—even international civil servants. In national systems, it is, in different measure, according to varying traditions, a matter for legislatures and the jurisprudence of courts. Naturally, private scholarship is always at liberty to help the process along, to point to new paths, to criticize, and encourage. But not the civil servants.

In the international community, the development of the law is a matter for states. They can act obliquely through their conduct, modifying practice and establishing custom, or intervene directly through the sponsorship or support of innovatory proposals. But this they need to do in a forum, whether within the standing organs of international organizations or agencies, or in the *ad hoc* multilateral conferences set up for specific subject areas. The great merit of the International Law Commission is to act as a bridge or two-way valve between the private scholars, who receive through their participation in the Commission's work an enhanced authority and status as international consultants, and the Sixth (Legal) Committee of the UN General Assembly where the representatives of states who understand the Commission's work meet to sift its proposals and take over the most approval-worthy as a basis for progressive development. That is how Article 13(1)(a) of the Charter, which revealingly associates such work in one seamless phrase with the promotion of 'international cooperation in the political field', is implemented in practice. This sub-paragraph has proved one of the most fruitful of the entire UN Charter.

4. The International Court of Justice

The International Court of Justice is open to all states members of the UN, and three other states (Liechtenstein, San Marino, and Switzerland) are also parties to the ICJ Statute. The jurisdiction of the ICJ depends on the consent of the states concerned. Such consent may take the form of a special agreement (or, occasionally, implied consent) to submit a particular dispute to the ICJ, or it may be a more general consent through a jurisdictional clause in a treaty, or a declaration accepting the compulsory jurisdiction of the Court. By June 1986, forty-six states had made such declarations, some four hundred treaties containing ICJ jurisdictional clauses were in force, and nine cases had been submitted to the ICJ by special agreement.

The ICJ may also give advisory opinions on legal questions to the General Assembly and twenty-one other UN organs and international agencies competent to request them. Such opinions are not generally binding, but nevertheless several of the eighteen opinions delivered by the ICJ from 1948 to 1986 have had considerable legal significance.

The case-law of the International Court of Justice is an important aspect of the UN's contribution to the development of international law. The modest number of its judgments and advisory opinions—these are listed in full in Appendix E to this volume—gives no inkling of the importance of its case-law, as this permeates into the international legal community not only through its decisions as such but through the wider implications of its methodology and reasoning. A few examples may be cited.

The dicta of the Court can be very general, and may flower greatly in the minds of legal advisers. It is impossible, for example, since the Court's *Barcelona Traction* judgment (1970) to maintain, before an international court, that risk capital placed abroad has any general right to diplomatic protection. The same judgment distinguished between obligations owed by states towards specific interests and their obligations towards the international community at large. The Court also observed:

In view of the importance of the rights involved, all States can be held to have a legal interest in their protection; they are obligations *erga omnes* . . . Such obligations derive, for example, in contemporary international law, from the outlawing of acts of aggression, and of genocide, as also from the principles and rules concerning the basic rights of the human person, including protection from slavery and racial discrimination.[18]

The implication is that any member of the world community is in principle entitled to call states to account for breaches of those obligations.

In the *Western Sahara* advisory opinion (1975), the Court struck a final blow against the notions of the 1885 Congress of Berlin which underlay the scramble for Africa, by finding that the concept of inhabited territory being *res nullius*—or territory belonging to no one, hence capable of being seized—no longer had any place in international law.[19] An earlier contribution to decolonization was the Court's *Namibia* opinion of 1971, which upheld the General Assembly's termination of South Africa's mandate to rule Namibia.[20]

In 1974 the Court might have had the opportunity to deal with the very thorny issue of responsibility for transboundary radioactive pollution, when Australia and New Zealand brought their *Nuclear Tests* cases against France.[21] But the French President declared before the cases were heard that France would cease atmospheric nuclear testing. The Court found this made the cases moot, and so judged. Its judgment nevertheless made a conspicuous contribution to the progressive development of international law, for never before had it so plainly been held that the high representative of a state could bind it with a public oral statement *erga omnes*. The Court has indeed consistently looked beyond formalities to the real substance and effect of

---

[18] *ICJ Reports*, 1970, p. 32. The Court went a step further when it observed later in the same case (p. 47) that 'with regard more particularly to human rights . . . it should be noted that these also include protection against denial of justice'.

[19] *ICJ Reports*, 1975, p. 30.

[20] *ICJ Reports*, 1971, p. 16.

[21] *ICJ Reports*, 1974, p. 257.

statements made in the context of international relations. As it observed in the *Nuclear Tests* cases:

The unilateral statements of the French authorities were made outside the Court, publicly and *erga omnes*, even though the first of them was communicated to the Government of Australia. As was observed above, to have legal effect, there was no need for these statements to be addressed to a particular State, nor was acceptance by any other State required. The general nature and characteristics of these statements are decisive for the evaluation of the legal implications, and it is to the interpretation of the statements that the Court must now proceed. The Court is entitled to presume, at the outset, that these statements were not made *in vacuo*, but in relation to the tests which constitute the very object of the present proceedings, although France has not appeared in the case.[22]

The successful resolution of the border dispute between Burkina Faso and Mali in the 1986 *Frontier Dispute* case illustrates the utility of judicial decision as a means of settlement in territorial disputes. The case was submitted to a Chamber of the ICJ pursuant to a special agreement concluded by the parties in 1983. In December 1985, while written submissions were being prepared, hostilities broke out in the disputed area. A cease-fire was agreed, and the Chamber by an Order of 10 January 1986 directed the continued observance of the cease-fire, the withdrawal of troops within twenty days, and the avoidance of actions tending to aggravate the dispute or prejudice its eventual resolution. The case proceeded, and in its judgment of 22 December 1986 the Chamber determined the overall course of the frontier line. The Presidents of Burkina Faso and Mali publicly welcomed the judgment and indicated their intention to comply with it.[23]

Several judgments of the Court have influenced the development of the law of the sea, and have been reflected in the work of conferences called by the United Nations to deal with this vital subject.

The Court's decision in the *Fisheries* case (1951) between the

[22] *ICJ Reports*, 1974, p. 269.

[23] *Frontier Dispute*: Provisional Measures Order of 10 Jan. 1986, *ICJ Reports*, 1986, p. 3; Judgment of 22 Dec. 1986, ibid., p. 554. The statements by Captain Thomas Sankara and General Moussa Traoré are annexed to ICJ Press Communiqué No. 87/1 of 16 Jan. 1987.

United Kingdom and Norway put an end to a long-standing controversy which had aroused considerable interest in maritime states. The Court held that the method adopted in a Norwegian decree of 1935 for calculating the baselines from which to measure the territorial sea was not contrary to international law. It laid down three criteria in this connection:

- that the baselines should not appreciably depart from the general direction of the coast;
- that the sea areas lying within these lines should be sufficiently closely linked to the land domain to be subject to the regime of internal waters; and
- that consideration should be given to the economic interests peculiar to the region in question, the reality and importance of which are clearly evidenced by a long usage.[24]

The Court rejected the view that, in international law, bays with an entrance more than ten miles wide could not, unless they were of the nature of so-called 'historic' bays, be regarded as internal waters.

In the *North Sea Continental Shelf* cases (1969), Denmark, the Netherlands, and the Federal Republic of Germany asked the Court to decide what principles of international law were applicable to the delimitation of that continental shelf. The Court rejected the contention that the delimitation in question had to be carried out in accordance with the principle of equidistance as defined in the 1958 Geneva Convention on the Continental Shelf. The Court took account of the fact that the Federal Republic of Germany had not ratified that Convention, and held that the equidistance principle was not inherent in the basic concept of continental shelf rights, that this principle was not a rule of customary international law. The Court promulgated the customary international law principles then applicable to delimitation of the continental shelf, enabling the parties to reach agreement on division of the contested shelf area.[25] This agreement was essential for drilling for oil and gas to proceed in these areas.

The Court has further elaborated the law on delimitation of

---

[24] *ICJ Reports*, 1951, p. 116.   [25] *ICJ Reports*, 1969, p. 3.

the continental shelf in the *Tunisia/Libya* case (1982) and the *Libya/Malta* case (1985). Similar issues were also considered by a Chamber of the ICJ in determining a single maritime boundary, applicable to the continental shelf and to the super-jacent waters between Canada and the United States in the *Gulf of Maine* case (1984). This series of maritime boundary cases has greatly enriched an increasingly important area of law, and has assisted other states seeking to delimit such boundaries through negotiation or arbitration.[26] In these three cases the Court took account of the 'new accepted trends' which appeared in the Third UN Conference on the Law of the Sea (1973–82) and in the resulting 1982 UN Convention on the Law of the Sea. Although that convention is not yet in force, the Court viewed certain of its provisions as evidence of new customary inter-national law. Thus the Court held that claims to Exclusive Economic Zones of up to 200 miles are now permissible, and noted the significance for maritime boundary delimitations of the automatic entitlement to a 200-mile continental shelf.

In the *Fisheries Jurisdiction* case (*United Kingdom* v. *Iceland*, 1974) the International Court of Justice contributed to the firm establishment in law of the idea that mankind needs to conserve the living resources of the sea and must respect these resources. The Court observed:

It is one of the advances in maritime international law, resulting from the intensification of fishing, that the former *laissez-faire* treatment of the living resources of the sea in the high seas had been replaced by a recognition of a duty to have due regard to the rights of other States and the needs of conservation for the benefit of all. Consequently, both Parties have the obligation to keep under review the fishery resources in the disputed waters and to examine together, in the light of scientific and other available information, the measures required for the conservation and development, and equitable exploitation, of these resources, taking into account any international agreement in force between them, such as the North-East Atlantic Fisheries Convention of 24 January 1959, as well as such other agreements as may be reached in the matter in the course of further negotiation.[27]

[26] *Continental Shelf (Tunisia/Libyan Arab Jamahiriya)*, Judgment, *ICJ Reports*, 1982, p. 18; *Continental Shelf (Libyan Arab Jamahiriya/Malta)*, Judgment, *ICJ Reports*, 1985, p. 13; *Delimitation of the Maritime Boundary in the Gulf of Maine Area*, Judgment, *ICJ Reports*, 1984, p. 246.
[27] *ICJ Reports*, 1974, p. 31.

The Court also held that the concept of preferential rights in fisheries limits is not static:

This is not to say that the preferential rights of a coastal State in a special situation are a static concept, in the sense that the degree of the coastal State's preference is to be considered as fixed for ever at some given moment. On the contrary, the preferential rights are a function of the exception dependence of such a coastal State on the fisheries in adjacent waters and may, therefore, vary as the extent of that dependence changes.[28]

The Court's judgment in the *Fisheries Jurisdiction* case contributes to the development of the law of the sea by recognizing the concept of the preferential rights of a coastal state in the fisheries of the adjacent waters, particularly if that state is in a special situation with its population dependent on those fisheries. Moreover, the Court proceeds further to recognize that the law pertaining to fisheries must accept the primacy of the requirement of conservation based on scientific data. The exercise of preferential rights of the coastal state as well as the historic rights of other states dependent on the same fishing grounds, have all to be subject to the overriding consideration of proper conservation of the fishery resources for the benefit of all concerned. The Court held:

In the fresh negotiations which are to take place on the basis of the present Judgment, the Parties will have the benefit of the above appraisal of their respective rights, and of certain guide-lines defining their scope. The task before them will be to conduct their negotiations on the basis that each must in good faith pay reasonable regard to the legal rights of the other in the waters around Iceland outside the 12-mile limit, thus bringing about an equitable apportionment of the fishing resources based on the facts of the particular situation, and having regard to the interests of other States which have established fishing rights in the area. It is not a matter of finding simply an equitable solution, but an equitable solution derived from the applicable law.[29]

(c) The Role of the UN Specialized Agencies

Any assessment of the efforts of the UN in the development of international law must give a prominent place to the

---

[28] Ibid., p. 30.   [29] Ibid., p. 33.

contribution of the specialized agencies. Some of the agencies of
the UN system have revolutionized international law in their
own domain and even established a full legal regime with its own
sanctions to enforce obedience to the laws generated in that
particular field. This observation applies particularly to the
International Maritime Organization (IMO), the International
Telecommunication Union (ITU), the International Labour
Organization (ILO), the International Civil Aviation
Organization (ICAO), and other organizations in technical
spheres. But important legal instruments have also been
adopted by Unesco, the World Health Organization (WHO),
the Office of the United Nations High Commissioner for
Refugees (UNHCR), and other bodies. Some of this work
merits particular attention here.

1. *Universalism of domestic standards through inter-state regulation*

We may take for example the world-wide regulation promoted
by the ILO. Its conventions and recommendations cover such
matters as hours of work, manning, and wages for factory and
other workers. Each state has its own laws to regulate the hours
of work or wages of the labour so employed, but the ILO has set
uniform minimum standards to which most states have adhered.

2. *Automatic ratification of amendments*

Problems occur where urgently required amendments to
existing conventions are negotiated, but do not come into force
for some or all states owing to slowness of ratification processes.
In the maritime field, the IMO has made path-breaking progress towards overcoming such problems. Certain conventions
concluded or administered by the IMO now compel state
parties to accept in a limited way the principle of automatic
acceptance of amendments after the lapse of a certain period of
time. Thus, for example, Article XV(2) of the 1972 Convention
on the Prevention of Marine Pollution by Dumping of Wastes
and Other Matter provides that amendments of a scientific and
technically specialized nature, if approved by a two-thirds
majority of those present and voting at a meeting called in
accordance with the provisions of the Convention, 'shall enter
into force for each Contracting Party immediately on notifica-

tion of its acceptance to the Organization and 100 days after approval by the meeting for all other parties except for those which before the end of 100 days make a declaration that they are not able to accept the amendment at that time'. This formulation does away with the need for a prescribed number of ratifications prior to entry into force of the amendments, and throws the burden on the dissenting minority to assert itself if it wishes to prevent the amendment from coming into force.

The 1974 Safety of Life at Sea (SOLAS) Convention also provides for automatic adoption of certain types of amendments six months after acceptance by two-thirds of the contracting states. Amendments adopted by the Maritime Safety Committee come into force two years after being communicated to the contracting states, unless rejected by either one-third of them, or by contracting states responsible for half of the world's gross tonnage of merchant shipping.

Similarly, the 1973 International Convention for the Prevention of Pollution from Ships (the MARPOL Convention), adopts in its Article 16(d), (e), (f), and (iii) the method of accepting an amendment to an Appendix by fixing a period of time 'not less than 10 months' after the lapse of which the amendment would come into force 'unless within that period an objection was communicated to the Organization by not less than one-third of the parties whose combined fleets constitute not less than 50 per cent of the gross tonnage of the world merchant fleets'.

This is in sharp contrast to the classical concept of sovereignty of states in international law, according to which a two-thirds majority could not, as a matter of right, bind the one-third minority since the consent of each state was essential to create binding obligations.

3. Effective enforcement in particular fields

Most of the main maritime conventions, including the 1974 SOLAS Convention and the 1966 International Convention on Load Lines, are enforced by the port authorities of the countries visited by the ships for trade and commerce. There are no protests from the foreign-flag ships that are penalized by the port authorities for having violated the Plimsoll mark by overloading.

What is still more significant is that even the 'non-convention' ships, that is ships flying the flag of countries that have not
ratified the maritime conventions, have to obey the law of the
conventions because most port states have ratified these conventions. The non-convention ships thus have no option but to
comply with the conventions, because they cannot avoid visiting
the ports of convention states. This ensures virtually universal
obedience to the convention laws.

(d) Legal Innovation under UN Auspices

The contributions of the UN, surveyed in the preceding parts of
this chapter, have assisted the development and promotion of
several new international legal concepts. Many of these spring
from the UN's global character, which promotes a global
approach to problems. Hence, for example, the genuine universalism of much contemporary international law, enabling the
law to avoid more regional or parochial lines of development
which would have been a disaster; hence also the concept of
human rights as rights of the entire human kind, both individually and collectively, irrespective of national boundaries, and
without discrimination as to race, religion, or sex. Two of the
new concepts with a strong universalist character merit further
consideration here: the concept of 'global commons' (or
common heritage of mankind), and proposals for a 'New International Economic Order'.

1. *'Global commons' and environmental protection*

The territorial jurisdiction of the state—whether on land, sea, or
air—is by and large well established. But technology is opening
up areas beyond the traditional terrestrial jurisdiction of states.
These areas, often described as 'international commons' or
'extraterritorial spaces', are increasingly the subject of international legal regulation. The *high seas*, as an international
highway for the passage of merchant ships, was the first recognized common space legally beyond the territorial sovereignty of
any state. A legal regime for the sea-bed beyond the limits of
national jurisdiction was formulated in the 1982 Law of the Sea
Convention. However, the Convention has yet to come into
force, and this regime has not attracted universal support.

There are other extraterritorial spaces, such as outer space or the atmosphere, which are neither fully nor effectively covered by an up-to-date legal system. Environmentalists are attempting to secure the protection, care, and conservation of the *atmosphere* as a 'common heritage of mankind', while *outer space* is regulated by specific rules rather than a codified general regime. *Antarctica* is regulated by a limited group of states under the 1959 Antarctic Treaty: the General Assembly began to take an interest in Antarctica in the early 1980s.

Mankind's principal use of another common resource, the earth's *electromagnetic environment*, is in the field of communications. An international organization, the International Telecommunication Union (ITU), has been created to facilitate international cooperation in this whole field. In a world which is increasingly connected and automated by means of electronics, major fluctuations in the electromagnetic environment may have serious international consequences, particularly during times of diplomatic or military crisis.

The concept of global commons carries with it common sharing, with common benefits and common costs. If it is a key characteristic of the concept of global commons that they cannot be appropriated by a single state, it follows that there must not only be common sharing in the name of humanity as a whole, but also respect for the needs of future generations.

2. The 'New International Economic Order'

The classical principles and standards of international treaty practice—such as national treatment, preferential treatment, fair treatment, reciprocity, and the international minimum standard—continue to develop and form part of many international economic treaties and organizations. Owing to their applicability to states with different economic systems, they reconcile the need for international cooperation with the diversity of national economic and legal systems. On the other hand, the various levels of private and public national and international economic law are slowly being integrated into a comprehensive 'international economic law' with mutually interacting and complementary structures and developments, such as the distinct tendency in both national and international economic law to supplement the classical principles of freedom and formal equality by new principles of substantive equality and solidarity.

The main contribution to the concept of the New International Economic Order was the 1974 General Assembly resolution on the Charter Economic Rights and Duties of States.[30] This was adopted by a vote of 120 in favour, six against and ten abstentions. Further developments in state practice, spurred in part by the work of the UN and its agencies, have aided the legal development of many aspects of the NIEO, although other aspects depend on further negotiations in the political sphere.

(e) Conclusions: Problems of Contemporary International Law

Although international law has developed markedly since 1945, both within and without the auspices of the UN, several fundamental problems remain unsolved. These relate especially to conflicts between international law principles, to gaps within the current body of international law, to regrettably frequent divergences between principles and practice, and to problems of implementation and enforcement. These are complex matters which cannot be treated extensively here. What follows will simply touch lightly on some areas of difficulty, without attempting to do so in a formal legal way, still less to propose solutions.

1. Conflict between principles

The content of international law is very much influenced by the practice and interests of states. International law rules are often formed as a compromise between different interests, whether economic, military, social, or other interests. General principles are agreed and applied, but in difficult or unusual cases it is not uncommon for them to appear to conflict. In many cases such apparent conflict can be resolved by detailed examination of all the legally relevant material germane to the case in hand. At the political level, however, there are often disputes as to which principle is applicable. There may be, for instance, tension between the principle of human rights and that of non-interven-

---

[30] GA Res. 3281 (XXIX) of 12 Dec. 1974, *GAOR*, 29th session, supplement no. 31 (UN doc. A/9631).

tion, or between the principle of self-determination of peoples
and that of the territorial integrity of states, or between the
principle of freedom of the high seas and that of the common
heritage of mankind.

A different dichotomy has occasionally been perceived
between regionalism and universalism in international law. To
a large extent this tension is illusory. Regional mechanisms for
implementing and enforcing law can be very successful, as is
evident for instance in the human rights field. The Court and
Commission established under the European Convention on
Human Rights are good examples which increasingly have
parallels in other regions. Regional institutions may also use law
to regulate local arrangements for navigation, carriage of goods,
customs, fisheries, and a myriad of other matters. Such institutions do not affect the universality of general international law,
which continues to apply in all regions. The fragmentation of
universal international law into different bodies of law applying
in different regions, without unifying principles or institutions,
would be a disastrous regression; fortunately, there is little
sign of this happening, and the trend is towards the further
strengthening of general international law.

2. *Gaps and ambiguities in international law*

The progressive development of international law is a continuing process, and there remain a number of areas in which
agreement on more detailed legal regimes is still needed. In
some cases this is because international opinion is only just
becoming seriously interested in particular problems. Rigorous
international regulation of environmental pollution has begun
in many areas, but, for instance, the problem of acid rain awaits
strict legal control. Similarly, international law does not yet
have an explicit means of taking into account the interests of
future generations in their environment. Another area of
increasing international activity concerns the protection of the
rights of indigenous peoples: the UN Working Group on Indigenous Populations is busy formulating appropriate international standards in response to growing recognition of the
importance of this issue. A third problem of mounting contemporary urgency is the problem of mass exodus of persons, whether spurred by war, natural disaster, or economic

deprivation. The existing international law on refugee status was not devised to deal with mass exodus, but it has not yet proved possible to adopt a comprehensive new legal regime in this difficult but vital area. A fourth problem is whether international law needs to be further developed in response to the complex issues raised by terrorism.

Other alleged gaps in international law relate to subjects which may not, or not yet, be so well suited to international legal regulation. Thus contemporary international law does not explicitly address the existence of so-called 'spheres of influence', of the sort associated (rightly or wrongly) with the 1945 Yalta Agreement, although the anti-imperialist principles of decolonization, non-intervention, and sovereign equality are formally opposed to spheres of influence. Similarly, general international law has relatively little impact on national immigration policies, although immigration matters are dealt with in many bilateral and other treaties. Views also differ on the international legality of certain forms of military activity, including the circumstances in which military interventions of various kinds may or may not be reconcilable with fundamental principles of international law.

3. Discrepancies between principles and practice

The practice of states and of international bodies conforms to international law in the vast majority of cases. Discrepancies may nevertheless appear on occasion. In some instances this is because international treaty standards are set at very high levels of attainment, and perfect universal compliance cannot be achieved instantly. Thus the growing body of human rights treaties does not instantly bring an end to all violations of human rights, much as the criminal law does not easily put an end to organized crime. Similarly, war has remained a feature of international life, despite the fundamental prohibitions on resort to aggressive war and the provisions for peaceful settlement of disputes contained in the UN Charter.

If humanity is to make progress, aspirational standards must often be set above the lowest common denominator—although not so far above as to flaw their efficacy. International legal standards will often be inconvenient to the short-term ends of a particular government. What is essential is that the international rule of law be effectively implemented and enforced.

4. *Implementation and enforcement*

The effectiveness of the law depends in part on the effectiveness of sanctions and recourses suitable for the protection of the victims of its violation. Without sanctions and without recourses, a legal regulation, as perfect as it may seem with regard to its content, risks remaining just empty words. Sanctions and recourses have developed considerably in the period since 1945, as indicated by the survey in this chapter. Further progress must still be made; the work of the International Law Commission in codifying the principles of state responsibility, when complete, will make an important contribution in this sphere.

More important than new formal procedures, however, is the task of increasing among states the habit of compliance with law. This cannot be left entirely to the states themselves. It is the responsibility of international organizations, of non-governmental organizations, of the news media, of individuals, and of international public opinion to castigate those who violate international law and to ensure better observance of it. The UN has an important role in coordinating these efforts as well as in facilitating the further development of international law. I am confident that future generations will be equal to this task.

Can the United Nations be Reformed?

MAURICE BERTRAND

THE United Nations has not lived up to the ideal envisioned at its origin: its role in the maintenance of peace is minor and its influence on the solution of global economic and social problems very limited. However, while scepticism may prevail as to the effectiveness of the institution, there is growing interest in considering the possibility of its revitalization. Its financial crisis, in large part the result of an anti-UN mood in the American Congress,[1] has encouraged the acceptance of the need for reform. In December 1985 the General Assembly created a group of eighteen 'intergovernmental experts' with a mandate to examine ways in which the 'effectiveness of the UN in dealing with political, economic and social issues' could be

---

[1] This mood in the US Congress led to the approval of: (a) the Kassebaum Amendment of August 1985, which was intended to force a 20 per cent cut in the US contribution to the UN budget, unless a system of weighted voting for financial decision-making was introduced. This would entail a reduction in the US contribution to the UN budget from 25 per cent down to 20 per cent. And (b) the Sundquist Amendment of October 1985, intended to deny the US contribution to the salaries of Soviet bloc UN staff members, in protest against their having to relinquish part of their pay cheques to their own governments. Another piece of legislation bearing on the level of the US contribution to the UN was the Gramm–Rudman Act (the Balanced Budget and Emergency Deficit Control Act) of Dec. 1985 which provided for reduced federal deficits over the following five years, with the intention of achieving a balanced budget in 1991. This Act provides that, if deficits are expected to be higher than those specified, starting in the 1986 fiscal year, funds are to be cut from most federal programmes, including those concerning payments to the UN regular budget and to forty-three other international organizations. The combination of these measures led to a reduction of approximately 50 per cent in the US contribution to the UN in 1986. The larger scale withholdings of assessed payments by the US over several years precipitated the UN financial crisis. Already by the end of 1985, eighteen member states, including four of the five permanent members of the Security Council, had combined withholdings of about US $120 million; unpaid dues for 1985 and earlier years had reached a grand total of $225 million. The UN regular budget is approximately $800 million per year. The only flexibility is provided by the UN's working capital fund of $100 million, and this has already been exhausted. The UN has no borrowing power, if not expressly authorized by the General Assembly. On withholdings, see also Zoller, *AJIL*, 81 (1987), p. 610.

strengthened.[2] The recommendations of the Group of Eighteen were considered by the General Assembly at its regular session of 1986: these are discussed below.

Outside of the UN, in the United States as well as in Europe, the clinical examination of the UN, in seminars, symposia, conferences, articles, books, research projects, and panels of 'wise men', increases every day.[3] The patient is moribund, but the physicians are numerous—some of them proposing panaceas, while others try with difficulty to establish a diagnosis.

Is the UN facing an exceptional situation or just a temporary crisis? Can it really be reformed? Opinions differ in this regard. But there are numerous indications that the problems faced by the UN today are indeed very serious, and that their real meaning has yet to be perceived.

(a) The Nature of the UN Crisis

Many arguments support the contention that the present crisis is temporary. The crisis alarm has often been sounded in the past, and in each case the UN has, after some cosmetic changes, survived. The organization has since its inception been periodically submitted to examination. Studies, reform projects, and restructuring operations are permanent items on its agenda.

1. Past proposals for reform

In the League of Nations, the need continually to adapt the structure of the political international organization was recognized from the outset. The last study bearing on reform of the League of Nations became famous, probably due to the date at which its conclusions were published. The group of experts

[2] GA Res. 40/237 of 18 Dec. 1985 entitled 'Review of the Efficiency of the Administrative and Financial Functioning of the UN'.

[3] In the USA, one of the main adversaries of the UN is the Heritage Foundation, which over several years has published numerous anti-UN pamphlets and has influenced the US Congress. Reacting against this trend, other foundations have sponsored studies on reform of the UN, inspired by a philosophy of constructive criticism. The 'UN management and decision-making project', organized by the UN Association of the USA, and financed by the Ford Foundation, is one example. In its report, published in September 1987, a diverse panel, including Nancy Kassebaum, Cyrus Vance, and Robert McNamara, called for far-reaching structural changes similar to those mentioned on p. 206 below. There have also been many academic symposia on the UN in the USA, Europe, and elsewhere.

chaired by the Australian Stanley Bruce finalized its report in 1939. It recommended the creation of a central committee for economic and social questions with the mission to direct and control the 'technical activities' previously addressed by the Council and the Assembly of the League. It envisaged participation of states which were not members of the League, and decision-making by majority. This audacious reform project—which six years later suggested to the fathers of the UN Charter the idea of the Economic and Social Council—was the outcome of reflections which had continued throughout the League's life: the Brussels Conference of September–October 1920; the preparation for the establishment of the Economic and Financial Committee by the Under-Secretary-General Jean Monnet;[4] the Geneva Economic Conference of 1927; and the work of the Committee of Twenty-Eight in 1936.

As for the United Nations, it would be overly fastidious to enumerate all the intergovernmental committees and groups of experts which have examined such issues as methods of work, financial difficulties, personnel policy, salaries, budgets, plans, economic and social programmes, decentralization, coordination, structure of the Secretariat, functioning of the intergovernmental machinery, and evaluation of results.

Initiatives for reform of the UN fall into two distinct periods. In the first, which lasted until the mid-1960s, initiatives for reflection and change mainly came from the Secretary-General, who proposed that the General Assembly create committees to help him in his task: for example the Group of Three Experts appointed by Trygve Lie in 1954, the Salaries Survey Committee of 1957, and the Group of Eight Experts approved by the General Assembly in 1960 to help Dag Hammarskjöld to define the Secretariat's structure. This Group of Eight, chaired by Guillaume Georges Picot, considered and rejected

[4] Jean Monnet (1888–1979) was one of the main initiators of the European Economic Community. After leaving the League of Nations in 1923, he was in private business until 1938. In 1939 he was chairman of the Franco-British Economic Coordination Committee, and later served as a member of the French Committee of National Liberation in Algiers. From 1947 to 1952 he was Commissioner of the first French Development Plan. He originated the Schuman Plan (1950), and was first President of the High Authority of the European Coal and Steel Community. In 1956 he became chairman of the Action Committee for the United States of Europe, which helped to prepare the Treaty of Rome of 1957.

Khrushchev's proposal for a 'troika' of three Secretaries-General.[5]

The second period began after Hammarskjöld's death. Henceforth the initiative was taken by member states, and the process of reflection and reform became a permanent function. From that time onward the number of committees and surveys on reform increased exponentially. In 1966, as a consequence of the financial crisis which resulted from the refusal by the USSR and France to pay their share of the expenses of ONUC in the Congo, a report of the Committee of Fourteen proposed measures concerning planning, programming, monitoring, evaluation, budgetary presentation, economic and social programmes and so on.[6] In 1969 a study on the capacity of the UN development system, concentrating on UNDP, was completed.[7] In 1975 the report of a Group of (twenty-five) Experts on the Structure of the United Nations System recommended the creation of the post of Director-General for Development, and the extension of the role of the Committee for Programme and Coordination (CPC).[8] Finally, throughout the whole period, numerous other studies by various special committees dealt with the financial situation and other administrative problems.[9]

In 1968 the Joint Inspection Unit (JIU) undertook on a per-

[5] 'Review of the Activities and Organization of the Secretariat: Report of the Committee of Experts Created by Resolution 1446 (XIV)', UN doc. A/4776 of 14 June 1961. Khrushchev had made his 'troika' proposal at the General Assembly in 1960.

[6] 'Second Report of the *Ad hoc* Committee of Experts to Examine the Finances of the United Nations and the Specialized Agencies (Committee established by Resolution 2049 (XX) of 13 Dec. 1965)', UN doc. A/6343 of 19 July 1966.

[7] *A Study of the Capacity of the United Nations Development System*, vols. 1 and 2 (UN, Geneva, 1969), sales no. E 70.1.10. The main author of the study is Sir Robert Jackson.

[8] 'A New United Nations Structure for Global Economic Cooperation: Report of the Group of Experts on the Structure of the UN System' (New York, 1975), UN doc. E/AC.62/9.

[9] Among others: Report of the Committee on the Reorganization of the Secretariat (Committee of Seven), Nov. 1968; Report of the Special Committee on the Financial Situation of the UN (Committee of Fifteen), 1972; Report of the Working Group on the UN Programme and Budget Machinery, 1975; Report of the Negotiating Committee on the Financial Emergency of the UN (Committee of Fifty-four), 1976; Report of the *Ad hoc* Committee on the Restructuring of the Economic and Social Sectors of the UN System (Committee of the Whole), Dec. 1977; Report of the Committee of Governmental Experts to Evaluate the Present Structure of the Secretariat in the Administrative, Finance and Personnel Areas (Committee of Seventeen), Nov. 1982. For details of these reports see the relevant volumes of the *Yearbook of the United Nations*.

manent basis consideration of how to improve the functioning of all the agencies of the UN system. The JIU has published approximately two hundred reports, dealing with administrative, financial, and structural aspects of the activities of these organizations. The JIU has secured implementation of a number of recommendations for reform, particularly in the recruitment of personnel, the adoption of medium-term plans and programme budgets, and improvement of methods of monitoring and evaluation.[10]

The lessons to be drawn from this experience are clear: the process of reform has in the past been fostered by financial difficulties, the cyclical worsening of which is a permanent feature of the life of the organization. Reform proposals have always been vigorously resisted by the Secretariat. Some measures aiming at modernization have been attempted:[11] but any limited results of these efforts have rapidly been eroded. It has never been really possible to revitalize the organization, which—buffeted by successive crises and efforts at reform—has become more and more marginalized.

[10] The Joint Inspection Unit was established on an experimental basis by General Assembly resolutions 2150 (XXI) of 4 Nov. 1966, 2360 (XXII) of 19 Nov. 1967, 2735 (XXV) of 17 Dec. 1970, and 2924 B (XXVII) of 24 Nov. 1972. It was established on a permanent basis, from 1 Jan. 1978, by GA Res. 31/192 of 22 Dec. 1976, the annex of which contains the Statute of the Unit. The JIU is composed of eleven Inspectors, who have the status of officials of the UN but are not staff members. The Inspectors 'have the broadest powers of investigators in all matters having a bearing on the efficiency of the services and the proper use of funds'; 'they make on the spot inquiries and investigations . . . as and when they themselves may decide, in any of the services of the organizations' of the UN system; they 'may propose reforms or make recommendations they deem necessary to the competent organs of the organizations'; they 'draw up, over their own signature, reports for which they are responsible and in which they state their findings and propose solutions to the problems they have noted . . . Upon receipt of reports, the executive head or heads concerned shall take immediate action to distribute them, with or without their comments, to the States members of their respective organizations.'

[11] For example, the development of a sophisticated system of planning, programming, budgeting, and evaluation, the adoption of precise regulations and rules on this topic, and the establishment of competitive examinations for recruitment of junior professionals. In each case, despite unanimous approval by member states, implementation has been greatly hindered by resistance from the Secretariat. On programming cf. JIU report 79/5 (UN doc. A/34/84) of 26 Mar. 1979, on 'Medium-term Planning in the United Nations'; and UN doc. A/36/171 'The Setting of Priorities and Identification of Obsolete Activities in the United Nations'. On personnel matters, see the first, second, and third reports of the JIU on the implementation of the personnel policy reforms approved by the General Assembly in 1974 (UN doc. A/31/264; JIU report 78/4; and UN doc. A/35/418); and the JIU report on 'Competitive Examinations in the United Nations' (JIU report 84/11 of Aug. 1984).

2. Diagnoses and proposals in the 1980s

The crisis in the mid-1980s seems to be similar in every respect
to the previous crises. The most recent popular proposals for
reform do not seem very different from what has been proposed
in the past. It would be difficult to present the creation of the
Group of Eighteen as an exceptional or new phenomenon. Its
report, presented in 1986, contains numerous recommendations which are simply repetitions of past proposals concerning
the functioning of intergovernmental organs, personnel policy,
coordination, methods of inspection, planning, programming,
and evaluation.[12]

Nevertheless, a relatively new tone was identifiable in the
consensus report of the Group of Eighteen. Several abusive
practices and problems of mismanagement affecting the Secretariat were confronted directly for the first time, including the
harmful proliferation of the posts of Under-Secretary-General
and Assistant Secretary-General, the inadequacy of qualifications of staff, particularly in these top posts, and the complex,
fragmented, and top-heavy structure of the Secretariat. The
report represented a sincere effort to reverse past tendencies
in recommending reducing the number of Under-Secretary-
General and Assistant Secretary-General posts by 25 per cent
over a period of three years, and in acknowledging the necessity
of pursuing in-depth studies of the structure of the intergovernmental machinery, a subject until now shielded from critical
investigation.

An important sign of a sincere desire for change was the particular attention paid by the Group of Eighteen to reform of the
intergovernmental mechanisms which prepare the decisions on
budgets, even if the Group was not able to reach a consensus on
this subject. Many experts advocate the creation of a Committee
of Programme and Budget, with a limited membership, a geographical distribution ensuring that the 'major contributors'
have reasonable representation, consensus decision-making,
and a mandate to advise the General Assembly on the content of
the UN's programme and the size of the budget. But despite the
fact that such a proposal has often been made in the past and

---

[12] Report of the Group of High-Level Intergovernmental Experts to Review the
Efficiency of the Administrative and Financial Functioning of the UN, *GAOR*, 41st
session, supplement no. 49 (UN doc A/41/49).

would be the logical conclusion of the adoption in 1974 of medium-term planning and programme budgeting, even the 1986 reforms did not put it fully into effect.[13]

The Group of Eighteen's report and the ensuing debates in the General Assembly reflect the current accepted diagnosis of the UN's crisis. This diagnosis has three main components:

(i) The prime cause of the present crisis is the 'crisis of multilateralism', in other words the 'lack of political will' of member states.

(ii) There is a lack of effective management, a problem which can be rectified mainly by 'reinforcing the power' of the Secretary-General.

(iii) The UN suffers from some structural deficiencies, mostly in the Secretariat and in some subsidiary intergovernmental organs which deal with programme and budget, which could be greatly ameliorated by the creation of a special committee to deal with these problems.

Such a diagnosis leads naturally to the conclusion that some minor changes and improved management will solve the UN's present crisis, but that a change in the political climate is needed before a real revitalization of the UN can be achieved.

The evolution of US policy in 1986 seemed to confirm this analysis. The US administration, which from early 1985 had pressed forcefully for major changes in the UN's decision-making process, softened its policy. On the US contribution for 1986, a payment of US $100 million was made at the end of November 1986, thus allowing the organization to survive

---

[13] By its resolution 41/213 of 19 Dec. 1986, the General Assembly finally approved, with a number of reservations, the recommendations of the Group of Eighteen concerning the structure of the Secretariat, reduction of staff, personnel policy, inspection, coordination, etc. On the budgetary process, the General Assembly decided to request the Secretary-General to prepare an outline of the programme budget one year in advance, and to give the existing Committee for Programme and Coordination the mandate to consider this outline. The CPC will 'continue its existing practice of reaching decisions by consensus', and will transmit its conclusions and recommendations to the General Assembly. The General Assembly will continue to decide on the programme-budget in conformity with Articles 17 and 18 of the Charter. In response, the US administration indicated that it would recommend to Congress that it be more positive in its financial support of the UN. It is still difficult to judge whether the passage of GA Res. 41/213 represents real long-term progress in the direction of a better mutual understanding of the role of the UN; at present it seems unlikely that it will permanently alleviate the financial and political crisis.

through the end of the year; and the Administration gave a commitment to request Congress to revise the amendments which were severely reducing the amount of the American contribution, if the reforms proposed by the Group of Eighteen were accepted. Finally, the unanimous and harmonious re-election of the Secretary-General in October 1986 confirmed the renewed confidence of member states in the future of the United Nations. The timely convergence of these events lend support to the customary belief that all immediate problems will eventually be settled, and that the UN will somehow continue its business as usual.

(b) The Political Framework of an Increasingly Interdependent World

1. *An illusion of specialists*

It is obviously possible that, for some years to come, the situation will not change greatly. But to believe that it could endure for a long period is pure illusion, and this illusion is in fact an 'illusion of specialists'. The United Nations is a far too complex world to allow laymen to make their own diagnoses, but the specialists—diplomats, civil servants, professors, or experts—have a tendency, due to the complexity of the subject, to limit their examination to the organization itself, and to forget the rest of the world. Their examination is made through the filter of collective vested interests, closely related to the main-tenance of the status quo, and they live in an environment of received ideas that the force of habit renders difficult to question.

Diplomats, for example, like the idea that they really contribute to the 'maintenance of peace' through the debates of the Security Council, or that they deal usefully with the main global economic questions in the Economic and Social Council. This overstates the importance of a profession which is losing ground in international relations, due to the active involvement both of the government ministers themselves and of the special-ists in economy, finance, trade, or arms control.[14]

Consequently, it is particularly hard for diplomats to question

---

[14] Indeed, UN diplomacy adds lustre to the profession of diplomats.

the idea—however false—that the 'maintenance of peace' can be brought about through an international organization in a politically divided world; or the illusion that it is possible for 159 member states, ranging from major powers to a large assortment of micro-states, to negotiate usefully on the major economic problems of the world.

International civil servants and experts have similar reasons for assuming that the present structure of the organization is fitted to the needs of the modern world, and for attributing the ineffectiveness of the UN to the 'lack of political will', or to some form of mismanagement. Public opinion has nothing to rely upon other than the advice of specialists: it is consequently natural that the public finds it difficult to gauge this complex problem, or even to be interested in it.

The 'illusion of specialists' obscures the real world, the world outside the organization.

2. A more and more interdependent world

The first important phenomenon of the real world relevant to the UN is the growth of interdependence among all countries. Acknowledgement of interdependence has now become a commonplace. Since the first oil crisis, governments and public opinion have learned to recognize that there is no way to establish independent national strategies in the economic and social fields, or to ignore the strategies, methods, and principles accepted by the rest of the world. Third World debt, international migrations, nuclear accidents, the spread of international terrorism, drugs, exchange-rate variations, and the activities of transnational corporations have permanently demonstrated that countries are no longer protected by their borders.

What is even more important is that the good fortune of any country can no longer be built exclusively on the misfortune of others, and that the need for economic solidarity has become more important than the advantages of competition. The prosperity of the USA is indispensable for the prosperity of Europe and Japan, and the reverse is true as well. No major creditor-country, international bank, or large corporation can accept the bankruptcy of a major debtor. The principles on which international economic relations were based are in a process of radical modification. The priority that a government is ready to accord to obtaining the establishment of, and respect for, common rules—for arms control, or for the equilibrium of external trade—is now often higher than the one it attaches to monopolizing its own resources to ensure its security or its prosperity.

3. The search for a world political framework

The direct consequence of these new principles is the need for reliable political institutions at the international and global level. Such institutions have to provide for medium-term commitments to implement common economic policies, as those agreed in the decisions of the Western summits; and, in the field of arms control, for international treaties which incorporate precise systems of verification and inspection. The collective decisions of such institutions tend to be more credible than the resolutions of the UN General Assembly or Security Council.

In other words, as the phenomenon of interdependence gains greater acceptance and acknowledgement, the need is created for a solid world political framework, which does not exist at present. Such a political framework is in the process of being established, but *outside* the United Nations. The rapid development of international intergovernmental organizations, which began in the middle of the nineteenth century, has spawned many institutions outside the UN, thus reducing its relative importance. Despite their theoretical membership in the UN system, the financial world organizations—the International Monetary Fund, the World Bank and GATT—have in fact operated as independent branches in which national ministries of Finance, Economy, and Trade are represented without being really connected with the Ministries of Foreign Affairs. The growing emphasis, particularly in Western Europe, on economic cooperation and progressive integration at the regional and even the intercontinental level has reduced considerably the interest of the major powers in the UN as a forum for discussing economic matters. Finally, particularly since 1970, regular summits have been instituted, both between the two superpowers to discuss arms control, and between the major Western powers—the United States, Europe, and Japan—to address the harmonization of their monetary and economic strategies. The experimental meeting at Cancún (Mexico) in 1981, which involved fourteen developing countries and eight industrialized states, indicated a possible future model for such consultations.

Clear trends which can be identified in these new political institutions include representation at the highest level;[15] and the limitation of membership to the most important countries—which means the exclusion of small countries and (despite the exception of Cancún) of the Third World.

(c) The UN is Not Able to Reform Itself

Despite the fact that increasing marginalization continues to reduce the role of the organization and even threatens its very existence, the UN appears totally unable to reform itself.

Defenders of the UN stress that it has rendered, and still renders, precise and limited services: the facilitation of decolonization, the success of some peacekeeping operations, the influence exercised for a better understanding of population and environment problems, the establishment of the law of the sea, the defence of human rights, the development of international law, the provision of a forum for discussion and diplomacy, the services rendered in the humanitarian field, especially to refugees, the modest but significant role of multilateral technical cooperation, and so on. But similar advocacy could equally enumerate the positive concrete contributions of the World Health Organization, the Arab League, or the Organization of American States. In other words, the UN, whose main mission is to foster peace and cooperation among nations, has not succeeded in performing its essential mandated service: to be *a centre offering a political framework* necessary to deal with international conflicts and to harmonize the actions of states in other areas of international concern.

Not only has the UN no chance today of fulfilling the role

---

[15] The main levels of representation one can distinguish are: Prime Minister and Heads of State (as in the East–West summits, the Western and European summits, etc.); Ministers (as in the Council of the European Community); Ambassadors (as in the Security Council); Diplomats below the rank of ambassador (as in the majority of the UN committees, the Economic and Social Council, the Trade and Development Board, and the Main Committees of the General Assembly).

which is played in this political field by a set of other institutions, but it is obviously unable even to correct its own managerial and structural deficiencies. The constraints which in the past have hampered complete recovery still remain. These include the structural decentralization of the UN system which still forbids any coordination between agencies; the continuing resistance of the Secretariat to any innovation; the concentration of the Secretary-General on political matters, which prevents him from giving sufficient attention to managerial and economic problems; the pressures from the foreign ministries of all countries which press for recruitment of their own nationals to high-level posts, whatever their qualifications; and the divergent interests of member states, which continue to render impossible any modification of the Charter.

Any small steps which are now taken in the right direction will almost certainly be rendered useless by deficient implementation. Long before any concrete results can be obtained, the UN will have reached such a level of marginality that its elimination would go unnoticed.

If there is any possibility of genuine reform, it will not originate inside the UN. In fact, only a constitutional reform could reinstate the organization in its legitimate and natural role. Although the majority of specialists believe that this is impossible, it is in fact the only serious reform which has any chance of success.

Both the UN crisis and the marginality of the UN reflect a problem which goes beyond the UN itself. These are only symptoms of a more serious malaise: *the unsatisfied need for an institutional framework suited to a more and more interdependent world.*

(d) World Constitutional Structure and Levels of World Consensus

It is clear from the style and the ambitious objectives of the Charter that its authors felt they were drafting a World Constitution. The distribution of powers and responsibilities between the principal organs, particularly the General Assembly, the Security Council, the Economic and Social Council, and the Secretariat, is comparable to the distribution of powers under a national constitution between an executive and a legislature composed of several 'houses' with different methods of representation.

To some extent the concept of drafting a world constitution overwhelmed the drafters. The enthusiasm brought about by the Allied victory fostered the belief that there existed a sufficient level of consensus between member states (and particularly among the most powerful member states) to enable the organization to undertake such ambitious missions as the 'maintenance of international peace and security' and the 'solution' of world economic and social problems. In many respects, the Charter is more the constitution of a federal state than a text regulating the functioning of an international organization.

Forty years of experience have shown that this was a mistaken conception and an impossible mission. But, on the other hand, the world has moved towards a more and more compelling economic interdependence, so that the need for a constitution for the 'political space' this has created becomes increasingly urgent. We are consequently facing a paradoxical situation: at the very time when the type of political framework the world needs grows clearer, received ideas and prevalent 'taboos' prevent it from gaining substance and becoming a reality.

The level of consensus presently existing between states is not sufficient to facilitate organized world political cooperation, so a Utopian system such as the one embodied in the Charter cannot succeed. On the other hand, we know that different levels of consensus exist in different fields: a relatively high level in technical fields (transport, communications, meteorology, etc.), and in respect of certain humanitarian activities; an intermediate but developing level in the field of economic relations, particularly between rich countries; and a very low—sometimes even non-existent—level in the ideological and political fields. The notion that these different levels of consensus allow, or require, different types of institutions has begun to find acceptance.[16]

In those fields where a high level of consensus exists, it is fairly easy to organize and manage concerted actions. In fields where the consensus level is very low, it is practically impossible to organize any activity. Areas where a moderate level of

---

[16] See JIU report 85/9 (UN doc. A/40/988), 'Some Reflections on Reform of the United Nations' by Maurice Bertrand, especially paras. 65–70 on 'Nature of the Activities of the System and the Notion of a World Consensus'.

consensus exists require particular attention, because activity in these fields depends on the existence of an effective negotiating system. Negotiations on a world scale work best if the number of participants is limited to not more than about twenty persons, if each of the participants represents a noticeable share of the world's population and economic power, and if a system for identifying world problems and negotiation opportunities is effective in providing the negotiators with relevant studies and information.

The UN currently offers the exact opposite of such a system. At the political level, where there is no consensus, a negotiating forum of reasonable size exists in the Security Council. But at the economic level, where negotiations may prove more fruitful, nothing comparable exists. Instead of a high-level and compact Economic Council, combining representation of great powers with a reasonable representation of Third World countries, the UN offers three different complex aggregates of intergovernmental organs: an Economic and Social Council of fifty-four members, a General Assembly of 159 members, and a Trade and Development Board of more than 100 members, each organ having numerous subsidiary bodies. The studies and reports provided to these bodies deal with the world economy in a purely descriptive manner, and the identification of problems to be examined does not entail any identification of opportunities for negotiations. One proposal for drastic reform in this field is for the creation of an Economic Security Council.[17] But a set of preconceived ideas, firmly established—and resulting in the acceptance of 'taboos'—has hampered any possibility of change in this area. Three of these ideas deserve particular mention.

The first such idea is that since the main mission of the UN is the 'maintenance of peace', attention should be focused on the reinvigoration of the Security Council and the restoration of powers to enforce its decisions. This naïve and Utopian idea is unfortunately very often shared by experienced diplomats.[18]

The second idea is that no important structural reform is possible since the Charter cannot be modified: any attempt to

---

[17] Bertrand, n. 16 above, Ch. V, and especially paras. 178–85.
[18] Ibid., paras. 77–88 on 'Collective Security and the Search for Peace'; and Maurice Bertrand, *Refaire l'ONU: Un Programme pour la Paix* (Geneva, 1986).

change it means opening a 'Pandora's box' with no possibility of reaching agreement. The main reply to this is that it would be possible to restructure the whole machinery of intergovernmental organs without touching the Charter. It is also important to note that the only amendments made to the Charter—apart from those relating to a slight change in the membership of the Security Council—have precisely concerned the increase of the membership of the Economic and Social Council from eighteen to twenty-seven and then from twenty-seven to fifty-four, a change which has destroyed the possibility of the Economic and Social Council becoming the forum for economic negotiations which is so badly needed.

The third idea is that the principle of sovereign equality of states stipulates that the only legitimate system of state representation is the 'one country, one vote' system, such as has always applied in the General Assembly. This idea is contrary to the constitutional practice applied in most federal states, including the United States, where a bicameral system comprises a Senate in which each state has the same number of representatives, and a House of Representatives where representation takes into account population and other facts. Such a system exists presently under the Charter in the political field, where the Security Council with the veto system counterbalances the power of the General Assembly. But it does not exist in the economic field, which is precisely where it would be most useful.

It will be necessary to eliminate these false but fixed ideas before real reform of the United Nations is possible. The prospects for reform thus depend on the effective evolution of ideas concerning the type of global organization the world needs at present.[19]

For governments to begin seriously to consider these questions, the numerous analyses of management, personnel coordination, plans, and budgets must be extended to a study of workable constitutional systems for the UN. It is also essential that world public opinion becomes interested in this problem.

It is far from certain that the fundamental problems at issue

---

[19] In para. 1 of the report 'Some Reflections', n. 16 above, the formulation used is that reflection on reform 'must focus, following the two unfinished experiments of the League of Nations and the United Nations, *on a third generation world organization*, genuinely in keeping with the needs of the modern world'. (Emphasis added.)

will be solved through a reform of the UN. It is perfectly possible that the solution could come, for example, from a better co-ordinated and structured organization of the summit meetings. It is not Utopian to imagine that a 'Cancún system' will eventually be systematized and that at some date the Soviet Union will become eager to participate in it. The creation of a permanent secretariat for such an institution would call into question the very need for the UN to exist. One can only hope that the evolution of ideas will be rapid enough to avoid such a situation.

In Chapter 25 of the First Book of the *Discourses*, Machiavelli writes that 'who wants to change the constitution of a free state—in order that this change be welcome and that it could last with everyone's agreement, must retain at least the shadow of the ancient forms in order that the people do not notice the change—even if the new institutions are in fact radically different from the previous ones.'

If this advice is followed by those who will have one day to define the new constitution of the world political space, the UN will be in a position to offer at least the shadow of its structures. If not, it will be necessary to invent something new.

Conclusion: The Contemporary Role of the United Nations

EVAN LUARD

(a) The United Nations Then and Now

THOSE who assembled at San Francisco in 1945 to finalize the United Nations Charter (and finalization was the only task conceded to them since its main outline had already been agreed between the principal Allied powers in advance) were hoping to create a structure that would transform international relations in the post-war world.

They were determined to learn the lessons of the League's failure and to create an institution that would be more effective than its predecessor in maintaining world peace. They had drawn certain conclusions from the League's sorry record. The new world body should be comprehensive, as the League had never been (the US had never been a member, and Germany, Italy, the Soviet Union, and Japan were members only for limited periods). Its Charter should recognize, as the League Covenant had only partially done, the special responsibility of the larger powers for maintaining world peace and security: by according them permanent membership in the body primarily responsible, the Security Council, and allowing them a veto over decisions of that body that were totally unacceptable to them. The Security Council should have a far greater authority than its predecessor, the League Council: every member would be obliged to 'accept and carry out' decisions of the Security Council, including any decisions it might make to use armed force against aggressors. The United Nations would be endowed with the 'teeth' that the League had always lacked: by arrangements under which member states would contribute contingents to serve as a permanent military force under the control of the Security Council. The new organization would also be given new responsibilities extending far beyond the peace and security field. It would, for example, unlike its predecessor, seek to secure respect for human rights in each of the member states, through new UN institutions established for that purpose. And it would exercise wide-ranging functions in the economic and social fields, including the coordination of the activities of a family of specialized agencies, some still to be created.

Within little more than a year the permanent members had failed to agree on the composition and functioning of a Security Council force. It had become equally clear that the great powers could rarely agree on the actions the organization ought to take to meet breaches of the peace. The idea that the great powers would be able to take action together to maintain world peace—or that they would at least refrain from *preventing* such action being taken by others—was based on the premise that local conflicts could be insulated from rivalries among the great powers themselves. That hope had quite often been fulfilled during the days of the League. In that earlier period, it had proved possible for disputes between Albania and Yugoslavia, Greece and Bulgaria, Turkey and Iran, Poland and Lithuania, Peru and Colombia to be resolved by that means. After 1945 the world was far smaller. Almost every issue, all over the world, was seen as being of direct concern to the two dominant powers. On most issues they took opposing viewpoints. It was not a case of a vast majority of detached bystanders acting together to knock sense into two unruly schoolboys. The entire body of bystanders was divided into supporters of one contestant or the other. The veto was used innumerable times to prevent any decision from being reached. It was thus impossible for the world body to act, as had been hoped, to deter the use of force. Even the great powers themselves, on which the peace of the world was supposed to depend, were willing to make use of force if their interests appeared to them to demand it: as was vividly demonstrated, little more than ten years after the organization's foundation, in November 1956, when three of the five were simultaneously engaged in acts of force against smaller and weaker countries.

Some adjustments were made to meet these problems. Even without a permanent Security Council force, an operation was undertaken in Korea which successfully protected a state under attack: an operation nominally under the UN umbrella, even if in practice it was dominated and controlled by the United States. To overcome the paralysing effect of the veto, the Assembly was given greater responsibility in dealing with threats to peace and security: especially in the Uniting for Peace procedure. Later the Secretary-General too came to be given a greater authority, enabling him to play a central role in many crises over the following years. After the 1956 Suez crisis, the organization for the first time created a peacekeeping force to facilitate and supervise the withdrawal of the invading forces, which helped to keep the peace between the principal antagonists for the next ten years. In the Congo in 1960–4 the organization attempted the still more ambitious task of maintaining law and order in a country rent with civil war. And further peacekeeping forces were established later: in Yemen, India–Pakistan, Cyprus, West Irian, Sinai (again), the Golan Heights, and south Lebanon. But the most important thing was that the organization remained, for its first twenty years, at the centre of the world stage: each time a new crisis arose it was still to meetings of the Security Council—and occasionally the General Assembly—that the world looked for an authoritative international response.

From about the middle of the 1960s even this degree of UN authority declined. Most states, and international opinion generally, no longer looked to the organization for effective action. In particular the Western powers, above all the United States, which were no longer able to rely on majority support in the organization, became increasingly reluctant to work with and through it, as they had in earlier days. Far from mobilizing and leading such a majority as before, they now saw themselves increasingly threatened by it. More and more it was the United States rather than the Soviet Union which found itself in a minority and under attack.

By the 1970s, therefore, it was no longer one superpower only that was negative in its approach to the UN and the procedures which it offered. Both equally preferred, on all of the most important questions, to deal directly with each other, outside the ambit of the organization: in negotiating on strategic weapons for example, or on the regional conflicts in which both had an interest. As a result the UN came to appear increasingly marginal to the task of maintaining world peace. Today its capacity to influence most international events is widely doubted.

When a major crisis occurs, it is no longer expected that the UN will be able to take effective action in response. It will be taken for granted that the Security Council will meet to discuss the question; but such a meeting will now—unlike twenty or thirty years ago—rarely even be reported in the world's press, since there will be little hope of any substantial outcome. It will be assumed that a ritual resolution will be passed; an imploring plea for a cease-fire, or for resumed negotiations, will be issued; at the very best the Secretary-General will appoint a 'special representative' to shuffle to and from between the combatants in the hope, usually vain, that this will produce a settlement. There is no general belief that the reality of warfare will be significantly affected. At the beginning of 1987, for example, there were over twenty wars taking place in different parts of the world, some of which had been going on for many years. Many of these had not even been discussed at the UN. Such discussions as there were had no significant influence. It is certainly not easy to point to any recent war that has been stopped as a result of UN action: whereas a measure of success was achieved several times in the first thirty years of the organization, for example, after the Arab–Israel wars of 1948, 1956, and 1973, after the India–Pakistan war of 1965, and twice during the conflict between the Dutch and the nationalist Indonesian forces in 1947–8.

The role currently fulfilled by the UN, therefore, falls far short of what was hoped in 1945. But if the organization has failed to transform international relationships in the way its founders hoped, is this because of defects in the organization and its members, in particular those who constitute a majority, as the UN's critics maintain? Or is it because the initial conception was itself flawed? It can plausibly be argued that the type of system that is set out in the Charter could never have come about, whatever the character of the member states, since it bore no relationship to the reality of international relations and state power. Was it ever reasonable to believe, for example, that the permanent members, which themselves wielded dominant power, would be able to agree both on the creation of a collec-tively controlled international force which could decisively influence events, and on the way such a force should be authorized and controlled? Was it realistic to believe that member states would always be willing submissively to obey, as they undertook to do, the 'decisions' of a small and not very representative body calling on them to send their forces to the far side of the world to meet some crisis which might appear of no immediate importance to them? Would states which disagreed so fundamentally on so many vital political issues really be able to form a common view on the many acute political conflicts of the age and work together to maintain the peace? In a word, were altogether excessive expectations focused on an institution that had been founded in the first place on overly optimistic premisses?

Much of the disillusionment that is frequently expressed about the 'failure' of the organization is the effect of these unrealistic expectations. The fairy godmothers who assembled at the organization's birth in San Francisco could endow their offspring with numerous assets, but they could not bequeath a magic wand. However enlightened the member states, however godlike the Secretary-General, it was never going to be possible for the new organization, by the ritual incantation of skilfully compounded resolutions, to cause nations engaged in conflict immediately to abandon that strife: to kiss and make up, and become good little boys again. If the UN was to be regarded as a failure because it failed to abolish war, then it was clearly doomed to failure from the beginning.

If more modest expectations are placed in the organization, however, the degree of disillusion that is now so widely expressed may be misplaced. Unhappily the idea that the United Nations could solve all problems has been replaced by the equally erroneous idea that it can do nothing. But the belief that it has no role at all to play in contemporary international relations is as misguided as the previous belief that its role would be decisive. If the organization is not performing its role in the way that many anticipated at San Francisco, or even as effectively as in the first decade or two of its life, this is not a reason for turning away in despair, and pronouncing its life at an end. It is a reason for giving careful thought to the ways in which it could be enabled to play a part which, though perhaps more modest than many dreamed of when it came into existence, could none the less be an important and constructive one; to consider whether, operated in a different way, it might indeed be enabled to play a valuable part in moderating national behaviour and reducing conflict among states.

(b) Current Criticisms of the UN

There are some in the West, even if at present a minority, who would declare that the idea of seeking to restore the effectiveness of the UN is a misguided task. In their eyes the organization is lost beyond redemption.

Probably the UN has never been under such a savage and sustained attack as that mounted in some Western countries over recent years. The most virulent onslaught has been that launched in the United States (for example, by the Heritage Foundation); but even among those who do not share the paranoid image of the organization which that body has sought to disseminate, there are a number of criticisms which (whether or not as the result of this campaign) have become widely prevalent and therefore deserve examination.

The first charge, which is perhaps the most widely made, is that the majority which controls the UN is biased in its approach to world problems: biased against the West as a whole, and against the US in particular. The bias attributed to the organization is often not simply a partiality in favour of the Third World but, more damagingly, a partiality in favour of the Soviet Union and the communist bloc as well. The UN is often said to apply 'double standards', making it unduly indulgent to the Soviet bloc and unduly harsh towards the West, or towards the United States. In fact the voting record of the UN bodies over recent years does not sustain this thesis.[1] For example, repeated resolutions of the General Assembly have, year by year, called unequivocally for the withdrawal of foreign forces from Afghanistan (since the Soviet intervention in 1979), and from Cambodia (since the Vietnamese invasion of December 1978). These votes follow the equally forthright condemnation of Soviet action in Hungary in 1956. These resolutions, passed by large majorities, are scarcely evidence of undue indulgence towards the Soviet Union. The same is true of the Assembly's action on one of the most important political issues arising within the organization over recent years: the question of the representation of Cambodia. Despite the fact that since 1979 the country has been largely under the control of the new government installed, with Vietnamese assistance, after the overthrow of Pol Pot, the Assembly has continued to recognize the credentials of the outsted regime (for all its appalling quasi-genocidal record), even while it controls almost no Cambodian territory.

The Assembly cannot even be accused of undue partiality towards Third World countries, despite the fact that over three-quarters of its membership consists of such countries. For example, the General Assembly consistently criticized both Indonesia's invasion of East Timor (1975), and Morocco's invasion of Western Sahara in the same year. The UN has continued on occasion to take positions more favourable to a Western state than to a Third World country: for example, at the time of the 1982 Falklands/Malvinas War, when the resolution carried by the Security Council, demanding Argentine withdrawal, was closer to the British view than to that of Argentina.

It is true that UN bodies can sometimes also be highly critical of the United States: for example, in the General Assembly resolution deploring the US-led intervention in Grenada in 1983 (a similar resolution in the Security Council was vetoed by the United States), and in the Council's resolution—also vetoed—condemning the US raid on Libya in April 1986 (though it is worth noting that the Council had decided to take no action on Libyan complaints against 'provocative' naval manœuvres off the Libyan coast in 1983). But these actions reflected the tendency of both bodies to condemn the unilateral use of force by states: not a surprising, nor a shameful, position for a peacekeeping organization to adopt. On many economic and social questions the majority in the Assembly have taken up positions which are closer to the US than to the Soviet Union. In 1986 the Assembly was equally scathing about the human rights records of Afghanistan, Iran, Chile, and El Salvador: not an unbalanced judgement. It would be difficult, on an objective reading of all the resolutions carried in the Assembly over the 1977–86 decade, to show any evidence of consistent bias against the US. This is demonstrated by the fact that the great majority of resolutions have secured US support, even if some may have been formulated in different terms from those which the US government itself would have chosen.

Another widespread charge is that the UN is financially irresponsible. It is complained that a majority of small states, which contribute little to the budget, vote for ambitious programmes of expenditure, which then have to be financed by a small number of larger and wealthier countries which are the major contributors. It is true that under the Charter (under provisions which Western states supported at the time of the organization's foundation) budgetary resolutions can be passed in the Assembly with only a two-thirds majority; and that permanent members, whatever the size of their own contribution, possess no veto over such a resolution. But it is sometimes forgotten that in 1964 the Western countries themselves, led by the United States, sought to compel the Soviet Union, under threat of losing its voting rights in the Assembly, to contribute to the cost of peacekeeping operations, which were not even part of the regular budget of the organization, and to the conduct of which she had strongly objected. Nor is it always realized that, even under the procedures followed until 1986, the budget of the organization increased more slowly than that of most national governments; and that the mandatory amounts contributed to the organization, even by major contributors, are a tiny fraction of their total public expenditures (little more than £30 million for Britain in 1985 against a defence budget about 600 times as large). Most of the large spending within the UN system is undertaken by bodies such as the World Bank—which is not financed from the UN budget nor from government contributions at all, but by raising money on financial markets—and by other development programmes which are voluntarily financed. In any case since the autumn of 1986 the budgetary system of the UN has been radically changed, so that budget decisions are to be reached by 'consensus'. This should mean that the major contributors have a veto over increases in spending which they disapprove. Agreement has also been reached on economy measures, including substantial reductions in the number of meetings held, documentation provided, and subsidiary bodies established. It seems likely that in future years, as a result of these decisions, the UN's budget will be allowed to increase only as fast as, or very little above, the rate of inflation.

Another charge widely made is that the UN is only a talking shop, in which windbags, often from tiny and insignificant states, declaim impassioned orations that have no impact whatever on world affairs. It cannot be denied that the organization is one in which a great many speeches are made, some more concise and relevant than others. But the same charge could be made of many national parliaments where a great deal of rhetoric is to be heard. In a political organization, whether domestic or international, one must expect to hear speeches. The UN is above all a forum in which the representatives of many states can express their views: as was often said in its early years, a town meeting of the world. For many small states, which cannot afford representation in any but a handful of other countries, it is the principal means of making their views known, of strutting, for even a brief moment, on the world stage. To afford such states the luxury of a few impassioned speeches (even if to a largely empty hall) is a small price to pay for maintaining an institution within which all states of the world can come together to discuss their problems. Fortunately many of the smaller and poorer states have themselves come to realize that excessive verbiage can be counter-productive, and now accept the need to curtail the number of useless speeches, resolutions, committees, studies, and bureaucrats, which add greatly to the cost of running the organization, often for very little practical result.

Again, it is complained that the distribution of votes within the organization bears no relation to effective power. It is said that the fact that the United States has an equal voice in the General Assembly with the Maldive Islands or Dominica, that the billion people of China have an equal voice with the 50,000 of St Christopher and Nevis, devalues Assembly votes. Resolutions can be passed which may be opposed by the ten largest states of the world, with a population two-thirds that of the world, because they are supported by 120 small states with a population that is far less. But however absurd this situation may sometimes appear, it conforms with the principle, universally accepted for the Assembly at the time the organization was created, of 'sovereign equality'. In practice even the smaller states which control the Assembly are aware of the emptiness of voting victories which ignore the reality of power. Precisely because it is the quality rather than the quantity of the support which is significant, there is now usually little effort to steamroller resolutions through against the opposition of the most important countries. On the contrary, the need for compromise is universally accepted, and the content of resolutions is considerably watered down for the sake of winning support which is as broadly based as possible, and which includes, above all, the votes of the major powers. Even in the few cases where this does not happen and a resolution is carried against the strongly held views of the major power, it can be nothing more than a non-binding recommendation in the Assembly; while in the Security Council it can be vetoed (for this reason the search for compromise is particularly pronounced in the Security Council, since a resolution can only have value if it secures adoption). Given the huge disparity in the size and importance of states, and because many of the governments represented are unelected, there has never been any possibility that Assembly votes could be regarded as representing the view of the peoples of the world. At best they should be seen as the expression of views which are widely held among governments representing states of widely varying size and significance. The weighting of votes in the Assembly, which is frequently recommended, would be one way of remedying the unrepresentative character its pronouncements have at present; but such a change is most unlikely to be implemented, if only because of the obvious self-interest of the majority in preventing it. In the meantime the plenary meetings of the Inter-Parliamentary Union are a somewhat more representative forum than the General Assembly (since opposition parties as well as government parties are normally represented there): though, given the nature of many parliaments at the present time, that too still falls far short of a genuinely representative body.

A final and more general criticism of the United Nations today is simply that it is ineffective in fulfilling its primary responsibility to maintain world peace; and therefore that it no longer needs to be taken seriously. It cannot be denied that, as we have already seen, the UN has been much less successful in this respect than many had hoped when it was founded. It was intended to prevent war, and war has remained widespread. But if, as we have argued, the original ambition was a quite unrealistic one, it is not logical to condemn the organization out of hand for its failings in this respect. Moreover, if it has failed in that respect (which is not beyond dispute) who should take the responsibility? If wars have continued to occur, despite the efforts of the world organization, this must surely be laid at the door not of a vague corporate entity existing somewhere out there, but of the member states of which it is constituted. Only a belief that the 'United Nations' has an existence independent of nations makes it possible to shift responsibility for its actions from states themselves to the joint undertaking of which they form a part. The General Assembly and the Security Council are only the sum of their parts. In blaming the organization, therefore, observers are only blaming the states of which it is constituted.

Sometimes it is the very states which have done most to prevent the organization becoming effective that are most strident in denouncing its failings. Many in Britain were most passionately hostile to the UN at the time when Britain herself was openly defying it and violating its principles in the Suez operation. Many in the US are equally free in condemning the UN today at a time when the US herself has openly and publicly defied the ruling of the International Court of Justice that assistance to the Nicaraguan Contras was contrary to international law, and has vetoed a Security Council resolution which merely drew attention to that judgment (although the US herself invoked the jurisdiction of the ICJ in the Iran hostages crisis in 1979). These are only particular examples of a phenomenon which is widespread, if not universal. Every member of the organization is willing to demand respect for the UN's pronouncements in cases where other states are involved; but where it is itself directly concerned it is able to find convincing reasons why the majority view is misguided and must, exceptionally, be defied. It will inevitably be difficult to build up the authority of the organization in the way that its critics demand so long as its leading members reserve for themselves the right to defy it when they believe their own national interests dictate this.

This is the fundamental difficulty which the UN now faces. States which almost universally pay lip-service to the ideal of respect for international law and the authority of the UN are unwilling, in particular cases, to accept the sacrifice of sovereignty and uninhibited freedom of action which collective decision-making requires. The members have created an organization to which they attribute authority but deny power. But the organization itself—the states and officials which make decisions within it—has not yet found the technique required to make its authority effective without the sanction of armed force.

(c) Can the United Nations be Made More Effective?

If the United Nations is not at present able to play the role in world affairs which many had hoped, are there changes in its procedures or institutions which might enable it to enjoy a more effective influence?

Many proposals have been made over the years for changes in the structure and practices of the UN system to enable it to perform its tasks more effectively (or as the authors of these schemes would like to see them performed). Some of the suggestions for change are more realistic than others. A number offer Utopian blueprints for a totally different kind of world from that which we live in today; and, whether or not they could work effectively if they were to be brought into being, there is not the remotest chance that the states, especially the most powerful states, which can alone determine whether or not they are put into effect, will consent to their realization (if only because in many cases their main purpose is to limit the power of such states). It seems, therefore, more sensible, in examining the way the organization may evolve over the next decade or so, to confine ourselves to considering the changes which look to have at least some chance of being accepted by important sections of the membership.

First, perhaps the most striking inadequacy of the UN as it operates today is the spasmodic and unpredictable way in which it works. Article 34 of the Charter provides that 'The Security Council may investigate any dispute, or any situation which might lead to international friction or give rise to a dispute, in order to determine whether the continuance of the dispute or situation is likely to endanger the maintenance of international peace and security.' In other words, it is empowered to examine situations which have not yet reached the stage of open conflict, or even given rise to a dispute. Indeed an entire chapter of the Charter (Chapter VI) sets out a long series of procedures which may be put into effect by the Council for this purpose. These include investigation (Article 34), consideration (Article 35), recommendation of appropriate procedures or methods of adjustment (Article 36(1)), reference to the International Court of Justice (Article 36(3)), and the recommendation, if a dispute is thought likely to endanger international peace and security, of 'such terms of settlement as it may consider appropriate' (Article 37). All of these are measures which the Council may take to deal with situations before they reach the stage of armed conflict; and which are designed, precisely, to prevent them reaching that stage.

The Security Council today almost never makes use of any of these procedures. In effect it ignores Chapter VI of the Charter altogether. In most cases it does nothing at all until a conflict has reached the stage of open war. To give an example, the Security Council (as Sir Anthony Parsons points out above) made no effort whatever to discuss the Iraq–Iran dispute during the summer of 1980, even though recurrent armed clashes were already taking place along their border and though it was apparent that open warfare must break out in the near future. In 1982, before the second Israeli invasion of Lebanon, the Security Council took no steps, despite having a peacekeeping force in the area, to stabilize the situation in southern Lebanon and make the invasion less likely. Such examples could be multiplied. In other words, the Council does not begin to consider the major issues of the day until they have already reached a stage when it is extremely difficult, if not impossible, for them to be effectively dealt with: after fighting has already broken out. But by that time it is too late. It is not reasonable to expect the belligerent nations, in which warlike passions have become aroused, will, after they have already embarked on war, meekly agree to recall their tanks and planes and return their troops to barracks, simply because the Council has carried an imploring call for a cease-fire. It was of course precisely for this reason that the organization's founders, with wisdom, provided that the UN should be concerned at an earlier stage: to *prevent* wars, rather than to confront them after they had occurred. But the powers given to the Council for the purpose are simply not used by it. Is it surprising that the UN is widely regarded as a failure?

A major reason for the organization's failure to fulfil its constitutional function is the convention that disputes and threatening situations are to be raised in the Security Council only by the parties which are directly involved. This is contrary to the express terms of Article 35 of the Charter, which lays down that 'any Member of the United Nations may bring any dispute, or any situation [which might lead to international friction or give rise to a dispute] to the attention of the Security Council or of the General Assembly'. The convention now adopted has the effect that if the parties to a dispute, for whatever reason, are not anxious for the question to come under its scrutiny (as, for example, was the case with both the US and the Soviet Union at the time of the Vietnam war, and with both Iran and Iraq in 1980) the matter is not discussed at all. This means that the principal mechanism on which the founders of the UN relied—the exertion of third-party pressures on the countries directly involved in conflict to reach a settlement—is never brought into use. Not only do many conflicts not reach the Council until war has already broken out—a number do not do so (as in the case of Vietnam) even after major armed conflict has begun because the principal protagonists choose not to raise them.

Second, not only are members of the Security Council reluctant to bring disputes in which they are not involved to its attention: so too have been successive Secretaries-General. Yet, given the hesitancy of the Council itself, it was, one might have hoped, precisely the task of the Secretary-General to ensure that situations which could lead to war were considered by the Council at an early stage. Under Article 99 the Secretary-General may 'bring to the attention of the Security Council any matter which in his opinion may threaten the maintenance of international peace and security'. But throughout the organization's history that power has only been used very infrequently. Its most conspicuous use was in July 1960, when Hammarskjöld raised the question of the Congo in the Security Council mainly because the Congo itself, not being a member, was unble to do so. Dr Pérez de Cuéllar, in his chapter in this book, describes some of the reasons for the hesitation that has been shown. He suggests, for example, that some situations may be aggravated and not eased if the Secretary-General draws attention to them and the Council then does nothing. But the fact of the Secretary-General bringing such a matter to its attention would in most cases stimulate the Council to take action. And even if this does not happen, the mere fact that international public attention has been focused on a dispute may often have a moderating influence. Fortunately successive Secretaries-General have been willing, as Professor Franck points out in his chapter, to take other steps, often on their own authority: for example, to appoint Special Representatives to establish contact with the parties and to try to promote a settlement between them. U Thant was perhaps the most daring in this respect, being willing, for example, to send an observer force to Yemen and to dispatch a mission to test the wishes of the people of Sabah and Sarawak, even without any authority from the Security Council. But this function too is one that could be better performed at an earlier stage than has normally been the case: it is not easy for even the most skilful negotiator (as Pérez de Cuéllar himself found over a number of years in Cyprus) to persuade states already engaged in active war—as in the Gulf and Afghanistan wars—to accept some proposal for peaceful settlement put forward on behalf of the Secretary-General.

Third, if the Secretary-General is to play a more active, and a more timely, role in seeking to resolve disputes, he needs to be better equipped for that task than he is today. Above all, he needs better sources of information and advice. It has often been suggested in the past that to perform his task effectively the Secretary-General requires facilities for acquiring and evaluating information about the political situation in many parts of the world, comparable to those at the disposal of the foreign minister of a national state (this is discussed by both Professor Franck and M. Bertrand above). The scale of representation could be relatively modest: perhaps a dozen representatives, with appropriate staff, stationed in the most important capitals and each covering a region or sub-region, providing regular detailed apppreciations of any crisis situation; together with appropriate 'desks' in New York to process the reports and draft evaluations and recommendations for the Secretary-General himself (and in some cases for the Council as a whole). The missions abroad would not be so much embassies—since they would have few representative functions—as local offices of the Secretary-General, though they should be accorded diplomatic privileges and courtesies and should normally expect to be able to enjoy access to the foreign ministers of the countries in each area they cover. The information they provide should make it easier for the UN and its chief executive to play a more active and positive role, instead of the essentially passive and reactive role they play today. This capability would also be improved if the Council were more often to appoint, as it used to do, sub-committees of three or four representatives of member states, to undertake fact-finding or mediatory tasks when disputes arise. These sub-committees would have an authority and a visibility that the anonymous 'personal representative' of the Secretary-General today often lacks, and so would probably have more influence on governments.

Fourth, the Security Council could itself exercise more influence if more of its meetings were held in private. It is true that the formal public meetings of the Council are only the tip of the iceberg; they are normally preceded by a considerable amount of confidential discussion in the corridor. But the value of this is often destroyed when all know that they are preparing for a public confrontation, under the glare of the television lights, at which the advantage of scoring well-publicized debating points off opponents will usually outweigh that of arriving at agreement on collective action or a compromise proposal. The Council is therefore seen as an arena of conflict, rather than a chamber for conciliation; an instrument for winning national advantage rather than for seeking international settlements. It is unable to acquire a sense of collective purpose, of 'collegiality', and remains in the eyes of the world merely a cockpit for disputatious diplomats, without authority or influence. The General Assembly has long ago, as Sir Michael Howard points out, been reduced to 'eloquent impotence' by its preference for empty rhetoric over practical decision-making. There is every likelihood that, without a change in its procedures, the Security Council will be reduced to equal impotence.

Fifth, if they are to acquire greater authority, UN bodies will need to develop, more deliberately and self-consciously than

they have in the past, a consistent set of principles of international behaviour. Since the organization is likely to remain,
within the foreseeable future, without the forcible sanctions
which its founders envisaged for it, it will continue to be dependent on intangible influence: the influence of the collective
judgements of a representative and authoritative body. These
are sanctions comparable to those wielded by other authorities
which cannot exercise superior physical power—the village
elders, the schoolmaster in a rowdy class, or the parents of
unruly children: the authority of consistent principles impartially applied. While the organization has on the whole, as
pointed out above, been reasonably consistent in condemning
the more blatant uses of armed force, it has not developed a
consistent set of principles governing some of the more ambiguous uses of force. This applies particularly to the most widespread, and most disputed, use of force in the modern world:
intervention by outside powers in the domestic conflicts of other
states. No clear doctrine has been formulated to enable the
reaching of judgements on such cases, or on the justifications
widely used in defence of such actions (for example, the need to
protect the nationals of the intervening state, the maintenance of
law and order, the defence of a constitutional government, or
the overthrow of a tyrannical one). If it is effectively to exercise
authority without power, the United Nations will have to
develop and to win support for far more clear-cut and consistent
positions on these and other questions than it has been able to do
so far.

Sixth, the organization may need to build on its acknowledged achievements in the field of peacekeeping. The range of
situations in which such operations can be effectively carried out
is limited: essentially where two combatants, who have already
agreed to stop fighting, need to be kept apart (as in Cyprus);
where a cease-fire line must be controlled (as on the Golan
Heights); or where elections need to be impartially supervised
(as in Namibia). But such situations will none the less continue
to be encountered at regular intervals. The better the organization and its members are prepared—in logistics, training, and
coordination—the more member states will be inclined to
respond positively when crisis situations arise. It is unlikely that
the twenty-five-year-old theological argument about the

authorization and control of such forces will be resolved. Adequate precedents have already been built up, through the accumulated experience of the UN, to provide reasonable guide-lines on any future operations. In comparable situations, it is to be hoped that the precedent set for the UN Emergency Force in Sinai in 1974 will be followed: when it was accepted in principle that all members would share in contributing to the cost of the force, outside the regular UN budget but on an agreed scale. Under such an arrangement a peacekeeping operation becomes, as most of the earlier operations cannot be claimed to have been, a genuinely collective enterprise, undertaken on behalf of the membership as a whole.

Seventh, both for peacekeeping and for other purposes, the UN needs to establish a more secure financial foundation. The 1986 financial crisis of the organization—itself but one of a series of such crises—only brought to the surface unsatisfactory features of the UN financial regime which have always existed. The main source of these has been that subsidiary bodies—not only the main Assembly committees but other bodies of various kinds—have effectively had the power to embark on programmes which the membership as a whole were then, on the basis of the system of assessment in force, bound to finance. Though theoretically any proposal for expenditure must be examined by the Advisory Committee on Administrative and Budgetary Questions (the ACABQ), the Assembly's Fifth (Budgetary) Committee, and finally be endorsed by the Assembly in plenary, in practice these have usually been little more than formalities. The Assembly in its final days, when delegates are anxious to get home for Christmas, has been willing (even though reminded, as constitutionally they must be, of the 'financial implications' of any such vote) to endorse almost every proposal put before them. In the early years it was the Soviet Union which most frequently complained of this procedure, refusing to pay for various programmes (and not only peacekeeping operations) which it regarded as outside the normal administrative expenses of the organization; and was roundly denounced by its opponents for that attitude. But in recent years it has been above all the US, and to a lesser extent the industrialized countries generally, which have become increasingly unwilling to be compulsorily assessed for programmes they believe are unnecessary, and which they them-selves may have opposed. Whether the 1986 agreement—under which 'consensus' will be required for all budgetary decisions—will permanently resolve these difficulties remains to be seen. The consensus requirement means in effect that each state has a veto. All will depend, as usual with compromises, on the way the agreement is applied in practice. If the developed states choose to use their veto power unreasonably, to prevent even moderate rates of UN budget growth—or if developing countries continually try to force through unreasonable expansion—the problem will not be removed, though the obligation on developed countries to contribute to programmes they have opposed will arguably be ended. As M. Bertrand points out in his chapter, it has been manifest for many years that what is required is a powerful budgetary committee: one which is not (like the Fifth Committee today) a cumbrous replica of the Assembly as a whole, nor (like the Committee for Programme and Coordination) a small sub-committee of little influence, but a powerful and representative body which, like a cabinet within the state, can impose discipline and coherence on the insatiable demands of individual spending departments. If the financial problems of the UN are to be more permanently overcome, therefore, a further reform on these lines is likely to be necessary.

Eighth, if the UN is to command the respect of international public opinion, as well as perform the task which it was set up to perform, it will need to strengthen its activities in the human rights field. In so far as international bodies have succeeded in protecting human rights over the period since 1945, this has mainly been achieved not by UN bodies but by regional com-missions, such as the European Commission on Human Rights and the Inter-American Commission. For the first thirty years of the UN's life its human rights bodies contented themselves with formulating a vast body of conventions, covenants, declarations, and other formal instruments, the influence of which on the governments that ratified them was not always obvious. No attempt was made directly to influence the human rights situation in any particular country. Such action would have been seen as a breach of sovereignty, and of Article 2(7) of the Charter, which excludes the UN from intervening in the

domestic affairs of a state. Over the last two decades or so, with
the development of the Resolution 1503 procedure described by
Professor Farer, this situation has changed. Although, as he
points out, this is a disastrously slow and cumbrous procedure,
and though it loses much of its impact from the fact that it
must remain confidential (confidentiality that, happily, is often
breached), it has allowed the Commission on Human Rights to
exercise influence in some cases where human rights violations
are particularly serious. Unfortunately, the commitment of
most member states to this procedure is only lukewarm; and it is
a sad commentary on the values which prevail in the Assembly
that the Sub-Commission on Prevention of Discrimination and
Protection of Minorities, which plays a leading role in the
examination of such cases and is by far the most effective and
hard-hitting body working in this field (because composed of
individual experts rather than government representatives),
was unable to meet in 1986 as a result of financial cuts. If the UN
is to be seen as a body that is concerned about human rights, and
to be taking active steps to protect them, it is important that
the Sub-Commission's activities should be maintained and
extended. Better still (though less likely because more radical)
would be the creation, after more than twenty-five years of discussion, of the post of UN High Commissioner for Human
Rights.

Ninth, it is necessary to improve the capacity of the United
Nations to coordinate the huge proliferation of economic and
social activities now being undertaken, not only by its own subsidiary organs but by the specialized agencies. The latter are in
practice independent bodies. The independence they enjoy is in
part a historical accident. While it may have been influenced by
the theory of 'functionalism' being propounded at the time of
the organization's foundation by such writers as David
Mitrany, it resulted primarily from the fact that a number of
important agencies were in existence before the UN was
formed. There was a good case for a reasonable degree of decentralization within the system: a situation in which all the multi-
farious activities of these agencies were directly controlled from
the centre would have established a bureaucratic monstrosity
even more unwieldy than that which now exists. It can, however, reasonably be maintained that decentralization is at

present excessive; and that at least more effective *coordination* of these wide-ranging activities is necessary. The existing coordinating bodies—principally the Administrative Committee on Coordination (ACC) and ECOSOC—have an influence that is only marginal. They may at best prevent the most glaring duplications of effort. They certainly do not affect the spending of each agency. Nor do they secure any overall balancing of effort. Ideally any new high-powered committee or council responsible for budgetary control would also be afforded the overall coordinating function within the UN (the two functions are almost inextricable). But this would not bring any integration of the programmes of the specialized agencies unless such a body was given some authority over the latter's budgets too: a revolutionary step, which could not be taken without a more radical change in thinking than appears likely at present. As Mr Dadzie points out, the largely 'unmanageable' intergovernmental bodies responsible for the different programmes are without 'systematic resource allocation procedures and effective accountability mechanisms'. In other words, what is really required is to establish, as M. Bertrand puts it, the political framework within which joint economic decisions can be taken. Perhaps the most likely embryo of such a mechanism is the system of economic 'summits'; but these could not perform the function here suggested unless they were opened to include representatives of the leading developing countries (as at Cancún) and brought into some relationship with the UN system.

Tenth, the last, and by far the most important, condition for making the UN a more effective institution is that its members, including above all its more powerful members, must really *want* it to work. What this implies is that they must be sufficiently committed to collective decision-making to be willing in some cases to accept decisions that are contrary to their own desires and interests. This in turn requires that the demands made of them, especially of the more powerful states, are not too far removed from their desires and interests. The surest recipe for a decline of the UN's influence is for it to become simply a pressure-group of small and powerless states, devoted to castigating and abusing the most powerful states of the world. For in that situation the latter could merely turn their backs on the organization altogether and pursue their own interests in their own way, paying no attention to its proceedings. If states which enjoy superior power outside the organization are to co-operate, they must be afforded within it a share in decision-making commensurate with that power. Conversely, however, the more powerful states, if allowed to play a leading role, must, in return, be willing not to abuse that influence, either by seeking to manipulate the organization for their own political purposes, or by trying to establish a great-power directorate to run the affairs of the world in the interests of the mighty. The interests of the strong and the weak, the rich and the poor, can, with sufficient effort, sometimes be reconciled. All at least share—most of the time—a common interest in peace.

By seeking to solve problems by consultation rather than con-frontation, by collective rather than unilateral action, the member states could even make the UN into the 'centre for har-monizing the actions of nations' which its founding fathers at San Francisco hoped to bring into being.

Appendix A

Charter of the United Nations

The UN Charter was signed on 26 June 1945 by the representatives of fifty states in San Francisco, at the conclusion of the United Nations Conference on International Organization. It came into force on 24 October 1945.

Four articles of the Charter have been amended: 23, 27, 61, and 109. In each case this has been to take account of the increased membership of the UN. All the amendments appear in italics in the text below. The footnotes, which have been added by the editors of this book, show what the previous versions were, and when each amendment came into force.

The Statute of the International Court of Justice was adopted at the same time as the UN Charter but is not included here.

Charter of the United Nations*

WE THE PEOPLES
OF THE UNITED NATIONS
DETERMINED

to save succeeding generations from the scourge of war, which twice in
our lifetime has brought untold sorrow to mankind, and
to reaffirm faith in fundamental human rights, in the dignity and
worth of the human person, in the equal rights of men and women
and of nations large and small, and
to establish conditions under which justice and respect for the obligations arising from treaties and other sources of international law can
be maintained, and
to promote social progress and better standards of life in larger
freedom,

AND FOR THESE ENDS

to practice tolerance and live together in peace with one another as
good neighbours, and
to unite our strength to maintain international peace and security, and

*Source: Yearbook of the United Nations 1982 (New York, 1986). There have been no
further amendments since this version was published.

to ensure, by the acceptance of principles and the institution of methods, that armed force shall not be used, save in the common interest, and

to employ international machinery for the promotion of the economic and social advancement of all peoples,

HAVE RESOLVED TO
COMBINE OUR EFFORTS TO
ACCOMPLISH THESE AIMS

Accordingly, our respective Governments, through representatives assembled in the city of San Francisco, who have exhibited their full powers found to be in good and due form, have agreed to the present Charter of the United Nations and do hereby establish an international organization to be known as the United Nations.

Chapter I
Purposes and Principles

ARTICLE 1

The Purposes of the United Nations are:

1. To maintain international peace and security, and to that end: to take effective collective measures for the prevention and removal of threats to the peace, and for the suppression of acts of aggression or other breaches of the peace, and to bring about by peaceful means, and in conformity with the principles of justice and international law, adjustment or settlement of international disputes or situations which might lead to a breach of the peace;

2. To develop friendly relations among nations based on respect for the principle of equal rights and self-determination of peoples, and to take other appropriate measures to strengthen universal peace;

3. To achieve international co-operation in solving international problems of an economic, social, cultural, or humanitarian character, and in promoting and encouraging respect for human rights and for fundamental freedoms for all without distinction as to race, sex, language, or religion; and

4. To be a centre for harmonizing the actions of nations in the attainment of these common ends.

ARTICLE 2

The Organization and its Members, in pursuit of the Purposes stated in Article 1, shall act in accordance with the following Principles.

1. The Organization is based on the principle of the sovereign equality of all its Members.

2. All Members, in order to ensure to all of them the rights and benefits resulting from membership, shall fulfil in good faith the obligations assumed by them in accordance with the present Charter.

3. All Members shall settle their international disputes by peaceful means in such a manner that international peace and security, and justice, are not endangered.

4. All Members shall refrain in their international relations from the threat or use of force against the territorial integrity or political independence of any state, or in any other manner inconsistent with the Purposes of the United Nations.

5. All Members shall give the United Nations every assistance in any action it takes in accordance with the present Charter, and shall refrain from giving assistance to any state against which the United Nations is taking preventive or enforcement action.

6. The Organization shall ensure that states which are not Members of the United Nations act in accordance with these Principles so far as may be necessary for the maintenance of international peace and security.

7. Nothing contained in the present Charter shall authorize the United Nations to intervene in matters which are essentially within the domestic jurisdiction of any state or shall require the Members to submit such matters to settlement under the present Charter; but this principle shall not prejudice the application of enforcement measures under Chapter VII.

Chapter II
Membership

ARTICLE 3

The original Members of the United Nations shall be the states which, having participated in the United Nations Conference on International Organization at San Francisco, or having previously signed the Declaration by United Nations of 1 January 1942, sign the present Charter and ratify it in accordance with Article 110.

ARTICLE 4

1. Membership in the United Nations is open to all other peace-loving states which accept the obligations contained in the present Charter and, in the judgment of the Organization, are able and willing to carry out these obligations.

2. The admission of any such state to membership in the United Nations will be effected by a decision of the General Assembly upon the recommendation of the Security Council.

ARTICLE 5

A Member of the United Nations against which preventive or enforce-
ment action has been taken by the Security Council may be suspended
from the exercise of the rights and privileges of membership by the
General Assembly upon the recommendation of the Security Council.
The exercise of these rights and privileges may be restored by the
Security Council.

ARTICLE 6

A Member of the United Nations which has persistently violated the
Principles contained in the present Charter may be expelled from the
Organization by the General Assembly upon the recommendation of
the Security Council.

Chapter III
Organs

ARTICLE 7

1. There are established as the principal organs of the United
Nations: a General Assembly, a Security Council, an Economic and
Social Council, a Trusteeship Council, an International Court of
Justice, and a Secretariat.

2. Such subsidiary organs as may be found necessary may be established in accordance with the present Charter.

ARTICLE 8

The United Nations shall place no restrictions on the eligibility of men
and women to participate in any capacity and under conditions of
equality in its principal and subsidiary organs.

Chapter IV
The General Assembly

Composition

ARTICLE 9

1. The General Assembly shall consist of all the Members of the
United Nations.

2. Each Member shall have not more than five representatives in
the General Assembly.

Functions and powers

ARTICLE 10

The General Assembly may discuss any questions or any matters within the scope of the present Charter or relating to the powers and functions of any organs provided for in the present Charter, and, except as provided in Article 12, may make recommendations to the Members of the United Nations or to the Security Council or to both on any such questions or matters.

ARTICLE 11

1. The General Assembly may consider the general principles of co-operation in the maintenance of international peace and security, including the principles governing disarmament and the regulation of armaments, and may make recommendations with regard to such principles to the Members or to the Security Council or to both.

2. The General Assembly may discuss any questions relating to the maintenance of international peace and security brought before it by any Member of the United Nations, or by the Security Council, or by a state which is not a Member of the United Nations in accordance with Article 35, paragraph 2, and, except as provided in Article 12, may make recommendations with regard to any such questions to the state or states concerned or to the Security Council or to both. Any such question on which action is necessary shall be referred to the Security Council by the General Assembly either before or after discussion.

3. The General Assembly may call the attention of the Security Council to situations which are likely to endanger international peace and security.

4. The powers of the General Assembly set forth in this Article shall not limit the general scope of Article 10.

ARTICLE 12

1. While the Security Council is exercising in respect of any dispute or situation the functions assigned to it in the present Charter, the General Assembly shall not make any recommendation with regard to that dispute or situation unless the Security Council so requests.

2. The Secretary-General, with the consent of the Security Council, shall notify the General Assembly at each session of any matters relative to the maintenance of international peace and security which are being dealt with by the Security Council and shall similarly notify the General Assembly, or the Members of the United Nations if the General Assembly is not in session, immediately the Security Council ceases to deal with such matters.

ARTICLE 13

1. The General Assembly shall initiate studies and make recommendations for the purpose of:

   (*a*) promoting international co-operation in the political field and encouraging the progressive development of international law and its codification;

   (*b*) promoting international co-operation in the economic, social, cultural, educational, and health fields, and assisting in the realization of human rights and fundamental freedoms for all without distinction as to race, sex, language, or religion.

2. The further responsibilities, functions and powers of the General Assembly with respect to matters mentioned in paragraph 1(b) above are set forth in Chapters IX and X.

ARTICLE 14

Subject to the provisions of Article 12, the General Assembly may recommend measures for the peaceful adjustment of any situation, regardless of origin, which it deems likely to impair the general welfare or friendly relations among nations, including situations resulting from a violation of the provisions of the present Charter setting forth the Purposes and Principles of the United Nations.

ARTICLE 15

1. The General Assembly shall receive and consider annual and special reports from the Security Council; these reports shall include an account of the measures that the Security Council has decided upon or taken to maintain international peace and security.

2. The General Assembly shall receive and consider reports from the other organs of the United Nations.

ARTICLE 16

The General Assembly shall perform such functions with respect to the international trusteeship system as are assigned to it under Chapters XII and XIII, including the approval of the trusteeship agreements for areas not designated as strategic.

ARTICLE 17

1. The General Assembly shall consider and approve the budget of the Organization.

2. The expenses of the Organization shall be borne by the Members as apportioned by the General Assembly.

3. The General Assembly shall consider and approve any financial

and budgetary arrangements with specialized agencies referred to in Article 57 and shall examine the administrative budgets of such specialized agencies with a view to making recommendations to the agencies concerned.

Voting

ARTICLE 18

1. Each member of the General Assembly shall have one vote.

2. Decisions of the General Assembly on important questions shall be made by a two-thirds majority of the members present and voting. These questions shall include: recommendations with respect to the maintenance of international peace and security, the election of the non-permanent members of the Security Council, the election of the members of the Economic and Social Council, the election of members of the Trusteeship Council in accordance with paragraph 1(c) of Article 86, the admission of new Members to the United Nations, the suspension of the rights and privileges of membership, the expulsion of Members, questions relating to the operation of the trusteeship system, and budgetary questions.

3. Decisions on other questions, including the determination of additional categories of questions to be decided by a two-thirds majority, shall be made by a majority of the members present and voting.

ARTICLE 19

A Member of the United Nations which is in arrears in the payment of its financial contributions to the Organization shall have no vote in the General Assembly if the amount of its arrears equals or exceeds the amount of the contributions due from it for the preceding two full years. The General Assembly may, nevertheless, permit such a Member to vote if it is satisfied that the failure to pay is due to conditions beyond the control of the Member.

Procedure

ARTICLE 20

The General Assembly shall meet in regular annual sessions and in such special sessions as occasion may require. Special sessions shall be convoked by the Secretary-General at the request of the Security Council or of a majority of the Members of the United Nations.

ARTICLE 21

The General Assembly shall adopt its own rules of procedure. It shall elect its President for each session.

ARTICLE 22

The General Assembly may establish such subsidiary organs as it deems necessary for the performance of its functions.

Chapter V
The Security Council

Composition

ARTICLE 23[1]

1. The Security Council shall consist of *fifteen* Members of the United Nations. The Republic of China, France, the Union of Soviet Socialist Republics, the United Kingdom of Great Britain and Northern Ireland, and the United States of America shall be permanent members of the Security Council. The General Assembly shall elect *ten* other Members of the United Nations to be non-permanent members of the Security Council, due regard being specially paid, in the first instance to the contribution of Members of the United Nations to the maintenance of international peace and security and to the other purposes of the Organization, and also to equitable geographical distribution.

2. The non-permanent members of the Security Council shall be elected for a term of two years. *In the first election of the non-permanent members after the increase of the membership of the Security Council from eleven to fifteen, two of the four additional members shall be chosen for a term of one year.* A retiring member shall not be eligible for immediate re-election.

3. Each member of the Security Council shall have one representative.

Functions and powers

ARTICLE 24

1. In order to ensure prompt and effective action by the United Nations, its Members confer on the Security Council primary res-

---

[1] Article 23(1) originally specified that the Security Council shall consist of *eleven* members, of whom *six* shall be elected by the General Assembly. Article 23(2), second sentence, originally read: 'In the first election of non-permanent members, however, three shall be chosen for a term of one year.' The current version came into force on 31 Aug. 1965.

ponsibility for the maintenance of international peace and security, and agree that in carrying out its duties under this responsibility the Security Council acts on their behalf.

2. In discharging these duties the Security Council shall act in accordance with the Purposes and Principles of the United Nations. The specific powers granted to the Security Council for the discharge of these duties are laid down in Chapters VI, VII, VIII, and XII.

3. The Security Council shall submit annual and, when necessary, special reports to the General Assembly for its consideration.

ARTICLE 25

The Members of the United Nations agree to accept and carry out the decisions of the Security Council in accordance with the present Charter.

ARTICLE 26

In order to promote the establishment and maintenance of international peace and security with the least diversion for armaments of the world's human and economic resources, the Security Council shall be responsible for formulating, with the assistance of the Military Staff Committee referred to in Article 47, plans to be submitted to the Members of the United Nations for the establishment of a system for the regulation of armaments.

Voting

ARTICLE 27[2]

1. Each member of the Security Council shall have one vote.

2. Decisions of the Security Council on procedural matters shall be made by an affirmative vote of *nine* members.

3. Decisions of the Security Council on all other matters shall be made by an affirmative vote of *nine* members including the concurring votes of the permanent members; provided that, in decisions under Chapter VI, and under paragraph 3 of Article 52, a party to a dispute shall abstain from voting.

Procedure

ARTICLE 28

1. The Security Council shall be so organized as to be able to function continuously. Each member of the Security Council shall for this purpose be represented at all times at the seat of the Organization.

---

[2] Article 27(2) and (3) originally specified affirmative votes of *seven* members. The current version came into force on 31 Aug. 1965.

2. The Security Council shall hold periodic meetings at which each of its members may, if it so desires, be represented by a member of the government or by some other specially designated representative.

3. The Security Council may hold meetings at such places other than the seat of the Organization as in its judgment will best facilitate its work.

ARTICLE 29

The Security Council may establish such subsidiary organs as it deems necessary for the performance of its functions.

ARTICLE 30

The Security Council shall adopt its own rules of procedure, including the method of selecting its President.

ARTICLE 31

Any Member of the United Nations which is not a member of the Security Council may participate, without vote, in the discussion of any question brought before the Security Council whenever the latter considers that the interests of that Member are specially affected.

ARTICLE 32

Any Member of the United Nations which is not a member of the Security Council or any state which is not a Member of the United Nations, if it is a party to a dispute under consideration by the Security Council, shall be invited to participate, without vote, in the discussion relating to the dispute. The Security Council shall lay down such conditions as it deems just for the participation of a state which is not a Member of the United Nations.

Chapter VI
Pacific Settlement of Disputes

ARTICLE 33

1. The parties to any dispute, the continuance of which is likely to endanger the maintenance of international peace and security, shall, first of all, seek a solution by negotiation, enquiry, mediation, conciliation, arbitration, judicial settlement, resort to regional agencies or arrangements, or other peaceful means of their own choice.

2. The Security Council shall, when it deems necessary, call upon the parties to settle their dispute by such means.

ARTICLE 34

The Security Council may investigate any disputes or any situation which might lead to international friction or give rise to a dispute, in order to determine whether the continuance of the dispute or situation is likely to endanger the maintenance of international peace and security.

ARTICLE 35

1. Any Member of the United Nations may bring any dispute, or any situation of the nature referred to in Article 34, to the attention of the Security Council or of the General Assembly.

2. A state which is not a Member of the United Nations may bring to the attention of the Security Council or of the General Assembly any dispute to which it is a party if it accepts in advance, for the purposes of the dispute, the obligations of pacific settlement provided in the present Charter.

3. The proceedings of the General Assembly in respect of matters brought to its attention under this Article will be subject to the provisions of Articles 11 and 12.

ARTICLE 36

1. The Security Council may, at any stage of a dispute of the nature referred to in Article 33 or of a situation of like nature, recommend appropriate procedures or methods of adjustment.

2. The Security Council should take into consideration any procedures for the settlement of the dispute which have already been adopted by the parties.

3. In making recommendations under this Article the Security Council should also take into consideration that legal disputes should as a general rule be referred by the parties to the International Court of Justice in accordance with the provisions of the Statute of the Court.

ARTICLE 37

1. Should the parties to a dispute of the nature referred to in Article 33 fail to settle it by the means indicated in that Article, they shall refer it to the Security Council.

2. If the Security Council deems that the continuance of the dispute is in fact likely to endanger the maintenance of international peace and security, it shall decide whether to take action under Article 36 or to recommend such terms of settlement as it may consider appropriate.

ARTICLE 38

Without prejudice to the provisions of Articles 33 to 37, the Security

Council may, if all the parties to any dispute so request, make recommendations to the parties with a view to a pacific settlement of the dispute.

Chapter VII
Action with Respect to Threats to the Peace, Breaches of the Peace, and Acts of Aggression

ARTICLE 39

The Security Council shall determine the existence of any threat to the peace, breach of the peace, or act of aggression and shall make recommendations, or decide what measures shall be taken in accordance with Articles 41 and 42, to maintain or restore international peace and security.

ARTICLE 40

In order to prevent an aggravation of the situation, the Security Council may, before making the recommendations or deciding upon the measures provided for in Article 39, call upon the parties concerned to comply with such provisional measures as it deems necessary or desirable. Such provisional measures shall be without prejudice to the rights, claims, or position of the parties concerned. The Security Council shall duly take account of failure to comply with such provisional measures.

ARTICLE 41

The Security Council may decide what measures not involving the use of armed force are to be employed to give effect to its decisions, and it may call upon the Members of the United Nations to apply such measures. These may include complete or partial interruption of economic relations and of rail, sea, air, postal, telegraphic, radio, and other means of communication, and the severance of diplomatic relations.

ARTICLE 42

Should the Security Council consider that measures provided for in Article 41 would be inadequate or have proved to be inadequate, it may take such action by air, sea, or land forces as may be necessary to maintain or restore international peace and security. Such action may include demonstrations, blockade, and other operations by air, sea, or land forces of Members of the United Nations.

ARTICLE 43

1. All Members of the United Nations, in order to contribute to the maintenance of international peace and security, undertake to make available to the Security Council, on its call and in accordance with a special agreement or agreements, armed forces, assistance, and facilities, including rights of passage, necessary for the purpose of maintaining international peace and security.

2. Such agreement or agreements shall govern the numbers and types of forces, their degree of readiness and general location, and the nature of the facilities and assistance to be provided.

3. The agreement or agreements shall be negotiated as soon as possible on the initiative of the Security Council. They shall be concluded between the Security Council and Members or between the Security Council and groups of Members and shall be subject to ratification by the signatory states in accordance with their respective constitutional processes.

ARTICLE 44

When the Security Council has decided to use force it shall, before calling upon a Member not represented on it to provide armed forces in fulfilment of the obligations assumed under Article 43, invite that Member, if the Member so desires, to participate in the decisions of the Security Council concerning the employment of contingents of that Member's armed forces.

ARTICLE 45

In order to enable the United Nations to take urgent military measures, Members shall hold immediately available national air-force contingents for combined international enforcement action. The strength and degree of readiness of these contingents and plans for their combined action shall be determined, within the limits laid down in the special agreement or agreements referred to in Article 43, by the Security Council with the assistance of the Military Staff Committee.

ARTICLE 46

Plans for the application of armed force shall be made by the Security Council with the assistance of the Military Staff Committee.

ARTICLE 47

1. There shall be established a Military Staff Committee to advise and assist the Security Council on all questions relating to the Security Council's military requirements for the maintenance of international

peace and security, the employment and command of forces placed at
its disposal, the regulation of armaments, and possible disarmament.

2. The Military Staff Committee shall consist of the Chiefs of Staff
of the permanent members of the Security Council or their representatives. Any Member of the United Nations not permanently
represented on the Committee shall be invited by the Committee to be
associated with it when the efficent discharge of the Committee's
responsibilities requires the participation of that Member in its work.

3. The Military Staff Committee shall be responsible under the
Security Council for the strategic direction of any armed forces placed
at the disposal of the Security Council. Questions relating to the command of such forces shall be worked out subsequently.

4. The Military Staff Committee, with the authorization of the
Security Council and after consultation with appropriate regional
agencies, may establish regional sub-committees.

ARTICLE 48

1. The action required to carry out the decisions of the Security
Council for the maintenance of international peace and security shall
be taken by all the Members of the United Nations or by some of them,
as the Security Council may determine.

2. Such decisions shall be carried out by the Members of the United
Nations directly and through their action in the appropriate international agencies of which they are members.

ARTICLE 49

The Members of the United Nations shall join in affording mutual
assistance in carrying out the measures decided upon by the Security
Council.

ARTICLE 50

If preventive or enforcement measures against any state are taken by
the Security Council, any other state, whether a Member of the United
Nations or not, which finds itself confronted with special economic
problems arising from the carrying out of those measures shall have the
right to consult the Security Council with regard to a solution of those
problems.

ARTICLE 51

Nothing in the present Charter shall impair the inherent right of
individual or collective self-defence if an armed attack occurs against a
Member of the United Nations, until the Security Council has taken
measures necessary to maintain international peace and security.

Measures taken by Members in the exercise of this right of self-defence shall be immediately reported to the Security Council and shall not in any way affect the authority and responsibility of the Security Council under the present Charter to take at any time such action as it deems necessary in order to maintain or restore international peace and security.

Chapter VIII
Regional Arrangements

ARTICLE 52

1. Nothing in the present Charter precludes the existence of regional arrangements or agencies for dealing with such matters relating to the maintenance of international peace and security as are appropriate for regional action, provided that such arrangements or agencies and their activities are consistent with the Purposes and Principles of the United Nations.

2. The Members of the United Nations entering into such arrangements or constituting such agencies shall make every effort to achieve pacific settlement of local disputes through such regional arrangements or by such regional agencies before referring them to the Security Council.

3. The Security Council shall encourage the development of pacific settlement of local disputes through such regional arrangements or by such regional agencies either on the initiative of the states concerned or by reference from the Security Council.

4. This Article in no way impairs the application of Articles 34 and 35.

ARTICLE 53

1. The Security Council shall, where appropriate, utilize such regional arrangements or agencies for enforcement action under its authority. But no enforcement action shall be taken under regional arrangements or by regional agencies without the authorization of the Security Council, with the exception of measures against any enemy state, as defined in paragraph 2 of this Article, provided for pursuant to Article 107 or in regional arrangements directed against renewal of aggressive policy on the part of any such state, until such time as the Organization may, on request of the Governments concerned, be charged with the responsibility for preventing further aggression by such a state.

2. The term enemy state as used in paragraph 1 of this Article applies to any state which during the Second World War has been an enemy of any signatory of the present Charter.

ARTICLE 54

The Security Council shall at all times be kept fully informed of activities undertaken or in contemplation under regional arrangements or by regional agencies for the maintenance of international peace and security.

Chapter IX
International Economic and Social Co-operation

ARTICLE 55

With a view to the creation of conditions of stability and well-being which are necessary for peaceful and friendly relations among nations based on respect for the principle of equal rights and self-determination of peoples, the United Nations shall promote:

(a) higher standards of living, full employment, and conditions of economic and social progress and development;

(b) solutions of international economic, social, health, and related problems; and international cultural and educational co-operation; and

(c) universal respect for, and observance of, human rights and fundamental freedoms for all without distinction as to race, sex, language, or religion.

ARTICLE 56

All Members pledge themselves to take joint and separate action in co-operation with the Organization for the achievement of the purposes set forth in Article 55.

ARTICLE 57

1. The various specialized agencies, established by intergovernmental agreement and having wide international responsibilities, as defined in their basic instruments, in economic, social, cultural, educational, health, and related fields, shall be brought into relationship with the United Nations in accordance with the provisions of Article 63.

2. Such agencies thus brought into relationship with the United Nations are hereinafter referred to as specialized agencies.

ARTICLE 58

The Organization shall make recommendations for the co-ordination of the policies and activities of the specialized agencies.

ARTICLE 59

The Organization shall, where appropriate, initiate negotiations among the states concerned for the creation of any new specialized agencies required for the accomplishment of the purposes set forth in Article 55.

ARTICLE 60

Responsibility for the discharge of the functions of the Organization set forth in this Chapter shall be vested in the General Assembly and, under the authority of the General Assembly, in the Economic and Social Council, which shall have for this purpose the powers set forth in Chapter X.

Chapter X
The Economic and Social Council

Composition

ARTICLE 61[3]

1. The Economic and Social Council shall consist of *fifty-four* Members of the United Nations elected by the General Assembly.

2. Subject to the provisions of paragraph 3, *eighteen* members of the Economic and Social Council shall be elected each year for a term of three years. A retiring member shall be eligible for immediate re-election.

3. *At the first election after the increase in the membership of the Economic and Social Council from twenty-seven to fifty-four members, in addition to the members elected in place of the nine members whose term of office expires at the end of that*

---

[3] Article 61 has been amended twice.

In the original version Article 61(1) specified that ECOSOC shall consist of *eighteen* members; 61(2) specified that *six* shall be elected each year; and 61(3) read as follows: 'At the first election, eighteen members of the Economic and Social Council shall be chosen. The term of office of six members so chosen shall expire at the end of one year, and of six other members at the end of two years, in accordance with arrangements made by the General Assembly.'

On 31 Aug. 1965 an amended version came into force, in which Article 61(1) specified that ECOSOC shall consist of *twenty-seven* members; 61(2) specified that *nine* shall be elected each year; and 61(3) read as follows: 'At the first election after the increase in the membership of the Economic and Social Council from eighteen to twenty-seven members, in addition to the members elected in place of the six members whose term of office expires at the end of that year, nine additional members shall be elected. Of these nine additional members, the term of office of three members so elected shall expire at the end of one year, and of three other members at the end of two years, in accordance with arrangements made by the General Assembly.'

The current version came into force on 24 Sept. 1973.

year, twenty-seven additional members shall be elected. Of these twenty-seven additional members, the term of office of nine members so elected shall expire at the end of one year, and of nine other members at the end of two years, in accordance with arrangements made by the General Assembly.

4. Each member of the Economic and Social Council shall have one representative.

Functions and powers

ARTICLE 62

1. The Economic and Social Council may make or initiate studies and reports with respect to international economic, social, cultural, educational, health, and related matters and may make recommendations with respect to any such matters to the General Assembly, to the. Members of the United Nations, and to the specialized agencies concerned.

2. It may make recommendations for the purpose of promoting respect for, and observance of, human rights and fundamental freedoms for all.

3. It may prepare draft conventions for submission to the General Assembly, with respect to matters falling within its competence.

4. It may call, in accordance with the rules prescribed by the United Nations, international conferences on matters falling within its competence.

ARTICLE 63

1. The Economic and Social Council may enter into agreements with any of the agencies referred to in Article 57, defining the terms on which the agency concerned shall be brought into relationship with the United Nations. Such agreements shall be subject to approval by the General Assembly.

2. It may co-ordinate the activities of the specialized agencies through consultation with and recommendations to such agencies and through recommendations to the General Assembly and to the Members of the United Nations.

ARTICLE 64

1. The Economic and Social Council may take appropriate steps to obtain regular reports from the specialized agencies. It may make arrangements with the Members of the United Nations and with the specialized agencies to obtain reports on the steps taken to give effect to its own recommendations and to recommendations on matters falling within its competence made by the General Assembly.

2. It may communicate its observations on these reports to the General Assembly.

ARTICLE 65

The Economic and Social Council may furnish information to the Security Council and shall assist the Security Council upon its request.

ARTICLE 66

1. The Economic and Social Council shall perform such functions as fall within its competence in connexion with the carrying out of the recommendations of the General Assembly.

2. It may, with the approval of the General Assembly, perform services at the request of Members of the United Nations and at the request of specialized agencies.

3. It shall perform such other functions as are specified elsewhere in the present Charter or as may be assigned to it by the General Assembly.

Voting

ARTICLE 67

1. Each member of the Economic and Social Council shall have one vote.

2. Decisions of the Economic and Social Council shall be made by a majority of the members present and voting.

Procedure

ARTICLE 68

The Economic and Social Council shall set up commissions in economic and social fields and for the promotion of human rights, and such other commissions as may be required for the performance of its functions.

ARTICLE 69

The Economic and Social Council shall invite any Member of the United Nations to participate, without vote, in its deliberations on any matter of particular concern to that Member.

ARTICLE 70

The Economic and Social Council may make arrangements for representatives of the specialized agencies to participate, without vote, in its deliberations and in those of the commissions established by it, and for its representatives to participate in the deliberations of the specialized agencies.

ARTICLE 71

The Economic and Social Council may make suitable arrangements for consultation with non-governmental organizations which are concerned with matters within its competence. Such arrangements may be made with international organizations and, where appropriate, with national organizations after consultation with the Member of the United Nations concerned.

ARTICLE 72

1. The Economic and Social Council shall adopt its own rules of procedure, including the method of selecting its President.

2. The Economic and Social Council shall meet as required in accordance with its rules, which shall include provision for the convening of meetings on the request of a majority of its members.

Chapter XI
Declaration regarding non-self-governing territories

ARTICLE 73

Members of the United Nations which have or assume responsibilities for the administration of territories whose peoples have not yet attained a full measure of self-government recognize the principle that the interests of the inhabitants of these territories are paramount, and accept as a sacred trust the obligation to promote to the utmost, within the system of international peace and security established by the present Charter, the well-being of the inhabitants of these territories, and, to this end:

(a) to ensure, with due respect for the culture of the peoples concerned, their political, economic, social, and educational advancement, their just treatment, and their protection against abuses;

(b) to develop self-government, to take due account of the political aspirations of the peoples, and to assist them in the progressive development of their free political institutions, according to the particular circumstances of each territory and its peoples and their varying stages of advancement;

(c) to further international peace and security;

(d) to promote constructive measures of development, to encourage research, and to co-operate with one another and, when and where appropriate, with specialized international bodies with a view to the practical achievement of the social, economic, and scientific purposes set forth in this Article; and

(e) to transmit regularly to the Secretary-General for information purposes, subject to such limitation as security and constitutional considerations may require, statistical and other information of a technical nature relating to economic, social, and educational conditions in the territories for which they are respectively responsible other than those territories to which Chapters XII and XIII apply.

ARTICLE 74

Members of the United Nations also agree that their policy in respect of the territories to which this Chapter applies, no less than in respect of their metropolitan areas, must be based on the general principle of good-neighbourliness, due account being taken of the interests and well-being of the rest of the world, in social, economic, and commercial matters.

Chapter XII
International Trusteeship System

ARTICLE 75

The United Nations shall establish under its authority an international trusteeship system for the administration and supervision of such territories as may be placed thereunder by subsequent individual agreements. These territories are hereinafter referred to as trust territories.

ARTICLE 76

The basic objectives of the trusteeship system, in accordance with the Purposes of the United Nations laid down in Article 1 of the present Charter, shall be:

(a) to further international peace and security;

(b) to promote the political, economic, social, and educational advancement of the inhabitants of the trust territories, and their progressive development towards self-government or independence as may be appropriate to the particular circumstances of each teritory and its peoples and the freely expressed wishes of the peoples concerned, and as may be provided by the terms of each trusteeship agreement;

(c) to encourage respect for human rights and for fundamental freedoms for all without distinction as to race, sex, language, or religion, and to encourage recognition of the interdependence of the peoples of the world; and

(*d*) to ensure equal treatment in social, economic, and commercial matters for all Members of the United Nations and their nationals, and also equal treatment for the latter in the administration of justice, without prejudice to the attainment of the foregoing objectives and subject to the provisions of Article 80.

ARTICLE 77

1. The trusteeship system shall apply to such territories in the following categories as may be placed thereunder by means of trusteeship agreements:

(*a*) territories now held under mandate;

(*b*) territories which may be detached from enemy states as a result of the Second World War; and

(*c*) territories voluntarily placed under the system by states responsible for their administration.

2. It will be a matter for subsequent agreement as to which territories in the foregoing categories will be brought under the trusteeship system and upon what terms.

ARTICLE 78

The trusteeship system shall not apply to territories which have become Members of the United Nations, relationship among which shall be based on respect for the principle of sovereign equality.

ARTICLE 79

The terms of trusteeship for each territory to be placed under the trusteeship system, including any alteration or amendment, shall be agreed upon by the states directly concerned, including the mandatory power in the case of territories held under mandate by a Member of the United Nations, and shall be approved as provided for in Articles 83 and 85.

ARTICLE 80

1. Except as may be agreed upon in individual trusteeship agreements, made under Articles 77, 79, and 81, placing each territory under the trusteeship system, and until such agreements have been concluded, nothing in this Chapter shall be construed in or of itself to alter in any manner the rights whatsoever of any states or any peoples or the terms of existing international instruments to which Members of the United Nations may respectively be parties.

2. Paragraph 1 of this Article shall not be interpreted as giving grounds for delay or postponement of the negotiation and conclusion of agreements for placing mandated and other territories under the trusteeship system as provided for in Article 77.

ARTICLE 81

The trusteeship agreement shall in each case include the terms under which the trust territory will be administered and designate the authority which will exercise the administration of the trust territory. Such authority, hereinafter called the administering authority, may be one or more states or the Organization itself.

ARTICLE 82

There may be designated, in any trusteeship agreement, a strategic area or areas which may include part or all of the trust territory to which the agreement applies, without prejudice to any special agreement or agreements made under Article 43.

ARTICLE 83

1. All functions of the United Nations relating to strategic areas, including the approval of the terms of the trusteeship agreements and of their alteration or amendments, shall be exercised by the Security Council.

2. The basic objectives set forth in Article 76 shall be applicable to the people of each strategic area.

3. The Security Council shall, subject to the provisions of the trusteeship agreements and without prejudice to security considerations, avail itself of the assistance of the Trusteeship Council to perform those functions of the United Nations under the trusteeship system relating to political, economic, social, and educational matters in the strategic areas.

ARTICLE 84

It shall be the duty of the administering authority to ensure that the trust territory shall play its part in the maintenance of international peace and security. To this end the administering authority may make use of volunteer forces, facilities, and assistance from the trust territory in carrying out the obligations towards the Security Council undertaken in this regard by the administering authority, as well as for local defence and the maintenance of law and order within the trust territory.

ARTICLE 85

1. The functions of the United Nations with regard to trusteeship agreements for all areas not designated as strategic, including the approval of the terms of the trusteeship agreements and of their alteration or amendment, shall be exercised by the General Assembly.

2. The Trusteeship Council, operating under the authority of the General Assembly, shall assist the General Assembly in carrying out these functions.

Chapter XIII
The Trusteeship Council

Composition

ARTICLE 86

1. The Trusteeship Council shall consist of the following Members of the United Nations:

   (*a*) those Members administering trust territories;
   (*b*) such of those Members mentioned by name in Article 23 as are not administering trust territories; and
   (*c*) as many other Members elected for three-year terms by the General Assembly as may be necessary to ensure that the total number of members of the Trusteeship Council is equally divided between those Members of the United Nations which administer trust territories and those which do not.

2. Each member of the Trusteeship Council shall designate one specially qualified person to represent it therein.

Functions and powers

ARTICLE 87

The General Assembly and, under its authority, the Trusteeship Council, in carrying out their functions, may:

   (*a*) consider reports submitted by the administering authority;
   (*b*) accept petitions and examine them in consultation with the administering authority;
   (*c*) provide for periodic visits to the respective trust territories at times agreed upon with the administering authority; and
   (*d*) take these and other actions in conformity with the terms of the trusteeship agreements.

ARTICLE 88

The Trusteeship Council shall formulate a questionnaire on the political, economic, social, and educational advancement of the inhabitants of each trust territory, and the administering authority for each trust territory within the competence of the General Assembly shall make an annual report to the General Assembly upon the basis of such questionnaire.

Voting

ARTICLE 89

1. Each member of the Trusteeship Council shall have one vote.

2. Decisions of the Trusteeship Council shall be made by a majority of the members present and voting.

Procedure

ARTICLE 90

1. The Trusteeship Council shall adopt its own rules of procedure, including the method of selecting its President.

2. The Trusteeship Council shall meet as required in accordance with its rules, which shall include provision for the convening of meetings on the request of a majority of its members.

ARTICLE 91

The Trusteeship Council shall, when appropriate, avail itself of the assistance of the Economic and Social Council and of the specialized agencies in regard to matters with which they are respectively concerned.

Chapter XIV
The International Court of Justice

ARTICLE 92

The International Court of Justice shall be the principal judicial organ of the United Nations. It shall function in accordance with the annexed Statute, which is based upon the Statute of the Permanent Court of International Justice and forms an integral part of the present Charter.

ARTICLE 93

1. All Members of the United Nations are *ipso facto* parties to the Statute of the International Court of Justice.

2. A state which is not a Member of the United Nations may become a party to the Statute of the International Court of Justice on conditions to be determined in each case by the General Assembly upon the recommendation of the Security Council.

ARTICLE 94

1. Each Member of the United Nations undertakes to comply with the decision of the International Court of Justice in any case to which it is party.

2. If any party to a case fails to perform the obligations incumbent upon it under a judgment rendered by the Court, the other party may have recourse to the Security Council, which may, if it deems necessary, make recommendations or decide upon measures to be taken to give effect to the judgment.

ARTICLE 95

Nothing in the present Charter shall prevent Members of the United Nations from entrusting the solution of their differences to other tribunals by virtue of agreements already in existence or which may be concluded in the future.

ARTICLE 96

1. The General Assembly or the Security Council may request the International Court of Justice to give an advisory opinion on any legal question.

2. Other organs of the United Nations and specialized agencies, which may at any time be so authorized by the General Assembly, may also request advisory opinions of the Court on legal questions arising within the scope of their activities.

Chapter XV
The Secretariat

ARTICLE 97

The Secretariat shall comprise a Secretary-General and such staff as the Organization may require. The Secretary-General shall be appointed by the General Assembly upon the recommendation of the Security Council. He shall be the chief administrative officer of the Organization.

ARTICLE 98

The Secretary-General shall act in that capacity in all meetings of the General Assembly, of the Security Council, of the Economic and

Social Council, and of the Trusteeship Council, and shall perform such other functions as are entrusted to him by these organs. The Secretary-General shall make an annual report to the General Assembly on the work of the Organization.

ARTICLE 99

The Secretary-General may bring to the attention of the Security Council any matter which in his opinion may threaten the maintenance of international peace and security.

ARTICLE 100

1. In the performance of their duties the Secretary-General and the staff shall not seek or receive instructions from any government or from any other authority external to the Organization. They shall refrain from any action which might reflect on their position as international officials responsible only to the Organization.

2. Each Member of the United Nations undertakes to respect the exclusively international character of the responsibilities of the Secretary-General and the staff and not to seek to influence them in the discharge of their responsibilities.

ARTICLE 101

1. The staff shall be appointed by the Secretary-General under regulations established by the General Assembly.

2. Appropriate staffs shall be permanently assigned to the Economic and Social Council, the Trusteeship Council, and, as required, to other organs of the United Nations. These staffs shall form a part of the Secretariat.

3. The paramount consideration in the employment of the staff and in the determination of the conditions of service shall be the necessity of securing the highest standards of efficiency, competence, and integrity. Due regard shall be paid to the importance of recruiting the staff on as wide a geographical basis as possible.

Chapter XVI
Miscellaneous Provisions

ARTICLE 102

1. Every treaty and every international agreement entered into by any Member of the United Nations after the present Charter comes into force shall as soon as possible be registered with the Secretariat and published by it.

2. No party to any such treaty or international agreement which has not been registered in accordance with the provisions of paragraph 1 of this Article may invoke that treaty or agreement before any organ of the United Nations.

ARTICLE 103

In the event of a conflict between the obligations of the Members of the United Nations under the present Charter and their obligations under any other international agreement, their obligations under the present Charter shall prevail.

ARTICLE 104

The Organization shall enjoy in the territory of each of its Members such legal capacity as may be necessary for the exercise of its functions and the fulfilment of its purposes.

ARTICLE 105

1. The Organization shall enjoy in the territory of each of its Members such privileges and immunities as are necessary for the fulfilment of its purposes.

2. Representatives of the Members of the United Nations and officials of the Organization shall similarly enjoy such privileges and immunities as are necessary for the independent exercise of their functions in connexion with the Organization.

3. The General Assembly may make recommendations with a view to determining the details of the application of paragraphs 1 and 2 of this Article or may propose conventions to the Members of the United Nations for this purpose.

Chapter XVII
Transitional Security Arrangements

ARTICLE 106

Pending the coming into force of such special agreements referred to in Article 43 as in the opinion of the Security Council enable it to begin the exercise of its responsibilities under Article 42, the parties to the Four-Nation Declaration, signed at Moscow, 30 October 1943, and France, shall, in accordance with the provisions of paragraph 5 of that Declaration, consult with one another and as occasion requires with other Members of the United Nations with a view to such joint action on behalf of the Organization as may be necessary for the purpose of maintaining international peace and security.

ARTICLE 107

Nothing in the present Charter shall invalidate or preclude action, in relation to any state which during the Second World War has been an enemy of any signatory to the present Charter, taken or authorized as a result of that war by the Governments having responsibility for such action.

Chapter XVIII
Amendments

ARTICLE 108

Amendments to the present Charter shall come into force for all Members of the United Nations when they have been adopted by a vote of two thirds of the members of the General Assembly and ratified in accordance with their respective constitutional processes by two thirds of the Members of the United Nations, including all the permanent members of the Security Council.

ARTICLE 109[4]

1. A General Conference of the Members of the United Nations for the purpose of reviewing the present Charter may be held at a date and place to be fixed by a two-thirds vote of the members of the General Assembly and by a vote of any *nine* members of the Security Council. Each Member of the United Nations shall have one vote in the conference.

2. Any alteration of the present Charter recommended by a two thirds vote of the conference shall take effect when ratified in accordance with their respective constitutional processes by two-thirds of the Members of the United Nations including all the permanent members of the Security Council.

3. If such a conference has not been held before the tenth annual session of the General Assembly following the coming into force of the present Charter, the proposal to call such a conference shall be placed on the agenda of that session of the General Assembly, and the conference shall be held if so decided by a majority vote of the members of the General Assembly and by a vote of any seven members of the Security Council.

[4] Article 109(1) originally specified a vote of any *seven* members of the Security Council. The current version came into force on 12 June 1968.

Chapter XIX
Ratification and Signature

ARTICLE 110

1. The present Charter shall be ratified by the signatory states in accordance with their respective constitutional processes.

2. The ratifications shall be deposited with the Government of the United States of America, which shall notify all the signatory states of each deposit as well as the Secretary-General of the Organization when he has been appointed.

3. The present Charter shall come into force upon the deposit of ratifications by the Republic of China, France, the Union of Soviet Socialist Republics, the United Kingdom of Great Britain and Northern Ireland, and the United States of America, and by a majority of the other signatory states. A protocol of the ratifications deposited shall thereupon be drawn up by the Government of the United States of America which shall communicate copies thereof to all the signatory states.

4. The states signatory to the present Charter which ratify it after it has come into force will become original Members of the United Nations on the date of the deposit of their respective ratifications.

ARTICLE 111

The present Charter, of which the Chinese, French, Russian, English, and Spanish texts are equally authentic, shall remain deposited in the archives of the Government of the United States of America. Duly certified copies thereof shall be transmitted by that Government to the Governments of the other signatory states.

IN FAITH WHEREOF the representatives of the Governments of the United Nations have signed the present Charter.

DONE at the city of San Francisco the twenty-sixth day of June, one thousand nine hundred and forty-five.

Appendix B

Member States of the United Nations

The 159 states members of the UN are listed below with the dates on which they became members. (An asterisk denotes an original member, as per Article 110 of the Charter.)

Member	Date of admission
Afghanistan	19 November 1946
Albania	14 December 1955
Algeria	8 October 1962
Angola	1 December 1976
Antigua and Barbuda	11 November 1981
* Argentina	24 October 1945
* Australia	1 November 1945
Austria	14 December 1955
Bahamas	18 September 1973
Bahrain	21 September 1971
Bangladesh	17 September 1974
Barbados	9 December 1966
* Belgium	27 December 1945
Belize	25 September 1981
Benin[1]	20 September 1960
Bhutan	21 September 1971
* Bolivia	14 November 1945
Botswana	17 October 1966
* Brazil	24 October 1945
Brunei Darussalam	21 September 1984
Bulgaria	14 December 1955
Burkina Faso[2]	20 September 1960
Burma	19 April 1948
Burundi	18 September 1962
* Byelorussian Soviet Socialist Republic	24 October 1945

Note: The information was provided by the UN Office, London, and was correct as of July 1987.
[1] Formerly Dahomey.
[2] Formerly Upper Volta.

Member	*Date of admission*
Cameroon	20 September 1960
* Canada	9 November 1945
Cape Verde	16 September 1975
Central African Republic	20 September 1960
Chad	20 September 1960
* Chile	24 October 1945
* China[3]	24 October 1945
* Colombia	5 November 1945
Comoros	12 November 1975
Congo	20 September 1960
* Costa Rica	2 November 1945
Côte d'Ivoire	20 September 1960
* Cuba	24 October 1945
Cyprus	20 September 1960
* Czechoslovakia	24 October 1945
Democratic Kampuchea[4]	14 December 1955
·Democratic Yemen	14 December 1967
* Denmark	24 October 1945
Djibouti	20 September 1977
Dominica	18 December 1978
* Dominican Republic	24 October 1945
* Ecuador	21 December 1945
* Egypt[5]	24 October 1945
* El Salvador	24 October 1945
Equatorial Guinea	12 November 1968
* Ethiopia	13 November 1945
Fiji	13 October 1970
Finland	14 December 1955
* France	24 October 1945
Gabon	20 September 1960
Gambia	21 September 1965
German Democratic Republic	18 September 1973

[3] By resolution 2758 (XXVI) of 25 Oct. 1971, the General Assembly decided 'to restore all its rights to the People's Republic of China and to recognize the representatives of its Government as the only legitimate representatives of China to the United Nations, and to expel forthwith the representatives of Chiang Kai-shek from the place which they unlawfully occupy at the United Nations and in all the organizations related to it'.

[4] Formerly Cambodia.

[5] Egypt and Syria were original members of the UN from 24 Oct. 1945. Following a plebiscite on 21 Feb. 1958, the United Arab Republic was established by a union of Egypt and Syria and continued as a single member. On 13 Oct. 1961 Syria resumed its status as an independent state and simultaneously its UN membership. On 2 Sept. 1971 the United Arab Republic changed its name to Arab Republic of Egypt.

Member	*Date of admission*
Germany, Federal Republic of	18 September 1973
Ghana	8 March 1957
* Greece	25 October 1945
Grenada	17 September 1974
* Guatemala	21 November 1945
Guinea	12 December 1958
Guinea-Bissau	17 September 1974
Guyana	20 September 1966
* Haiti	24 October 1945
* Honduras	17 December 1945
Hungary	14 December 1955
Iceland	19 November 1946
* India	30 October 1945
Indonesia[6]	28 September 1950
* Iran (Islamic Republic of)	24 October 1945
* Iraq	21 December 1945
Ireland	14 December 1955
Israel	11 May 1949
Italy	14 December 1955
Jamaica	18 September 1962
Japan	18 December 1956
Jordan	14 December 1955
Kenya	16 December 1963
Kuwait	14 May 1963
Lao People's Democratic Republic	14 December 1955
* Lebanon	24 October 1945
Lesotho	17 October 1966
* Liberia	2 November 1945
Libyan Arab Jamahiriya[7]	14 December 1955
* Luxembourg	24 October 1945
Madagascar	20 September 1960
Malawi	1 December 1964
Malaysia[8]	17 September 1957

[6] By letter of 20 Jan. 1965, Indonesia announced its decision to withdraw from the UN 'at this stage and under the present circumstances'. By telegram of 19 Sept. 1966 it announced its decision 'to resume full cooperation with the United Nations and to resume participation in its activities'. On 28 Sept. 1966 the General Assembly took note of this decision, and the President invited the representatives of Indonesia to take seats in the Assembly.

[7] Formerly Libyan Arab Republic.

[8] The Federation of Malaya joined the UN on 17 Sept. 1957. On 16 Sept 1963 its name changed to Malaysia, following the admission to the new federation of Singapore, Sabah (North Borneo) and Sarawak. Singapore became an independent state on 9 Aug. 1965 and a UN member on 21 Sept. 1965.

Member	*Date of admission*
Maldives	21 September 1965
Mali	28 September 1960
Malta	1 December 1964
Mauritania	27 October 1961
Mauritius	24 April 1968
* Mexico	7 November 1945
Mongolia	27 October 1961
Morocco	12 November 1956
Mozambique	16 September 1975
Nepal	14 December 1955
* Netherlands	10 December 1945
* New Zealand	24 October 1945
* Nicaragua	24 October 1945
Niger	20 September 1960
Nigeria	7 October 1960
* Norway	27 November 1945
Oman	7 October 1971
Pakistan	30 September 1947
* Panama	13 November 1945
Papua New Guinea	10 October 1975
* Paraguay	24 October 1945
* Peru	31 October 1945
* Philippines	24 October 1945
* Poland	24 October 1945
Portugal	14 December 1955
Qatar	21 September 1971
Romania	14 December 1955
Rwanda	18 September 1962
Saint Christopher and Nevis	23 September 1983
Saint Lucia	18 September 1979
Saint Vincent and the Grenadines	16 September 1980
Samoa	15 December 1976
São Tomé and Príncipe	16 September 1975
* Saudi Arabia	24 October 1945
Senegal	28 September 1960
Seychelles	21 September 1976
Sierra Leone	27 September 1961
Singapore	21 September 1965
Solomon Islands	19 September 1978
Somalia	20 September 1960
* South Africa	7 November 1945
Spain	14 December 1955

Member	Date of admission
Sri Lanka	14 December 1955
Sudan	12 November 1956
Suriname[9]	4 December 1975
Swaziland	24 September 1968
Sweden	19 November 1946
* Syrian Arab Republic[5]	24 October 1945
Thailand	16 December 1946
Togo	20 September 1960
Trinidad and Tobago	18 September 1962
Tunisia	12 November 1956
* Turkey	24 October 1945
Uganda	25 October 1962
* Ukrainian Soviet Socialist Republic	24 October 1945
* Union of Soviet Socialist Republics	24 October 1945
United Arab Emirates	9 December 1971
* United Kingdom of Great Britain and Northern Ireland	24 October 1945
United Republic of Tanzania[10]	14 December 1961
* United States of America	24 October 1945
* Uruguay	18 December 1945
Vanuatu	15 September 1981
* Venezuela	15 November 1945
Viet Nam	20 September 1977
Yemen	30 September 1947
* Yugoslavia	24 October 1945
Zaïre	20 September 1960
Zambia	1 December 1964
Zimbabwe	25 August 1980

[9] Formerly Surinam.
[10] Tanganyika was a UN member from 14 Dec. 1961; Zanzibar was a member from 16 Dec. 1963. Following the ratification on 26 Apr. 1964 of Articles of Union between Tanganyika and Zanzibar, the United Republic of Tanganyika and Zanzibar continued as a single member, changing its name to United Republic of Tanzania on 1 Nov. 1964.

Appendix C

Secretaries-General of the United Nations

1 February 1946–10 April 1953	Trygve Lie, b. 1896, d. 1968. Norwegian. (Tendered resignation on 10 November 1952.)
10 April 1953–17 September 1961	Dag Hammarskjöld, b. 1905, d. 17 September 1961 in Northern Rhodesia. Swedish.
3 November 1961–31 December 1971	U Thant, b. 1909, d. 1974. Burmese. (Was Acting Secretary-General until 1 January 1962.)
1 January 1972–31 December 1981	Kurt Waldheim, b. 1918. Austrian.
1 January 1982–	Javier Pérez de Cuéllar, b. 1920. Peruvian.

Appendix D

List of UN Peacekeeping and Observer Forces

This is a quick-reference chronological list of UN peacekeeping and observer forces whose composition includes military or police units contributed for the purpose by member states. This list does not refer to smaller special missions, investigatory panels, or advisory groups. Information is given in the form: *Name of force (acronym), location, years of operation, a principal authorizing resolution. Maximum strength. Strength in October 1985 (if applicable).*

For further information, see: United Nations, *The Blue Helmets: A Review of United Nations Peacekeeping* (United Nations, New York, 1985); and Rosalyn Higgins, *United Nations Peacekeeping*, 4 vols. (Oxford, 1969–81).

(a) MAIN PEACEKEEPING AND OBSERVER FORCES

United Nations Truce Supervision Organization (UNTSO), Several areas in the Middle East, 1948–, SC Res. 54 of 15 July 1948. Maximum strength: 572 (1948). Strength in October 1985: 298.

United Nations Military Observer Group in India and Pakistan (UNMOGIP), Jammu and Kashmir, 1949–, SC Res. 47 of 21 April 1948. Maximum strength: 102 (October 1965). Strength in October 1985: 39.

United Nations Emergency Force (UNEF I), Suez Canal, Sinai, Gaza, 1956–67, GA Res. 1000 (ES–I) of 5 November 1956 and GA Res. 1001 (ES–I) of 7 November 1956. Maximum strength: 6,073 (February 1957).

United Nations Observer Group in Lebanon (UNOGIL), Lebanon, 1958, SC Res. 128 of 11 June 1958. Maximum strength: 591 (November 1958).

United Nations Operation in the Congo (Opération des Nations Unies pour le Congo = ONUC), Republic of the Congo, 1960–4, SC Res. 143 of 14 July 1960. Maximum strength: 19,828 (July 1961).

United Nations Security Force in West New Guinea (UNSF), established to assist the *United Nations Temporary Executive Agency (UNTEA)*, West Irian, 1962–3, GA Res. 1752 (XVII) of 21 September 1962. Maximum strength: 1,576.

United Nations Yemen Observation Mission (UNYOM), Yemen, 1963–4, SC Res. 179 of 11 June 1963. Maximum strength: 189.

United Nations Peacekeeping Force in Cyprus (UNFICYP), Cyprus, 1964–, SC Res. 186 of 4 March 1964. Maximum strength: 6,411 (June 1964). Strength in October 1985: 2,345.

Mission of the Representative of the Secretary-General in the Dominican Republic (DOMREP), Dominican Republic, 1965–6, SC Res. 203 of 14 May 1965. Strength: 2.

United Nations India–Pakistan Observation Mission (UNIPOM), India–Pakistan border, 1965–6, SC Res. 211 of 20 September 1965. Maximum strength: 96 (October 1965).

United Nations Emergency Force II (UNEF II), Suez Canal, Sinai, 1973–9, SC Res. 340 of 25 October 1973. Maximum strength: 6,973 (February 1974).

United Nations Disengagement Observer Force (UNDOF), Golan Heights, 1974–, SC Res. 350 of 31 May 1974. Authorized strength: 1,450. Strength in October 1985: 1,316.

United Nations Interim Force in Lebanon (UNIFIL), Southern Lebanon, 1978–, SC Res. 425 and 426 of 19 March 1978. Authorized strength: 7,000. Strength in October 1985: 5,773.

(b) A NOTE ON OTHER FORCES

Two earlier forces performed functions similar to those later fulfilled by UN observer forces, but are not treated as such because contingents remained under national command. These were:

United Nations Observers in Indonesia (the Consular Commission), Indonesia, 1947–50, SC Res. S/525 (I) and (II) of 25 August 1947.

United Nations Special Committee on the Balkans (UNSCOB), Balkans, 1947–52, GA Res. 109 (II) of 21 October 1947.

The *United Nations Force in Korea*, Korea, 1950–3, is not generally regarded as a peacekeeping or observer force, especially as it was under national rather than UN command, was not based on the consent of the parties to the conflict, and was fully engaged in active combat operations. It was authorized by SC Res. 84 of 7 July 1950.

Provision has been made for the creation of a new force: the *United Nations Transition Assistance Group (UNTAG)*, Namibia, not deployed, is envisaged in SC Res. 435 of 29 September 1978.

Appendix E

Judgments and Opinions of the International Court of Justice*

In the period from its foundation in 1946 up to 31 December 1986 the International Court of Justice in The Hague dealt with thirty-six contentious cases between states, and also delivered eighteen advisory opinions—making a total of fifty-four. These are listed below. Several of these involved more than one phase, and a number of the contentious cases involved more than two states parties.

The ICJ, which is a successor to the Permanent Court of International Justice (1922–46), was constituted by the Statute of the ICJ. This was adopted with the UN Charter by the San Francisco Conference on 26 June 1945. All UN member states are also parties to this Statute. The text of the Statute may be found in the *Yearbook of the United Nations* and in numerous other sources.

(a) Contentious Cases

1. CASES TERMINATED BY A JUDGMENT ON THE MERITS

	Reference to *ICJ Reports*
Corfu Channel	*1947–48,* p. 15
	1949, pp. 4, 244
Asylum (with *Haya de la Torre*)	*1950,* pp. 266, 395
	1951, p. 71
Fisheries	*1951,* p. 116
Rights of Nationals of the United States of America in Morocco	*1952,* p. 176
Ambatielos	*1952,* p. 28
	1953, p. 10
Minquiers and Ecrehos	*1953,* p. 47

* *Source*: ICJ, *The International Court of Justice* (3rd edn., The Hague, 1986), pp. 133–7.

Reference
to *ICJ Reports*

Application of the Convention of 1902 Governing the	
Guardianship of Infants	*1958*, p. 55
Sovereignty over Certain Frontier Land	*1959*, p. 209
Right of Passage over Indian Territory	*1957*, p. 125
	1960, p. 6
Arbitral Award Made by the King of Spain on	
23 December 1906	*1960*, p. 192
Temple of Preah Vihear	*1961*, p. 17
	1962, p. 6
North Sea Continental Shelf	*1969*, p. 3
Appeal Relating to the Jurisdiction of the ICAO Council	*1972*, p. 46
Fisheries Jurisdiction	*1972*, pp. 12, 30
	1973, pp. 3, 49
	1974, pp. 3, 175
United States Diplomatic and Consular Staff in Tehran	*1979*, pp. 7, 23
	1980, p. 3
	1981, p. 45
Continental Shelf (Tunisia/Libyan Arab Jamahiriya)	*1979*, p. 3
	1980, p. 70
	1981, p. 3
	1982, p. 18
Delimitation of the Maritime Boundary in the Gulf of	
Maine Area	*1982*, pp. 3, 557
	1983, p. 6
	1984, pp. 165, 246
Continental Shelf (Libyan Arab Jamahiriya/Malta)	*1982*, p. 554
	1983, p. 3
	1985, p. 13
Application for Revision and Interpretation of the	
Judgment of 24 February 1982 in the case concerning	
the Continental Shelf (Tunisia/Libyan Arab	
Jamahiriya) *(Tunisia* v. *Libyan Arab Jamahiriya)*	*1985*, p. 192
Military and Paramilitary Activities in and against	
Nicaragua (Nicaragua v. *United States of America)*	*1984*, pp. 169, 215, 392
	1985, p. 3
	1986, p. 14
Frontier Dispute (Burkina Faso/Mali)	*1985*, pp. 6, 10, 189
	1986, pp. 3, 554

2. CASES TERMINATED BY A JUDGMENT ON A PRELIMINARY OBJECTION OR OTHER INTERLOCUTORY POINT

	Reference to *ICJ Reports*
Anglo-Iranian Oil Co.	*1951*, p. 89
	1952, p. 93
Nottebohm	*1953*, p. 111
	1955, p. 4
Monetary Gold Removed from Rome in 1943	*1954*, p. 19
Certain Norwegian Loans	*1957*, p. 9
Interhandel	*1957*, p. 105
	1959, p. 6
Aerial Incident of 27 July 1955 (with two similar cases terminated by discontinuance)	*1959*, pp. 127, 264
	1960, p. 146
Northern Cameroons	*1963*, p. 15
South West Africa	*1962*, p. 319
	1966, p. 6
Barcelona Traction, Light and Power Company, Limited (with a first case terminated by discontinuance)	*1961*, p. 9
	1964, p. 6
	1970, p. 3
Nuclear Tests	*1973*, pp. 99, 135
	1974, pp. 253, 457
Aegean Sea Continental Shelf	*1976*, p. 3
	1978, p. 3

3. CASES TERMINATED BY DISCONTINUANCE PRIOR TO A JUDGMENT ON THE MERITS

Protection of French Nationals and Protected Persons in Egypt	*1950*, p. 59
Electricité de Beyrouth Company	*1954*, p. 107
Compagnie du Port, des Quais et des Entrepôts de Beyrouth and Société Radio-Orient ·	*1960*, p. 186
Trial of Pakistani Prisoners of War	*1973*, p. 347

(b) Advisory Opinions

1. UPON REQUEST BY THE GENERAL ASSEMBLY OF THE UNITED NATIONS

2. UPON REQUEST BY THE SECURITY COUNCIL OF THE UNITED NATIONS

3. UPON REQUEST OF THE UNITED NATIONS COMMITTEE ON APPLICATIONS FOR REVIEW OF ADMINISTRATIVE TRIBUNAL JUDGMENTS

Appendix F

Select Further Reading

The literature on the UN, like the literature produced by the UN, is prodigious in extent. We list here a very short selection of works on the UN which may serve as a starting-point for those interested in reading further on any of the subjects covered in this book. The list contains only books, and is largely confined to more recent works in the English language. More specialized reading-lists are included in some of these works; the reader may refer also to the footnotes of the various chapters in the present volume.

ABI-SAAB, GEORGES, *The United Nations Operation in the Congo 1960–1964*, Oxford University Press, Oxford, 1978.

ALLSEBROOK, MARY, *Prototypes of Peacemaking: The First Forty Years of the United Nations*, Longman, Harlow, 1986.

ARCHER, CLIVE, *International Organisations*, George Allen & Unwin, London, 1983.

BAEHR, PETER, and GORDENKER, LEON, *The United Nations: Reality and Ideal*, Praeger, New York, 1984.

BAILEY, SYDNEY, *The General Assembly of the United Nations*, rev. edn., Pall Mall Press, London, 1964.

—— *How Wars End: The United Nations and the Termination of Armed Conflict 1946–1964*, 2 vols., Oxford University Press, Oxford, 1982.

BARDONNET, DANIEL (ed.), *The Adaptation of Structures and Methods at the United Nations*, Hague Academy of International Law Workshop, Martinus Nijhoff, Lancaster, 1986.

BEIGBEDER, YVES, *Management Problems in United Nations Organizations*, Frances Pinter, London, 1987.

BERRIDGE, G.R., and JENNINGS, A. (eds.), *Diplomacy at the UN*, Macmillan, London, 1985.

BERTRAND, MAURICE, *Refaire l'ONU: Un programme pour la paix*, Zoé, Geneva, 1986.

BOWETT, DEREK W., *United Nations Forces: A Legal Study of United Nations Practice*, Stevens, London, 1964.

CASSESE, ANTONIO (ed.), *United Nations Peacekeeping: Legal Essays*, Sijthoff and Noordhoff, Alphen aan den Rijn, 1978.

—— (ed.), *UN Law/Fundamental Rights: Two Topics in International Law*, Sijthoff and Noordhoff, Alphen aan den Rijn, 1979.

—— (ed.), *The Current Legal Regulation of the Use of Force 40 Years after the UN Charter*, Martinus Nijhoff, Lancaster, 1986.

CASTANEDA, JORGE, *Legal Effects of United Nations Resolutions* (tr. Alba Amoia), Columbia University Press, New York, 1969.

CLAUDE, INIS, *Swords into Ploughshares: The Problems and Progress of International Organisation*, 4th edn., Random House, New York, 1971.

CORDIER, ANDREW *et al.* (eds.), *Public Papers of the Secretaries-General of the United Nations*, 8 vols., Columbia University Press, New York, 1969–77.

COT, JEAN-PIERRE, and PELLET, ALAIN (eds.), *La Charte des Nations Unies*, Economica, Paris, 1985.

ELMANDJRA, MAHDI, *The United Nations System: An Analysis*, Faber, London, 1973.

FELD, WERNER JACOB, *et al.* (eds.), *International Organization, a Comparative Approach*, Praeger, New York, 1983.

FRANCK, THOMAS M., *Nation Against Nation: What Happened to the UN Dream and What the US Can Do About It*, Oxford University Press, New York, 1985.

GATI, TOBI TRISTER (ed.), *The US, the UN, and the Management of Global Change*, New York University Press, London, 1983.

GOODRICH, L.M., *The United Nations in a Changing World*, Columbia University Press, New York, 1974.

—— HAMBRO, E., and SIMONS, A.P., *Charter of the United Nations: Commentary and Documents*, 3rd edn., Columbia University Press, New York, 1969.

HAMMARSKJÖLD, DAG, *The Servant of Peace: A Selection of the Speeches and Statements of Dag Hammarskjöld* (ed. by Wilder Foote), Bodley Head, London, 1962.

HANNUM, HURST (ed.), *Guide to International Human Rights Practice*, Macmillan, London, 1984.

HAZZARD, SHIRLEY, *Defeat of An Ideal: A Study of the Self-Destruction of the United Nations*, Little, Brown & Co., Boston, 1973.

HIGGINS, ROSALYN, *The Development of International Law through the Political Organs of the United Nations*, Oxford University Press, London, 1963.

—— *United Nations Peacekeeping*, 4 vols., Oxford University Press, Oxford, 1969–81.

HILL, M., *The United Nations System: Coordinating its Economic and Social Work*, Cambridge University Press, Cambridge, 1979.

HOGGART, RICHARD, *An Idea and its Servants: UNESCO From Within*, Chatto & Windus, London, 1978.

INTERNATIONAL COURT OF JUSTICE, *The International Court of Justice*, 3rd edn., ICJ, The Hague, 1986.

JACKSON, RICHARD, *The Non-Aligned, the UN and the Superpowers*, Praeger for the Council on Foreign Relations, Eastbourne, 1983.

JACKSON, ROBERT, *A Study of the Capacity of the United Nations Development System*, 2 vols., United Nations, New York, 1969.

JACOBSON, HAROLD KARAN, *The USSR and the UN's Economic and Social Activities*, University of Notre Dame Press, Indiana, 1963.

JAMES, ALAN, *The Politics of Peace-keeping*, Chatto and Windus, London, 1969.

JORDAN, ROBERT S. (ed.), *International Administration: Its Evolution and Contemporary Applications*, Oxford University Press, New York, 1971.

—— (ed.), *Dag Hammarskjöld Revisited: the UN Secretary-General as a Force in World Politics*, Carolina Academic Press, Durham NC, 1983.

JÜTTE, R., and GROSSE-JÜTTE, A. (eds.), *The Future of International Organization*, Frances Pinter, London, 1981.

KAPTEYN, P.J.G. *et al.* (eds.), *International Organization and Integration: Annotated Basic Documents and Descriptive Directory of International Organizations and Arrangements*, vol. 1A (*The United Nations Organization*), vol. 1B (*Organizations Related to the United Nations*), Martinus Nijhoff, The Hague, 1981 and 1982.

KAUFMAN, JOHAN, *United Nations Decision-Making*, Sijthoff & Noordhoff, Rockville, MI, 1981.

LIE, TRYGVE, *In the Cause of Peace: Seven Years with the United Nations*, Macmillan, New York, 1954.

LUARD, EVAN (ed.), *International Agencies: the Emerging Framework of Interdependence*, Macmillan, London, 1977.

—— *The United Nations: How It Works and What It Does*, Macmillan, London, 1979.

—— *A History of the United Nations*, vol. 1, Macmillan, London, 1982.

LYOU, BYUNG-HWA, *Peace and Unification in Korea and International Law*, University of Maryland School of Law, Baltimore, 1986.

MCWHINNEY, EDWARD, *United Nations Law Making: Cultural and Ideological Relativism and International Law Making for an Era of Transition*, Holmes & Meier, London, 1984.

MERON, THEODOR, *The UN Secretariat: the Rules and the Practice*, D.C Heath, Lexington, Mass., 1977.

—— (ed.), *Human Rights in International Law: Legal and Policy Issues*, Clarendon Press, Oxford, 1984.

MISRA, KASHI PRASAD, *The Role of the United Nations in the Indo-Pakistan Conflict of 1971*, Vikas, Delhi, 1973.

MOSKOWITZ, MOSES, *The Roots and Reaches of United Nations Actions and Decisions*, Sijthoff and Noordhoff, Alphen aan den Rijn, 1980.

MOYNIHAN, DANIEL PATRICK, *A Dangerous Place*, Secker & Warburg, London, 1979.

MURPHY, JOHN F., *The United Nations and the Control of International*

Violence: A Legal and Political Analysis, Manchester University Press, Manchester, 1983.

NICHOLAS, H.G., *The United Nations as a Political Institution*, 5th edn., Oxford University Press, Oxford, 1975.

O'BRIEN, CONOR CRUISE, *To Katanga and Back: a UN Case History*, Hutchinson, London, 1962.

—— and TOPOLSKI, FELIKS, *The United Nations: Sacred Drama*, Hutchinson, London, 1968.

PETERSON, M.J., *The General Assembly in World Politics*, Allen & Unwin, Boston, 1986.

PITT, DAVID and WEISS, THOMAS, *The Nature of United Nations Bureaucracies*, Croom Helm, London, 1986.

POGANY, ISTVAN, *The Security Council and the Arab–Israeli Conflict*, Gower, Aldershot, 1984.

RIKHYE, INDAR JIT, *The Theory and Practice of Peacekeeping*, Hurst, London, 1984.

ROVINE, ARTHUR, *The First Fifty Years: The Secretary-General in World Politics 1920–1970*, Sijthoff, Leyden, 1970.

ROYAL INSTITUTE OF INTERNATIONAL AFFAIRS, *United Nations Documents 1941–1945*, RIIA, London, 1946.

RUSSELL, RUTH, *The United Nations and United States Security Policy*, Brookings Institution, Washington DC, 1968.

—— and MUTHER, JEANETTE, *A History of the United Nations Charter: The Role of the United States 1940–1945*, Brookings Institution, Washington DC, 1958.

SAXENA, J.N., SINGH, GURDIP, and KOUL, A.K. (eds.), *United Nations for a Better World*, Lancers Books, New Delhi, 1986.

SCHIAVONE, G., *International Organisations*, Macmillan, London, 1987.

SEYERSTED, FINN, *United Nations Forces in the Law of Peace and War*, Sijthoff, Leiden, 1966.

SOHN, LOUIS B. (ed.), *Cases on United Nations Law*, Foundation Press, Brooklyn, 1967.

STONE, JULIUS, *Conflict Through Consensus: United Nations Approaches to Aggression*, Johns Hopkins University Press, London, 1977.

THANT, U., *Toward World Peace: Addresses and Public Statements, 1957–1963*, Thomas Yoseloff, New York, 1964.

—— *Portfolio for Peace: Excerpts from the Writings and Speeches of U Thant, 1961–1968*, 2nd edn., United Nations, New York, 1970.

—— *View From the UN*, David & Charles, Newton Abbot, 1978.

TWITCHETT, KENNETH J. (ed.), *The Evolving United Nations: A Prospect For Peace?*, Europa, London, 1971.

UNCTAD, *The History of UNCTAD 1964–1984*, United Nations, New York, 1985.

UNITED NATIONS, *The Blue Helmets: A Review of United Nations Peace-keeping*, United Nations, New York, 1985.

—— *Everyone's United Nations: A Handbook on the Work of the United Nations*, 10th edn., United Nations (Sales No. E.85.I.24), New York, 1986.

—— *Yearbook of the United Nations*, United Nations, New York, annually.

UNITED NATIONS CONFERENCE ON INTERNATIONAL ORGANISATION (San Francisco, 1945), *Documents*, 22 vols, United Nations and Library of Congress, London, 1945–66.

URQUHART, BRIAN, *Hammarskjöld*, Alfred A. Knopf, New York, 1972.

—— *A Life in Peace and War*, Weidenfeld & Nicolson, London, 1987.

WAINHOUSE, D.W. *et al.*, *International Peacekeeping at the Crossroads: National Support—Experience and Prospects*, Johns Hopkins University Press, Baltimore, 1973.

WALDHEIM, KURT, *Building the Future Order*, The Free Press, New York, 1980.

—— *The Challenge of Peace*, Weidenfeld & Nicolson, London, 1980.

—— *In the Eye of the Storm: the Memoirs of Kurt Waldheim*, Weidenfeld & Nicolson, London, 1985.

WEISS, THOMAS, *Multilateral Development Diplomacy in UNCTAD: the Lessons of Group Negotiations 1964–84*, Macmillan, London, 1986.

WELLS, CLARE, *The UN, Unesco and •the Politics of Knowledge*, Macmillan, London, 1987.

WILLIAMS, DOUGLAS, *The Specialized Agencies and the United Nations—the System in Crisis*, C. Hurst & Co., London, 1987.

WISEMAN, HENRY (ed.), *Peacekeeping: Appraisals and Proposals*, Pergamon Press, New York, 1983.

YESELSON, ABRAHAM, and GAGLIONE, ANTHONY, *A Dangerous Place: the United Nations as a Weapon in World Politics*, Grossman, New York, 1974.

INDEX

Colombia 121 n., 210
Colonial Countries, Declaration on the
  Granting of Independence to
  (1960) 172
Commission on Human Rights (UN):
  action and 101
  Bill of Rights and 103
  composition 113
  establishment 102, 113
  inactivity 121-2, 123, 124, 126, 128,
    130
  Poland and 85
  political nature 113
  special rapporteurs 110-11, 113
  Uganda and 130-1
  working groups 110-11, 113-14, 128
Committee on the Elimination of Racial
  Discrimination 174
Committee of Fourteen 196
Committee of Programme and Budget,
  proposed 198
Committee for Programme and
  Coordination 196, 199 n.
Committee of Twenty-Eight 195
Committee of Twenty-Four 114-15,
  124
Common Fund for Commodities 145
Congo 96-7, 222; see also UN Operation
  in the Congo
Continental Shelf, Geneva Convention
  on (1958) 181
Cordovez, Diego 82, 86
Council of Europe 137
Cuba 12, 52-3, 89, 121 n., 167
Cyprus 67, 80-1, 84, 85, 130, 223; see
  also UN Peacekeeping Force in
  Cyprus
Czechoslovakia 24, 38

debt bondage 118
Declaration on the Elimination of
  Discrimination against Women
  (1967) 115
decolonization 10, 14, 17, 24, 50,
  114-15, 141, 165, 172, 179, 190,
  203
de Gaulle, Charles 18 n.
Denmark 181
development:
  aid, effectiveness of 155-6
  bilateral assistance 154
  commitment to 147
  domestic measures 141

international development policy 152
  language of UN Charter on 148-9
  models of 149-52
  prospects for 152
  theory 150
  UN and 139-57
diplomatic and consular relations,
  conventions on 174-5, 176
diplomats, illusions of 200-1
Director-General for Development 196
disarmament 11, 17, 39-43, 73, 160-1;
  see also arms control
Disarmament Commission 41-2
Disarmament Decades 42
disasters 74-5
Division of Human Rights 100, 126
Dominican Republic 38, 268
Drummond, Sir Eric 64
Dulles, John Foster 121 n.
Dumbarton Oaks Conference
  (1944) 17 n.

East Timor 215
Economic and Social Council:
  Bill of Rights 103
  description 7
  human rights and 100, 101, 102, 105,
    112, 118, 121, 122, 123, 124, 125,
    126, 166
  membership 207
  origins 195
  political nature 112
  resolution 1235 125, 129, 131, 132
  resolution 1503 126, 127, 128, 129,
    131, 132, 133
Economic Commission for Latin
  America 142
Economic Security Council,
  proposed 149
Economic, Social, and Cultural Rights,
  Covenant on (1966) 107-8
economics, neo-classical 145
EEC (European Economic
  Community) 50, 51, 81
Egypt 24, 35; see also Suez crisis
electromagnetic environment 187
El Salvador 114, 121 n., 131 n., 133,
  215
environmental protection 187
Equatorial Guinea 131-2
Ethiopia 131 n.
European Commission on Human
  Rights 227

European Human Rights Convention
(1950) 137, 189
Exclusive Economic Zones 182

Falklands/Malvinas war 19, 47, 56–7,
60, 90, 215
First International 1
First World War 97–8
Fisheries case 180–1
Fisheries Jurisdiction case 182–3
Food and Agriculture Organization 7
force, use of 14, 15, 19, 20, 32, 38,
164–5, 225
Ford, President Gerald 134
Four Nations Declaration (1943) 9, 39
France:
development assistance 155
human rights and 136–7
nuclear weapons tests 81, 179, 180
Rainbow Warrior and 81
Revolution 97
UN and 35
see also Suez crisis
Frontier Dispute case 180

General Act for Pacific Settlement of
International Disputes (1928) 164
General Agreement on Tariffs and
Trade (GATT) 8, 143
General Assembly:
action, lack of power for 33
Antarctica and 187
Apartheid, Special Committee
against 174
budget 5
committees 174
Decolonization Committee 174
description 5
disarmament and 39
'double standards' 12, 13
Fifth Committee 226
Fourth Committee 7
human rights and 112, 118, 123
law and 167–74
non-intervention 169, 172
organizational responsibility 72
Outer Space Committee 167, 174
resolutions, law-making character
of 169–74
Sixth Committee 167, 174, 177
Special Sessions on Disarmament 11,
36–7, 42
terrorism and 22, 59

Third World and 215
women and 115, 116
General Treaty for the Renunciation of
War (1928) 164
Geneva Conventions 164
Geneva Economic Conference 195
'Geneva Group' 25
Genocide Convention (1948) 167–9
Germany, pre-1945 9, 98–9, 167
Germany, Democratic Republic
(East) 131 n.
Germany, Federal Republic (West) 181
Gobbi, Hugo 86
Golan Heights 225, 268
Gorbachev, Mikhail 28, 134–5
Gramm–Rudman Act (1985) 193 n.
Great Britain *see* United Kingdom
Greece 80–1, 87, 97, 127 n., 210
Grenada 18, 215
Group of 77 18, 143, 170
Group of Eight Experts 195
Group of Eighteen 73 n., 194, 198, 199,
200
Group of Three Experts 195
Group of Twenty-Five Experts on the
Structure of the UN, 196
Guatemala 49–50, 121 n., 131 n., 133
Guicciardi, Vittorio Winspeare 89
Gulf of Maine case 182
Gulf war *see* Iran–Iraq war
Guyana 90

Haiti 75, 121 n., 131 n.
Hammarskjöld, Dag 61, 87, 88, 195,
196, 222
Hau 82
Hassan II, King 82
High Commissioner for Human Rights,
proposed 228
high seas 186
Hoffmann, Stanley 134
Howard, Michael 224
humanitarian assistance 108–9
human rights:
ambivalence towards 101
conceptions of 16
history 95–9
liberalism and 135
machinery, activities 116–33
machinery, form of 108–16
national sovereignty and 102,104
protection problematics 119–28
states' inviolability and 14, 15–16